Microsoft® Manual of Style for Technical Publications Third Edition

Microsoft Corporation Editorial Style Board

PUBLISHED BY
Microsoft Press
A Division of Microsoft Corporation
One Microsoft Way
Redmond, Washington 98052-6399

Library of Congress Cataloging-in-Publication Data
Microsoft Manual of Style for Technical Publications / Microsoft Corporation Editorial
   Style Board.--3rd ed.
       p. cm.
   Includes index.
   ISBN 0-7356-1746-5
     1. Technical writing--Handbooks, manuals, etc.   2. Microsoft Corporation.   I. Microsoft
   Corporation. Editorial Style Board.

   T11.M467   2003
   808'.066005--dc22   2003065115

Printed and bound in the United States of America.

1 2 3 4 5 6 7 8 9   QWT   8 7 6 5 4 3

Distributed in Canada by H.B. Fenn and Company Ltd.

A CIP catalogue record for this book is available from the British Library.

Microsoft Press books are available through booksellers and distributors worldwide. For further information about international editions, contact your local Microsoft Corporation office or contact Microsoft Press International directly at fax (425) 936-7329. Visit our Web site at www.microsoft.com/learning/. Send comments to *mspinput@microsoft.com*.

Active Directory, ActiveX, DirectDraw, DirectX, Encarta, FrontPage, Home Essentials, IntelliMouse, JScript, Microsoft, Microsoft Press, MS-DOS, MSDN, MSN, Natural, Outlook, PowerPoint, Slate, Verdana, Visio, Visual Basic, Visual FoxPro, Visual Studio, Windows, Windows Media, Windows NT, Windows Server, and Xbox are either registered trademarks or trademarks of Microsoft Corporation in the United States and/or other countries. Other product and company names mentioned herein may be the trademarks of their respective owners.

The example companies, organizations, products, domain names, e-mail addresses, logos, people, places, and events depicted herein are fictitious. No association with any real company, organization, product, domain name, e-mail address, logo, person, place, or event is intended or should be inferred.

This book expresses the author's views and opinions. The information contained in this book is provided without any express, statutory, or implied warranties. Neither the authors, Microsoft Corporation, nor its resellers or distributors will be held liable for any damages caused or alleged to be caused either directly or indirectly by this book.

Acquisitions Editor: Alex Blanton
Project Editor: Kristine Haugseth and Sandra Haynes
Technical Editor: Jim Purcell
Indexer: Kari Kells
Body Part No. X10-08622

Contents

General Topics

1: Documenting the User Interface

2: Content Formatting and Layout

3: Global Content

4: Content for Software Developers

5: Web Content

6: Indexing and Attributing

7: Tone and Rhetoric

8: Accessible Content

9: Common Style Problems

10: Grammatical Elements

11: Punctuation

12: List of Acronyms and Abbreviations

Usage Dictionary

A

B

Contents

C

D

Contents

G

H

I

J

K

L

M

N

O

P

Q

R

S

T

U

V

W

X

Y

Z

Acknowledgments

MSTP has been the work of many hands. The first lead editor at Microsoft, Amanda Clark, provided a foundation without which the present edition is inconceivable. Her successor, Barbara Roll, maintained and added to the book over several years and has provided invaluable guidance, assistance, and encouragement, particularly in the area of global English. For the present edition, Stephanie Marr helped update the guidance on indexing. Karin Carter wrote the guidelines that became the Global Content section based on a presentation by Barbara Roll. Karen Strudwick and the Microsoft Accessibility Group provided much information about accessible content. Much of the new content was stolen shamelessly from various product groups' style sheets.

Special thanks to Anne Taussig and to Kristen Heller, Lynette Skinner, and the Training and Certification editorial team for their thorough, thoughtful content reviews, as well as to Annette Hall, Barbara McGuire, Sean Maguire, Dave Cash, and Melissa Bramble. Thanks, too, to Legal reviewers Marianne Moran Peterson, Sue Stickney, Diane Tibbott, and Judy Weston. Your comments made this a better book.

The editorial community at Microsoft does a wondrous job of discovering the limitations and internal contradictions of style guidance, the happy result of their commitment to standards and their enforcement. The sharp-eyed Matt Barry found many errors large and small. We can only hope he finds fewer in this edition. Shannon Evans covered me with a thoughtful and comprehensive review and revision of the version released to Microsoft editors. Kristine Haugseth lent her discerning eye to ensure that the version you hold in your hand is editorially sound. Many technical editors outside Microsoft generously shared their experiences with MSTP and offered suggestions for making it more useful.

At Microsoft, the Editorial Style Board discusses and decides issues as they come up, and the product of their deliberations finds its way into MSTP. The board consists of Sean Bentley, Meredith Kraike, Jim Purcell, Barbara Roll, Robin Lombard, Darla Crass, Paula Ladenburg Land, Hanne Smaadahl, Stephanie Morton, and June Thomas. The discussions are always collegial and usually virtual. This is, after all, a software company.

Jim Purcell
Lead Editor, Content Applications & Services
Microsoft Corporation

Introduction to the Third Edition

This third print edition of the *Manual of Style for Technical Publications* (MSTP) is something of a departure from earlier editions. As the manual has grown and evolved, it seemed to be the right time to overhaul its organization. General topics now make up the first part of the manual, organized by subject. The alphabetical usage dictionary follows with specific guidance about usage and spelling of general and computer-related terms.

Since the second edition, the language and concepts of software have changed a great deal. New technologies beget new technical terms. More people are writing content for information technology professionals and software developers. The Internet has become ubiquitous. The needs of the global audience are now a primary consideration, even (especially) for content that will not be localized. The third edition of MSTP reflects these changes, as well as the general evolution and simplification of language: At Microsoft *CD-ROM* as a general term has become *CD* and *blog* has entered our vocabulary. *E-mail*, however, is still *e-mail*.

Style is a matter of convention and consensus, and the guidance offered here does not describe the only correct way to write. Our primary aim is to help Microsoft writers and editors maintain consistency within and across products. MSTP is not a set of rules, but a set of guidelines that have been discussed and reviewed by experienced writers and editors across the company. These guidelines represent their expertise and opinions of what best serves Microsoft and its customers. If you do not work for Microsoft, we hope the decisions we have made will lighten the load of decisions you have to make in your workplace, but we do not presume to say that a different approach would be wrong. It just would not be Microsoft style.

This version of MSTP is also available as an e-book on the companion CD. For more information, see "About the CD" later in this chapter.

How to use this manual

Topics provide information ranging from a simple note on the correct spelling of a term to a thorough review of what to do, why, what to avoid, and what to do instead, with frequent correct and incorrect examples. Topic titles listing two or more terms connected by a comma, such as "expand, collapse," reflect correct usage for two similar terms. Topic titles listing terms connected by vs., such as "active vs. current" or "who vs. that," show that the two similar terms have different meanings in some contexts. Although topics separated by a comma or connected by vs. are alphabetized according to the first word, each term appears separately in the index for easier searching.

There are two kinds of cross-references: inline see reference, which notes the chapter topic where the information is covered, and *See also*, which notes terms with related information. Semi-colons have been used to separate term entries in See also because a number of entries include two or more terms connected by a comma. We have made an effort to minimize cross-references by including enough information within a short topic to answer the most basic questions.

MSTP does not cover all the terms or all the content issues specific to various Microsoft products. Individual product groups maintain their own project style sheets to deal with style issues that are not covered in this manual. In addition, because legal guidelines change quickly, MSTP does not include content on legal issues in this printed edition. Information about Microsoft trademarking, including the trademark list, guidelines for usage, and licensing can be found on www.microsoft.com/mscorp/ip/trademarks.

In the past, MSTP was targeted mainly at people who were writing and editing product documentation for "end users." With the growth of the Web, the scope of MSTP has broadened considerably. And that term, "end users," seems too broad in some cases. As you explore the manual, you will notice four primary audiences mentioned by name:

- **Home users.**   People who use their computer at home to send e-mail, browse the Internet, download music, display digital photos, and perform similar tasks. We make very few assumptions about home users' knowledge of, or comfort with, computers.

- **Information workers.**   People who use their computer at the office for word processing, e-mail, spreadsheet work, presentations, and other work-related tasks that do not involve programming or system administration.

- **Information technology professionals.**   People with a very sophisticated knowledge of system administration, including administration of enterprise-wide systems and database administrators.

- **Software developers.**   People who write computer programs professionally.

Unless a topic specifically addresses one or more of these audiences, it applies to all of them.

Italic is used to refer to words used as terms; examples of usage appear in quotation marks.

The comment *do not use* means just that; *avoid* means that you can use the term if no other word is suitable in context.

Other reference materials   The following reference materials are the authorities for issues not covered in this guide:

- *American Heritage Dictionary of the English Language*, 4th ed. Boston: Houghton Mifflin Company, 2000.

- *Associated Press Stylebook and Briefing on Media Law with Internet Guide and Glossary*, 37th ed. Cambridge, MA: Perseus Books Group, 2002.

- Brusaw, Charles T., Gerald J. Alred, and Walter E. Oliu. *Handbook of Technical Writing.* 6th ed. New York: St. Martin's Press, 2000.

- *Chicago Manual of Style*, 15th ed. Chicago: The University of Chicago Press, 2003.

- *Harbrace College Handbook*, 13th ed. Fort Worth: Harcourt Brace College Publishers, 1998.

- *Microsoft Press Computer Dictionary*, 5th ed. Redmond, WA: Microsoft Press, 2002.

- *Microsoft Windows User Experience*, Redmond, WA: Microsoft Press, 1999.

About the CD The CD that accompanies this book contains the e-book version of this book as well as e-book versions of the *Microsoft Computer Dictionary, Fifth Edition*, and the *Microsoft Encyclopedia of Networking, Second Edition*. To use the e-book files, you may need to install Adobe Acrobat or Adobe Reader and Microsoft Internet Explorer 5.01 or later. For further information, see the Readme on the CD.

To use the CD, insert it into your CD-ROM drive. If Autorun is not enabled on your computer, double-click the file StartCD.exe in the root folder of the CD. (You'll be presented with a licensing agreement that you need to accept before you can open the e-book.)

Support Information Every effort has been made to ensure the accuracy of the book and the contents of this Companion CD.

Microsoft Press provides corrections for books through the World Wide Web at *http://www.microsoft.com/learning/support/*. To connect directly to the Microsoft Press Knowledge Base and enter a query regarding a question or issue that you may have, go to *http://www.microsoft.comlearning/support/search.asp*.

If you have comments, questions, or ideas regarding the book or this CD, or questions that are not answered by querying the Knowledge Base, please send them to Microsoft Press via e-mail to:

mspinput@microsoft.com

or via postal mail to:

Microsoft Press
Attn: Microsoft Manual of Style for Technical Publications, Third Edition Editor
One Microsoft Way
Redmond, WA 98052-6399

Please note that product support is not offered through the above addresses.

Part 1

General Topics

This section provides guidelines that have been grouped thematically into twelve topics. They cover technical editing practices, such as the user interface, global content, software documentation, accessible content, and Web content as well as the more traditional areas of editorial focus such as formatting and layout, indexing, style, grammar, punctuation, and tone. The section ends with a list of acronyms and abbreviations.

Chapter 1
Documenting the User Interface

Understanding the user interface can be a confusing experience for customers. By using a consistent set of terminology and style, you can help customers navigate the product user interface successfully. Once customers become familiar with this system, they can jump seamlessly between content about different products.

This chapter contains the following sections:

- Screen Terminology
- Dialog Boxes and Property Sheets
- Unnamed Buttons
- Menus and Commands
- Control Panel
- Mouse Terminology
- Messages
- Key Names
- Command Syntax
- File Names and Extensions

Screen Terminology   The following illustrations show a Windows desktop, an open window, a browser window, a Web page, and a document window, with the various elements that appear on them called out. The callouts use usual capitalization style for callouts, which is sentence-style capitalization.

Elements that appear in more than one illustration are not necessarily called out on each illustration. For example, the scroll bar and the Close button appear in all windows, so they are called out only in the illustration of an open window.

For the names of dialog box elements, see *Dialog Boxes and Property Sheets* in this chapter. For the names of items on a menu, see *Menus and Commands* in this chapter.

1

Icon Desktop Submenu Open window

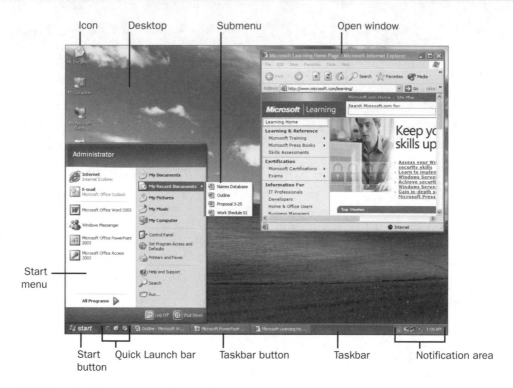

Start menu

Start button

Quick Launch bar

Taskbar button

Taskbar

Notification area

Windows desktop

Menu bar Title bar Maximize button

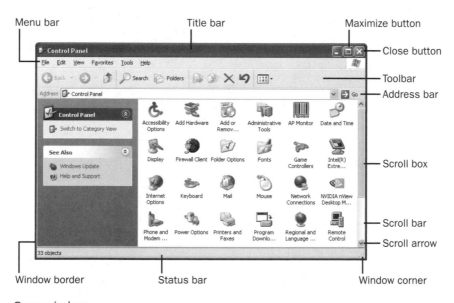

Close button

Toolbar

Address bar

Scroll box

Scroll bar

Scroll arrow

Window border Status bar Window corner

Open window

1

Close button

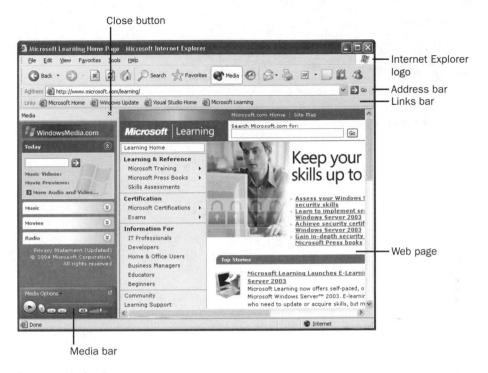

Internet Explorer logo

Address bar

Links bar

Web page

Media bar

Browser window

Banner

Navigation button

Link

Left navigation bar

Web page

1

Program icon

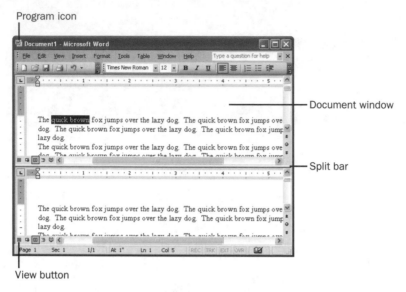

Document window

Split bar

View button

Document window

For more information, see the following section *Dialog Boxes and Property Sheets*, and the names of individual items in Part 2, "Usage Dictionary."

Dialog Boxes and Property Sheets

Dialog boxes contain command buttons and other options through which users can carry out a particular command or task. For example, in the **Save As** dialog box, the user must indicate in which folder and under what name the document should be saved. Toolboxes are simply dialog boxes with graphical options that are treated in the same way as other options.

Save As dialog box

A *property sheet* is a dialog box that displays information about an object (the object's properties). For example, the **System Properties** property sheet shows information regarding devices that are installed and how the system is performing. Property sheets have command buttons. When properties can be edited, property sheets can also contain options. Both dialog boxes and property sheets can have tabbed pages that group similar sets of options or properties.

System Properties property sheet

In most content, treat elements in dialog boxes and property sheets the same way. In general, avoid using *dialog box* or *property sheet* as a descriptor. If you cannot avoid a descriptor, use *dialog box* for both property sheets and dialog boxes unless your project style sheet provides different guidance. The distinction may be important for software developers and information technology professionals, but do not distinguish in content for home users or information workers.

In content for software developers, buttons and other dialog box elements are called *controls*, especially in discussions about creating them. Do not use *control* in content for home users or information workers.

> **Note:** In some hardware products, buttons, switches, and so on are called controls because they give the user control over various actions. For example, users use joystick controls to move around the screen, especially in action games. This usage is all right as long as the meaning is clear.

Dialog box syntax

These terms are most commonly used to describe user actions in dialog boxes:

- **Click:**   Use for commands, command buttons, option buttons, and options in a list, gallery, or palette.

- **Select and clear:**   Use for check boxes.

- **Type or select:**   Use to refer to an item (as in a combo box) that the user can either type or select in the accompanying text box. You can use *enter* instead if there is no possibility of confusion.

1

Except for the identifiers *box*, *list*, *check box*, and *tab*, the generic name of an item within a dialog box (*button*, *option*, and so on) should not follow the item's label, especially within procedures. *Check box* in particular helps localizers differentiate this item from other option boxes.

Use bold type in procedures for dialog box titles, labels, and options.

Correct

To view bookmarks

1. On the **Tools** menu, click **Options**, and then click the **View** tab.

2. Select the **Bookmarks** check box.

For more information, see *Procedures* in Chapter 9, "Common Style Problems."

Dialog box elements

In most content, especially for home users and information workers, do not differentiate between drop-down combo boxes, list boxes, and text boxes. Refer to such elements by their label, and use a descriptor only if necessary for clarity. If you must use a descriptor, use *list* or *box*. Do use the term *check box*, however.

The following table describes the various elements that can appear in dialog boxes. Except where noted, avoid using the element name except in a discussion about designing a user interface. Use lowercase for the name of the descriptor ("the **Spaces** check box"). In general, use sentence-style capitalization for the specific element.

Element name	Definition	Usage	Example
Check box*	Square box that is selected or cleared to turn on or off an option. More than one check box can be selected.	Select the **Spaces** check box. –or– Click to clear the **Bookmarks** check box. –or– Under **Show**, select the **Draft font** check box. **Note:** Always include *check box* with the label name.	Effects ☐ Strikethrough ☐ Shadow ☐ Small caps ☐ Double strikethrough ☐ Outline ☐ All caps ☐ Superscript ☐ Emboss ☐ Hidden ☐ Subscript ☐ Engrave

Element name	Definition	Usage	Example
Combo box	Text box with a list box attached. The list is always visible. Because users can either type or select their choice, you can use *enter* to describe the action. Follow your project style sheet.	In the **Font** box, type or select the font you want to use. –or– In the **File Name** box, enter a file name.	
Command button	Rectangular button that initiates an action. A command button label ending with ellipses indicates that another dialog box will appear: More information is needed before the action can be completed.	Click **Options**.	
Drop-down arrow	Arrow associated with a drop-down combo or list box or some toolbar buttons, indicating a list the user can view by clicking the arrow.	Click the **Size** arrow to see more options.	
Drop-down combo box	Closed version of a combo box with an arrow next to it. Clicking the arrow opens the list.	In the **Size** box, type or select a point size.	

1

Element name	Definition	Usage	Example
Drop-down list box	Closed version of a list box with an arrow next to it. Clicking the arrow opens the list. Depending on the type of list, use either *list* or *box*, whichever is clearer.	In the **Item** list, click **Desktop**.	
Group box	Frame or box that encloses a set of related options. In Windows XP, a group box can be indicated by a single line that unifies the options below it. The group box is a visual device only. If necessary for clarity, you can use either *under* followed by the label or *in the [name of group] area*.	Click **Small Caps**. –or– Under **Effects**, click **Small Caps**. –or– In the **Effects** area, click **Small Caps**.	
Label (do not use *caption*)	Text attached to any option, box, command, and so on. Refer to any option, box, and so on by its label.	In the **Font** list, click **Arial**.	

Element name	Definition	Usage	Example
List box	Any type of box containing a list of items the user can select. The user cannot type a selection in a list box. Depending on the type of list, use either *list* or *box*, whichever is clearer.	In the **Wallpaper** list, click the background wallpaper of your choice.	
Option button (avoid *radio button*)	Round button used to select one of a group of mutually exclusive options.	Click **Portrait**.	
Slider* (also called *trackbar control* in some developer content)	Indicator on a gauge that displays and sets a value from a continuous range, such as speed, brightness, or volume.	Move the slider to the right to increase the volume.	
Spin box (do not use *spinner* or other labels)	Text box with up and down arrows that the user clicks to move through a set of fixed values. The user can also type a valid value in the box.	In the **Date** box, type or select the part of the date you want to change.	
Tab* (also called *tabbed page* in technical documentation)	Labeled group of options used for many similar kinds of settings.	On the **Tools** menu, click **Options**, and then click the **View** tab. **Note:** Always include *tab* with the label name.	

1

Element name	Definition	Usage	Example
Text box	Rectangular box in which the user can type text. If the box already contains text, the user can select that default text or delete it and type new text.	In the **Size** box, select **10** or type a new font size. –or– In the **Size** box, enter a font size. **Note:** You can use *enter* if there is no chance of confusion.	Find what: [ ] File name: [Document1.doc ▼]
Title (do not use *caption*)	Title of the dialog box. It usually, but not always, matches the title of the command name. Refer to the dialog box by its title when necessary, especially if the user needs to go to a new tab.	In the **Options** dialog box, click the **View** tab.	Options [?][X]
Unfold button	Command button with two "greater than" signs (>>) that enlarges a secondary window to reveal more options or information.	Click **Profiles** for more information.	[Details >>]

Check box, *tab*, and *slider* are the only terms in this table that should typically be used in end-user documentation.

For more information, see *Document Conventions* in Chapter 2, "Content Formatting and Layout."

See Also: *dialog box*

Unnamed Buttons
If you refer to unnamed buttons that appear in the interface, use the syntax given in the example and insert a bitmap showing the button, if possible.

Correct

Click the **Minimize** button.

Most buttons are named in ToolTips, so if it is impossible to use inline graphics, use the name only.

For more information, see *Screen Terminology* in this chapter.

Menus and Commands
Menus contain commands. Dialog boxes contain command buttons and options. Do not refer to a command as a *menu item* (except in content for software developers about the user interface), a *choice*, or an *option*. Refer to a command button simply as a *button* in content for general audiences.

Users can customize the menu bar and toolbar by adding additional menus, by putting menus on toolbars, and by dragging toolbar buttons to a menu. Customization does not change the essential characteristics of these items, however. They should still be treated as menus, commands, and toolbar buttons.

Users *click* menu items. If you must refer to the user action of opening a menu, use *click*. To open a submenu, the user *points to* a command on the main menu, which causes the submenu to open, and then *clicks* the appropriate command.

Correct

On the **File** menu, click **Open**.

On the **View** menu, point to **Toolbars**, and then click **Formatting**.

The following illustration shows elements of menus. In most content, it should not be necessary to refer to user interface elements by their names; the usual practice, here as elsewhere in the user interface, is to refer to elements by their labels.

Note: The callouts in the illustration use callout style.

1

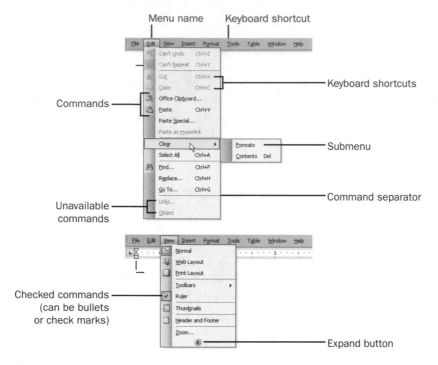

Menu elements

Menu terminology

- When referring to a specific menu, use lowercase for the word *menu*, as in "the **Edit** menu."

- Avoid the words *cascading*, *pull-down*, *drop-down*, or *pop-up* to describe menus except in some programming documents. For more information, see *Types of Menus* in this section.

- Refer to unavailable commands and options as *unavailable*, not as *dimmed*, *disabled*, or *grayed*. In programming contexts, however, it is all right to refer to unavailable commands as *disabled*. If you are describing the appearance of an unavailable command or option, use *dimmed*, but not *grayed* or *disabled*.

Correct

There are several unavailable commands on the **Edit** menu.

If the **Paste** command is unavailable, first select the text you want to paste, and then choose **Cut** or **Copy**.

The **Paste** command appears dimmed because it is unavailable.

A disabled control is unavailable to the user. [Content for software developers]

14

Incorrect

There are several dimmed commands on the **Edit** menu.

If the **Paste** command is disabled, first select the text you want to paste, and then choose **Cut** or **Copy**.

The **Paste** command appears grayed because it is unavailable.

- Names of menus and menu commands are distinct elements on the screen. Do not combine the two names into one.

Correct

On the **File** menu, click **Open**.

Incorrect

Click **File Open**.

- In general, mention the name of the menu the first time you refer to a particular command. However, if the location of the command is clear from the immediate context (for example, a topic about the **Edit** menu), you may not need to mention the menu name.

Correct

In Control Panel, click the **File** menu, and then click **Open**.

If the **Paste** command on the **Edit** menu is unavailable, first select the text you want to paste, and then choose **Cut** or **Copy**. You now should be able to choose **Paste** to insert the text in its new location.

Types of menus In content for home users and information workers, do not qualify the term *menu* with the adjective *drop-down*, *pull-down*, or *pop-up* unless the way the menu works needs to be emphasized as a feature of the product. *Shortcut menu* is acceptable, although in most cases you can avoid it. Do not use any of these terms as verbs.

Correct

Open the **File** menu.

When you click the right mouse button, a shortcut menu appears.

Incorrect

Drop down the **File** menu.

When you click the right mouse button, a shortcut menu pops up.

In technical material, however, you might need to detail these specific kinds of menus to differentiate their programming constructions:

- Drop-down menu
- Pop-up menu
- Shortcut menu
- Submenu

1

Style of menu names and commands   The following style guidelines apply to menu and command names:

- Always surround menu names with the words *the* and *menu* both in text and procedures.

  Correct

  On the **File** menu, click **Open**.

  Incorrect

  On **File**, click **Open**.

  From **File**, click **Open**.

- In procedures, do not surround command names with the words *the* and *command*. In text, you can use "the ... command" for clarity.

  Correct

  On the **File** menu, click **Open**.

  Incorrect

  On the **File** menu, click the **Open** command.

  On the **File** menu, choose the **Open** command.

- Do not use the possessive form of menu and command names.

  Correct

  The **Open** command on the **File** menu opens the file.

  Incorrect

  The **File** menu's **Open** command opens the file.

- Follow the interface for capitalization, which usually will be title caps, and use bold formatting. Do not capitalize the identifier such as *menu* or *command*.

  Correct

  On the **Options** menu, click **Keep Help on Top**.

  Incorrect

  On the Options menu, click Keep Help On Top.

Control Panel   Control Panel contains *icons* that represent different Control Panel *items*. Do not use *applets*, *programs*, or *control panels* to refer to either the icons or the items. Use bold text for the names of the icons and items.

If you cannot avoid identifying Control Panel by a category, use *the Control Panel application* in content for software developers or information technology professionals, or *the Control Panel program* in content for home users and information workers. For a mixed audience, use *program*.

1

When documenting an alternate path to Control Panel items, use *To open [name of item]*, with the name of the item in bold type.

When referring to Control Panel itself, use roman type except when you are referring to the command on the **Start** menu. In that case, use bold type.

Do not use *the* when referring to Control Panel.

Correct

In Control Panel, open Network Connections.

To open Network Connections, click **Start**, click **Control Panel**, and then double-click **Network Connections**.

Control Panel (Category View)

Mouse Terminology
These sections describe how to refer to the mouse itself; how to use verbs such as *click*, *point*, and *drag* that refer to mouse actions; and how to handle mouse procedures.

Referring to the mouse

- Avoid using the plural *mice*; if you need to refer to more than one mouse, use *mouse devices*.

- Do not use *cursor* or *mouse cursor* to refer to the pointer. Use *pointer* or *mouse pointer* instead.

1

- It is best to use a graphic to describe the various ways the mouse pointer can appear on the screen. If that is not possible, use descriptive labels for mouse pointers. Do not, however, use a graphic or a descriptive label as a synonym for *pointer*.

Correct

When the pointer becomes a ⁺‖⁺, drag the pointer to move the split line.

When the pointer becomes a double-headed arrow, drag the pointer to move the split line.

Incorrect

When the pointer becomes a double-headed arrow, drag the double-headed arrow to move the split line.

- Use *right mouse button*, not other terms such as *mouse button 2* or *secondary mouse button*. Regardless of accuracy, users understand this term and users who reprogram their buttons make the mental shift.

- The Microsoft mouse that includes a wheel and wheel button is the *IntelliMouse pointing device*. Note capitalization. Always use *IntelliMouse* as an adjective, but do not use *the IntelliMouse mouse*.

- Use *wheel button* to refer to the third (middle) button on the IntelliMouse pointing device. Use *rotate* to refer to movement of the wheel itself, and they *click* the wheel button.

Using mouse verbs

- In general, use *point to*, not *move the mouse pointer to*. The latter is acceptable only in teaching beginning skills.

Correct

Point to the window border.

- Use *click*, not *click on*.

Correct

Using the mouse, click the **Minimize** button.

- Use *click* with a file, command, or option name, as in *click **OK***; but use *in* to refer to clicking in a general area within a window or dialog box, not *click the window* or *click the **Styles** box*.

Correct

To see the **Control** menu, right-click anywhere in the window.

Click in the window to make it active.

Incorrect

To see the **Control** menu, right-click the window.

1

- Always hyphenate *double-click* and *right-click* as verbs.

  Correct

  Double-click the Word icon.

  Right-click to see the shortcut menu.

- Use *press and hold the mouse button* only to teach beginning skills.

- Use *drag*, not *click and drag*. Use *press and drag* only in entry-level products. The *drag* action includes holding down a button while moving the mouse and then releasing the button.

- Use *drag*, not *drag and drop*, for the action of moving a document or folder. It is all right to use *drag-and-drop* as an adjective, as in "moving the folder is a drag-and-drop operation."

  Correct

  Drag the folder to the desktop.

- Use *rotate*, not *roll*, to refer to rotating the IntelliMouse wheel.

  Correct

  Rotate the IntelliMouse wheel forward to scroll up in the document.

- In general, use *mouse button* to indicate the left mouse button. Use *left mouse button* only to teach beginning skills or in a discussion of more than one mouse button, when not referring to the *left mouse button* would create ambiguity.

- Use right-click to mean "click with the right mouse button" after you have clarified the meaning.

  Correct

  You can click with the right mouse button (called *right-click*) to see a shortcut menu.

- When more than one mouse button is used within a procedure, identify only the least commonly used button.

  Correct

  With the right mouse button, double-click the icon.

Documenting mouse procedures

- Be consistent in the way you list mouse procedures. For example, always list the mouse method before listing the keyboard method if you document both.

- Do not combine keyboard and mouse actions as if they were keyboard shortcuts.

  Correct

  Hold down SHIFT and click the right mouse button.

  Incorrect

  SHIFT+click the right mouse button.

1

Messages

In content for home users and information workers, messages are online descriptions, instructions, or warnings that inform the user about the product or about conditions that may require special consideration. Refer to these simply as *messages*, not *alerts*, *error messages*, *message boxes*, or *prompts*. Include the term *error message* in indexes, however.

Error message is acceptable in content for software developers to describe messages that indicate an error condition.

When explaining a message, include the situation in which the message occurs, the message text, and what the user should do to continue. If the wording of the message is not final in the product as you are writing, use a paraphrase. Do not use special formatting (such as monospace or bold) or title capitalization to set off messages from surrounding text. Set messages off on a separate line, or enclose them in quotation marks, as appropriate.

Interactive messages

An interactive message requires a response, such as clicking **OK**. For example, warning messages require the user to confirm an action before it is carried out. There are three types of interactive messages, which are described in the following table.

Symbol	Name	Description	Example
	Information	Provides information about the results of a command. Offers the user no choice.	Setup completed successfully.
	Warning	Informs the user about a situation that may require a decision, such as replacing an existing version of a document with a new one.	Do you want to save changes to Document 1?
	Critical	Informs the user about a situation that requires intervention or correction before work can continue, such as a network being unavailable. Also used as the **Stop** button in Microsoft Internet Explorer.	The computer or sharename could not be found. Make sure you typed it correctly and try again.

Note: Do not use the question mark symbol ( ) to indicate a message that appears in the form of a question. Users may confuse it with the Help symbol.

Informative messages

Informative messages can also appear in the status bar at the bottom of the screen, in balloons, or in desktop alerts (messages that pop up from the Windows notification area). A message in a program might tell the user the location within a document, for example. A

1

command message in the status bar tells the user what the selected command will do. A desktop alert might notify the user of new mail.

Use present tense for informative messages that explain what a command does. The following example describes the **New** command on the Word **File** menu.

Correct

Creates a new document or template.

Writing messages

Messages should be clear, concise, and specific. Whenever appropriate, they should describe an action the user should take. When you write error messages, do not make the reader feel stupid or at fault, even if the problem is a result of user error. It is all right to use the passive voice to describe the error condition. It is all right to make third-person reference to the operating system or the program.

When you write messages, follow these guidelines:

- Avoid vague wording. Give specific names and locations of the objects involved.

- Avoid "please." It can be interpreted to mean that a required action is optional.

- Avoid uppercase text and exclamation points.

- Do not refer to implementation details that are invisible to the user. For example, do not refer to the names of functions or objects in the program.

- Avoid phrasing that will seem silly to the user, such as "unexpected error."

- Avoid using placeholder variables in the middle of a message. They are very hard to localize.

Correct

The name of the object file conflicts with that of another program in the project. File name: %s

Works did not find a match for this term.

Incorrect

You have named the object file with the name of another program in the project. File name: %s

The term you typed does not appear in this Works file.

For warning or critical messages, include an action the user can take to remedy the situation. If that is not possible, the message should include a Help button that links to a Help topic written especially for the message. For example, the following message includes the compiler string, which can be useful to product support staff. The additional information gives users a possible way to solve the problem.

1

Useful message

502 Authentication error. Could not authorize your password with the News Server.

Try an anonymous connection by removing your user name and password from the Communications dialog box.

Providing only an **OK** button on messages annoys many readers. They may accept the situation, but they do not consider it "OK." Although some user action is required to close the message box, use a more friendly or logical term on the command button, such as "Close."

See Also: *message box; prompt*

Key Names   In general, spell key names as they appear in the following list, whether the name appears in text or in a procedure. Use all uppercase unless otherwise noted.

Note: This list applies to Microsoft and IBM-type keyboards unless otherwise noted. For more information about keys on the Microsoft Natural Keyboard, see Microsoft Natural Keyboard Key Names later in this section.

Correct

ALT

ALT GR

Application key [Microsoft Natural Keyboard only]

arrow keys [Do not use direction keys, directional keys, or

movement keys.]

BACKSPACE

BREAK

CAPS LOCK

CLEAR

CTRL

DELETE

DOWN ARROW [Use "the" and "key" with the arrow keys except in key combinations or key sequences. Always spell out. Do not use graphical arrows.]

END

ENTER

ESC [Always use ESC, not ESCAPE or Escape.]

F1–F12

HOME

INSERT

LEFT ARROW [Use "the" and "key" with the arrow keys except in key combinations or key sequences.]

NUM LOCK

PAGE DOWN

PAGE UP

PAUSE

PRINT SCREEN

RESET

RIGHT ARROW [Use "the" and "key" with the arrow keys except in key combinations or key sequences.]

SCROLL LOCK

SELECT

SHIFT

SPACEBAR [Precede with "the" except in procedures, key combinations, or key sequences.]

SYS RQ

TAB [Use "the" and "key" except in key combinations or key sequences.]

UP ARROW [Use "the" and "key" with the arrow keys except in key combinations or key sequences.]

Windows logo key

Spell key names that do not appear in this list as they appear on the keyboard.

When telling a user to "press" a key, format the key name in all uppercase. When telling a user to "type" a key, use lowercase bold, unless an uppercase letter is required.

Correct

Press Y.

Type **y**.

Note: Format punctuation according to intended use. If the user must type the punctuation, use bold. If not, use roman.

At first mention, you can use *the* and *key* with the key name if necessary for clarity—for example, "the F1 key." At all subsequent references, refer to the key only by its name—for example, "press F1."

For the arrow keys and the TAB key, list only the key name in key combinations without *the* and *key*.

Correct

To move the insertion point, use the LEFT ARROW key.

To extend the selection, press SHIFT+LEFT ARROW.

1

Special character names

Because these keys could be confused with an action (such as +) or be difficult to see, always spell out the following special character names: PLUS SIGN, MINUS SIGN, HYPHEN, PERIOD, and COMMA.

Correct

SHIFT+PLUS SIGN

Press ALT, HYPHEN, C.

Press COMMA.

Press COMMAND+PERIOD.

Type an em dash.

Press the PLUS SIGN (+).

Incorrect

SHIFT+ +

SHIFT+ -

Press +.

It is all right to add the symbol in parentheses after the special character, for example, PLUS SIGN (+), if necessary to avoid confusion. Use discretion in adding symbols, however. It may not be necessary for commonly used symbols such as PERIOD (.).

Microsoft Natural Keyboard key names

For conceptual topics and descriptions of programmable keys on the Microsoft Natural Keyboard, use the name of the key followed by its icon in parentheses at the first reference. For subsequent references, use the icon alone if possible. Note, however, that inline graphics affect line spacing, so using the name only may be preferable. The key name appears with an initial capital only, not in all uppercase.

Correct

You can define the Application key (▤) to open any program you want, and then

press ▤ to open that program.

Then press the Application key to open that program.

Incorrect

Press the WINDOWS LOGO key.

Names of keyboard "quick access" keys

Terms in current or recent use are listed in the following table. See the specific topics for more details.

Table 1.1: Keyboard "Quick Access" Keys

Name	Alternative name	Definition	Audience
Accelerator key		Now obsolete in all uses	Do not use.
Access key	Keyboard shortcut	Keyboard sequence corresponding to underlined letter on a menu name or command	Technical only. If a term is necessary, use *keyboard shortcut* in end-user documents.
Hot key		Key or key combination that activates a TSR (memory-resident program)	Obsolete. Use *keyboard shortcut.*
Quick key			Do not use.
Shortcut key		Key that corresponds to a command name on a menu, such as CTRL+Z	Technical only. If a term is necessary, use *keyboard shortcut* in end-user documents.
Speed key			Do not use.

Keyboard shortcuts

In most situations, it should be sufficient to refer to a *key combination* or *key sequence* by the keys that make it up. To specify a key combination, use the plus sign between the keys to be pressed. To specify a key sequence, use commas and spaces to indicate the sequence in which the keys must be pressed.

Correct

To undo the last action, press CTRL+Z.

To open a file, press ALT, F, O.

To show a key combination that includes punctuation that requires use of the SHIFT key, such as the question mark, add SHIFT to the combination and give the name or symbol of the shifted key. Using the name of the unshifted key, such as 4 rather than $, could be confusing to users or even wrong; for instance, the ? and / characters are not always shifted keys on every keyboard. Do, however, spell out the names of the plus and minus signs, hyphen, period, and comma.

Correct

CTRL+SHIFT+?

CTRL+SHIFT+*

CTRL+SHIFT+COMMA

1

Incorrect

CTRL+SHIFT+/

CTRL+?

CTRL+SHIFT+8

CTRL+*

If you must use a term to describe a keyboard shortcut, use *keyboard shortcut*. In content for software developers or in material that pertains to customizing the user interface, a more specific term such as *key combination* or *key sequence* may be needed.

See Also: key combination; key sequence; keyboard shortcut

Command Syntax   Although computer users today do most of their work with the graphical user interface, there are still many tasks that require typing commands or running programs at a command prompt.

For elements that the user must type as they appear in the text, use bold. For elements that are placeholders representing information the user must supply, use italic.

> **Note:** In text files where formatting is unavailable, substitute all uppercase for bold and all lowercase for italic.

The general form for presenting command syntax is as follows:

sample {**+r** | **−r**} *argument* ... [*option*]

where:

Element	Meaning
sample	Specifies the name of the command or utility.
{ }	Indicates a set of choices from which the user must choose one.
|	Separates two mutually exclusive choices in a syntax line. The user types one of these choices, not the symbol.
argument	Specifies a variable name or other information the user must provide, such as a path and file name.
...	Indicates that the user can type multiple arguments of the same type. The user types only the information, not the ellipsis (...).
[ ]	Indicates one or more optional items. The user types only the information within the brackets, not the brackets themselves.

1

Correct

chkdsk [*volume:*] [*Path*] [*FileName*] [**/v**] [**/r**] [**/x**] [**/i**] [**/c**] [**/l:***size*]

doskey {**/reinstall** | **/listsize=***size* | **/macros:**[{**all** | *exename*}] | **/history**
| **/insert** | **/overstrike** | **/exename=***exename* | **/macrofile=***FileName*
| **macroname=**[*text*]}

For more information, see *Document Conventions* in Chapter 2, "Content Formatting and Layout," and *Procedures* in Chapter 9, "Common Style Problems."

File Names and Extensions
For new and revised documentation for Windows, use title caps for file names and directory and drive names. Use all lowercase for extensions.

Correct

.htm file

C:\Taxes\April2003

My Tax File, 2003

It is all right to use internal caps for readability in concatenated file names if they cannot be confused with function names.

Correct

MyTaxFile

Mytaxfile

Avoid using the file name extension to identify the type of file under discussion. Use more descriptive language instead.

Correct

A Microsoft Excel workbook contains one or more worksheets. Store the result as a text file.

Incorrect

An .xls file contains one or more worksheets. Store the result as a .txt file.

If you must use the file name extension as a word, precede the extension with a period. Use the article (*a* or *an*) that applies to the sound of the first letter of the extension, as if the period (or "dot") is not pronounced, as in "a .com file" and "an .exe file." In a title or heading, capitalize as you would other common nouns.

Correct

Initialization information is stored in an .ini file.

Saving an .Rtf File as a .Doc File [heading]

1

Sometimes the file name extension corresponds to the abbreviation of the generic term for the file. For example, a .dll file contains a dynamic-link library (DLL). Do not confuse the abbreviation with the file name extension. For example, a .dll file (not DLL file) contains a DLL.

When instructing users to type literal file names and paths, use all lowercase and bold type. Use italic type for placeholders.

Correct

At the command prompt, type **c:\msmail\msmail.mmf** *password*

Note: Do not use *Foo, Fu, Foo.bar*, and the like as a placeholder for a file name. Use a substitute such as *Sample File* or *MySample* instead.

For more information, see *Document Conventions* in Chapter 2, "Content Formatting and Layout," and *Capitalization* in Chapter 9, "Common Style Problems."

See Also: *file name extension, extension*

Chapter 2
Content Formatting and Layout

An effective design can help customers in finding information quickly and efficiently. Essential to any design is the consistent application of standard formatting and layout. This chapter contains the following sections:

- Art, Captions, and Callouts
- Cross-References
- Document Conventions
- Headings and Subheadings
- Line Breaks
- Lists
- Marginal Notes
- Page Breaks
- Tables
- Notes and Tips

Art, Captions, and Callouts   Art can be most effective in providing an example of the topic under discussion or in showing hierarchies or complex relationships that are difficult to explain in words. Because art is expensive to localize and because it can take up a great deal of disk space and screen space, use art only if it is the best method for communicating a point.

Make sure that your art complements or supplements ideas that are also expressed in text. If you make your point only in art, blind and sight-impaired readers will not get the information. Provide alt text that is brief but as descriptive as possible.

Do not rely on color alone to communicate the point of an illustration. Readers who are colorblind will not see what you are highlighting.

Be aware of the impact of your art on the worldwide audience. Images that are perfectly innocuous for the U.S. audience may be deeply offensive elsewhere. Images and other elements of art, including color, can raise serious cultural or geopolitical issues.

For details on creating art that is suitable for the worldwide audience, see *Global Art* in Chapter 3, "Global Content."

If your content is being localized, avoid screen shots and illustrations that include text. Text in art is expensive to localize, and screen shots are unnecessary if the reader has access to the user interface.

The appearance and placement of art are determined by the specific design guidelines for your content. Consult your designer or any available documentation of your document template for guidelines on the placement and appearance of art, captions, and callouts.

Content

In printed content, information that appears in captions and callouts should also generally appear in text, unless there is no possibility of misreading or confusion and the art appears in the immediate textual context. However, online content and some printed documents require essential or procedural information to be placed solely in captions and callouts. This is acceptable, but doing so can affect accessibility.

Not all art needs captions or callouts, even within the same document. Use editorial judgment or see your project style sheet.

Always provide a brief description or a caption for a graphic on a Web page.

See Also: alt text

Cross-references to art

Make cross-references to untitled or unnumbered art only if the relation of the art to the text is not immediately apparent or the content of the art furthers the explanation found in the text. In that case, a reference to the art can be helpful; however, the art should appear as close to the reference as possible so that you can refer to the art with a phrase such as "the following illustration."

Avoid making cross-references to art unless the art immediately precedes or follows the reference within the Help topic or on the page.

Use *preceding* and *following* (or more specific references) when referring to art, not *above*, *below*, *earlier*, or *later*. End the introductory sentence with a period, not a colon.

Correct

The following illustration shows file sharing with user-level access control.

Captions

You can use both title captions and descriptive captions within the same document. Use sentence-style capitalization for both kinds of captions.

Title captions label a piece of art and should be concise. Do not use end punctuation. Some groups use numbered titles for art. In that case, the pieces are referred to as "figures," for example, Figure 7.1, Arcs.

Figure 10.1   The Internet Options dialog box

Descriptive captions explain something about the art, but do not necessarily point to or call out anything in particular about the art. Writers and editors determine how to write descriptive captions and when to use them. Use end punctuation only if the caption is a complete sentence or a mixture of fragments and sentences.

Beziers screen saver, just one of the screen savers included with Windows XP

Callouts

A callout points to a specific item that the reader should notice in an illustration. Observe the following rules when writing callouts:

- Capitalize each callout unless it begins with an ellipsis.

- End the callout with a period only if the callout is a complete sentence.

- Avoid mixing fragments and complete sentences as callouts for the same piece of art. If you must, use the end punctuation that is appropriate to each callout.

2

My Documents

① Double-click My Documents. Find the file or folder you want to send, and then click it.

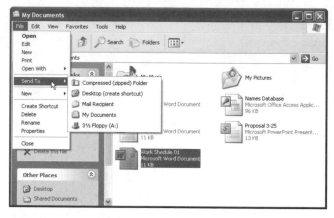

② On the File menu, point to Send To, and then click where you want to send the file or folder

Sample callouts

- For multiple-part callouts with ellipses, use lowercase for the first word in the second part of the callout. Leave one space between the ellipsis and the text that accompanies it, as shown in the example.

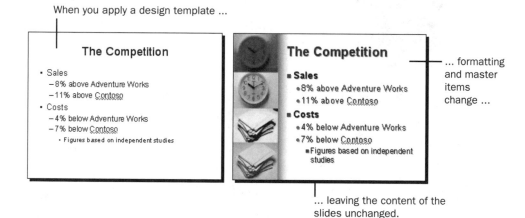

When you apply a design template ...

... formatting and master items change ...

... leaving the content of the slides unchanged.

Using ellipses in callouts

For more information, see *Headings and Subheadings* in this chapter and *Ellipses* in Chapter 11, "Punctuation."

Cross-References Use cross-references to direct users to related information that might add to their understanding of a concept.

Try to write and edit so that you use cross-references only for material that is not essential to the task at hand. For example, users should not have to look up material to complete a procedure. If the material has too many cross-references, consider restructuring it.

Material written for programmers or information technology professionals can have more cross-references than material written for home users or information workers.

Different products have different requirements and methods for referring to other material. Always consult your project style sheet for specific information about using and formatting cross-references.

Do not provide cross-references to a product, its user interface, or its application programming interface. Refer only to content about the product.

Correct

For information about available storage formats, see "Saving Your Document."

Incorrect

For information about available storage formats, see the **Save As** dialog box.

Avoid cross-references to material that is not within your control, especially hyperlinks. Web sites are always being modified and reorganized, and few things are as frustrating to the reader as an invalid cross-reference.

Blind cross-references

In text, avoid blind cross-references, which provide no information about why you are referring to the material. The reader should know whether it is worth interrupting the current topic for the cross-referenced material before following the reference.

Correct

For more information about modifying Visual Basic source code and installing Visual Basic forms, see Chapter 9, "Extending Forms."

Incorrect

See Chapter 9, "Extending Forms."

It is all right to use blind cross-references in a "See Also" or "Related Links" section or at the end of glossary entries.

Structure and style of cross-references

Information about why a cross-reference might be of interest should precede the cross-reference itself. That way, if the reason for following the cross-reference is not compelling, the reader can move on quickly.

Correct

For more information about modifying Visual Basic source code and installing Visual Basic forms, see Chapter 9, "Extending Forms."

Incorrect

See Chapter 9, "Extending Forms," for more information about modifying Visual Basic source code and installing Visual Basic forms.

For cross-references that provide additional information, say "For more information *about*," not "For more information *on*." Many international readers have trouble with the latter phrase.

If the cross-referenced material provides an extended discussion of the current topic, the introduction to the cross-reference can be general.

Correct

For details, see Chapter 9, "Extending Forms."

For cross-references to books or manuals, provide both a chapter number and title. If the reference is to material in the same chapter or short document (such as an article or white paper), provide a section title. In this case, explicitly note that the reference is to the current chapter or document. Use *earlier* or *later*, not *above* or *below*.

If a cross-reference refers to a section within a chapter or to a chapter in another publication, structure the cross-reference from the most specific to the most general reference; that is, section first, then chapter, then book title.

Correct

For information about creating new pages, see "Working with Page Files" in Chapter 6, "Creating Your Pages."

For information about arithmetic conversions, see "Usual Arithmetic Conversions" earlier in this white paper.

Incorrect

For details, see "Extending Forms."

For information about creating new pages, see Chapter 6, "Creating Your Pages," under the topic "Working with Page Files."

For online cross-references that are formatted as hyperlinks, use descriptive text for the hyperlink; do not use an empty expression, such as "Click here." Do not include ending punctuation in the hyperlink.

Correct

For more information about modifying Visual Basic source code and installing Visual Basic forms, see <u>Extending Forms</u>.

For details, see <u>Extending Forms</u>.

Incorrect

For more information about modifying Visual Basic source code and installing Visual Basic forms, <u>click here</u>.

Web-style hyperlinks, in which the reason for the cross-reference is implicit in the text, can be effective. Be sure, however, that the purpose of the link is clear.

Correct

You can save your document in a variety of <u>storage formats</u>.

Formatting of cross-references

Do not rely on color alone to indicate hyperlink text. Colorblind readers will not be able to see the links. Always provide a redundant visual cue, such as underlining.

When referring to a book, chapter, or section title, use title-style capitalization, even if the document you are referring to uses sentence-style capitalization.

Correct

For more information about modifying Visual Basic source code and installing Visual Basic forms, see <u>Extending Forms</u>.

Incorrect

For more information about modifying Visual Basic source code and installing Visual Basic forms, see <u>Extending forms</u>.

Cross-references in "See Also" sections

The style of providing "See Also" sections can vary a great deal, depending on the needs of the audience and the type of content that you are writing. For example, a "See Also" section in a programming reference is usually very basic, providing only blind cross-references to documentation for programming elements similar to the one under discussion. A "See Also" section in a white paper, by contrast, might provide extensive information about each cross-referenced item.

Titles of "See Also" sections can also vary. For example, such sections might be called "Related Topics" or, for cross-references that are exclusively hyperlinks, "Related Links." These sections can be formatted as pop-up windows, lists, or even margin text. Because such variations are project-specific, consult your project style sheet and be consistent in the way you format these sections.

Navigation tables

In printed content, you can provide a navigation table to direct the reader to information about a series of related tasks.

Correct

To	*See*
Route a Word document for review	"Have Your Group Review a Word Document," page 333
Fax a copy of a document	"Create a Fax Cover Sheet," page 157
Add fractions, exponents, integrals, and other mathematical elements to a document	"Equation Editor" in the Word online index

2

In general, table format is less useful in online content, in which the information in the left-hand column can simply be made into a hyperlink.

Correct

You can:

- Route a Word document for review.
- Fax a copy of a document.
- Add fractions, exponents, integrals, and other mathematical elements to a document.

Cross-references to art

Do not make cross-references to untitled or unnumbered art or tables unless the art or table immediately precedes or follows the reference.

Marginal cross-references

Cross-references that appear in the margin of a document can direct the reader to additional help or ideas without interrupting the flow of the main text. These marginal cross-references can follow standard cross-reference style, using a complete sentence and ending with a period, or they can include a graphic (such as the **Help** button) with a heading and the cross-reference. Use a consistent format within your group.

Correct

For more ideas, see "Writing and Correspondence" in *Getting Started*.

 See *Getting Started*

The following are some basic guidelines for marginal cross-references:

- Avoid cluttering a page with too many marginal cross-references; some groups limit notations to three per page.
- Try to limit marginal cross-references to about three or four lines. They expand when localized.
- Break lines so that they are about the same length.
- Follow the design for a specific project to determine whether to apply character formatting in marginal notations.

For more information, see *Marginal Notes*, *Notes and Tips*, and *Tables* in this chapter.

Document Conventions   Consistent text formatting helps users locate and interpret information easily. The following guidelines present some specific conventions for content.

In general, if you are asking the user to click an item, as in a procedure, apply bold text formatting to the item.

Note: Some elements may not appear here. Consult your project style sheet.

Item	Convention	Example
Accessory programs	Title caps.	Heap Walker Nmake Notepad
Acronyms	All uppercase; usually spelled out on first use.	common user access (CUA) first-in, first-out (FIFO)
Arguments (predefined)	Bold italic.	*expression*.**Add**(***Name, Range***)
Attributes	Bold; capitalization follows that of attribute name.	**IfOutputPrecision**
Book titles	Title caps, italic.	See the *Visual Basic Custom Control Reference*.
Chapter titles	Title caps, in quotation marks.	See Chapter 9, "Extending Forms."
Classes (predefined)	Bold; capitalization follows that of class name.	**ios** **filebuf**
Classes (user-defined)	Roman in text; capitalization follows that of class name. Monospace in code samples.	The class money consists ... `class money`

Code samples, including keywords and variables within text and as separate paragraphs, and user-defined program elements within text	Monospace.	`#include <iostream.h>`
		`void main ()`
		the pointer `psz`

Command-line commands and options (switches)	All lowercase, bold.	**copy** command **/a** option
Commands on menus and buttons	Bold in procedures; capitalization follows that of user interface.	**Date and Time** **Apply** **New Query** button
Constants	Normally bold; capitalization follows that of constant name. Treatment of constants can vary, so always consult your project style sheet.	**INT_MAX** **dbDenyWrite** **CS**

Item	Convention	Example
Control classes	All uppercase.	EDIT control class
Data formats	All uppercase.	CF_DIB
Data structures and their members (pre-defined)	Bold; capitalization follows that of the structure or member name.	**BITMAP** **bmbits** **CREATESTRUCT** **hInstance**
Data types	Bold; capitalization follows that of the application programming interface.	**DWORD** **float** **HANDLE**
Device names	All uppercase.	LPT1 COM1
Dialog box options	Bold in procedures; capitalization follows that of the user interface.	Click **Close all programs and log on as a different user?** **Find Entire Cells** Only check box
Dialog box titles	Bold; title caps.	**Protect Document** dialog box **Import/Export Setup** dialog box
Directives	Bold.	**#if** **extern "C"**
Directories	Initial caps (internal caps are acceptable for readability).	\\Irstaxforms\Public \\IRSTaxForms\Public
Environment variables	All uppercase.	INCLUDE SESSION_SIGNON
Error message names	Roman type; sentence-style capitalization.	Access denied
Event names	Bold; capitalization varies.	In the **OnClick** event procedure...
Extensions	All lowercase.	.mdb .doc
Fields (Members of a class or structure)	Bold; capitalization varies.	**IfHeight** **biPlanes**
File names	Title caps. Internal caps in short file names are acceptable for readability.	My Taxes for 1995 Msacc20.ini MSAcc20.ini

Item	*Convention*	*Example*
Folder and directory names	Bold in procedures if the user is to type the name as shown; title caps. Treatment may vary, so always consult your project style sheet.	My Documents Vacation and Sick Pay \\Accounting\Payroll\Vacpay
Functions (predefined)	Normally bold; capitalization follows that of function name. Treatment of function names can vary, so always consult your project style sheet.	**CompactDatabase** **CWnd::CreateEx** **FadePic**
Handles	All uppercase.	HWND
Hooks	All uppercase.	WH_CBT
Icon names	Bold in procedures if the user is to type the name as shown; title caps.	**Recycle Bin** In Control Panel, click **Add New Hardware.**
Indexes	All uppercase.	RASTERCAPS
Key names, key combinations, and key sequences	All uppercase.	CTRL, TAB CTRL+ALT+DEL SHIFT, F7 ALT, F, O
Keywords (language and operating system)	Bold; capitalization follows that of the user interface or the application programming interface.	**main** **True** **AddNew**
Logical operators	All uppercase, bold.	**AND** **XOR**
Macros	Normally all uppercase; bold if predefined; may be monospace if user-defined. Treatment of macro names can vary, so always consult your project style sheet.	**LOWORD** MASKROP
Members	Bold; capitalization follows that of the member name.	**ulNumCharsAllowed**
Members (fields)	Bold; capitalization follows that of the member or field name.	**lfHeight** **biPlanes**

2

Item	*Convention*	*Example*
Menu names	Bold in procedures; title caps.	**Insert** menu
Methods	Bold; capitalization follows that of the method name.	**OpenForm** **GetPrevious**
New terms or emphasis	Italic, unless your project style sheet specifies otherwise. **Note:** Italic type does not always show up well online. If necessary to accommodate low-resolution monitors, use quotation marks for new terms. Use italic type sparingly for emphasis.	Microsoft Exchange consists of both *server* and *client* components. You *must* close the window before you exit.
Operators	Bold.	**+, -** **sizeof**
Options (command-line)	Bold; case exactly as it must be typed.	**copy** command **/a** option **/Aw**
Parameters	Italic; capitalization varies from all lowercase to initial cap to lowercase with intermediate caps.	*hdc* *grfFlag* **ClientBinding**
Placeholders (in syntax and in user input)	Italic.	*[form] Graph.***Picture** Type *password*.
Programs, including utility and accessory programs	Usually title caps.	Microsoft Word Notepad Network Connections Lotus 1-2-3 for Windows Microsoft At Work Heap Walker Nmake
Properties	Normally bold. Capitalization follows that of the property name. Treatment of property names can vary, so always consult your project style sheet.	**M_bClipped** **AbsolutePosition** **Message ID**

Item	*Convention*	*Example*
Registers	All uppercase.	DS
Registry settings	Subtrees (first-level items): all uppercase, separated by underscores; usually bold. Registry keys (second-level items): capitalization follows user interface. Registry subkeys (below the second level): capitalization follows user interface, but consult your project style sheet.	**HKEY_CLASSES_ROOT HKEY_LOCAL_MACHINE SOFTWARE ApplicationIdentifier Microsoft**
Statements	All uppercase; bold.	**IMPORTS LIBRARY**
Strings	Sentence caps; enclosed in quotation marks.	"Now is the time"
Structures	All uppercase; usually bold.	**ACCESSTIMEOUT**
Switches	Usually lowercase; bold.	**build: commands**
System commands	All uppercase.	SC_HOTLIST
Toolbar button names	Usually title caps (follow the interface); bold.	**Format Painter Insert Microsoft Excel Worksheet**
URLs	All lowercase for fully specified URLs. Break long URLs before a forward slash, if necessary to break; do not hyphenate	*http://www.microsoft.com /seattle.sidewalk.com /music/* *www.microsoft.com*
User input	Usually lowercase (note also bold or italic, depending on element), unless to match standard capitalization conventions or if the user must match case exactly.	Type **-p** *password*
Utilities	Usually title caps.	Makefile RC Program
Values	All uppercase.	DIB_PAL_COLORS

Item	Convention	Example
Variables	Variable treatment; always consult your project style sheet for treatment of variables.	bEmpty **m_nParams** *file_name*
Views	Usually lowercase, but consult your product style sheet. Capitalize those based on proper names.	outline view chart view Gantt view Design view (Access)
Windows, named	Title caps.	Help window
Windows, unnamed	All lowercase.	document window

For more information, see *Command Syntax*, *File Names and Extensions*, *Key Names*, and *Menus and Commands* in Chapter 1, "Documenting the User Interface"; *Code Formatting Conventions* in Chapter 4, "Content for Software Developers"; *HTML Tag, Element, and Attribute Styling* and *XML Tag, Element, and Attribute Styling* in Chapter 5, "Web Content"; and *Urls, Addresses* in Chapter 9, "Common Style Problems."

See Also: *font and font style; registry, registry settings*

Headings and Subheadings

Headings should convey as much information as possible about the text that follows to help readers locate information quickly.

Heading style varies among groups. The guidelines in this section are widely used and can make it easier to share files across groups. If your group follows a different practice, however, use your group's style consistently.

Heading style and conventions

These guidelines apply to both online and printed content as much as is practicable:

- In the first sentence following any heading, do not assume that the reader has read the heading.

  Correct

  Finding Information in Help [Heading]

  When you click Help on the menu bar, Help commands appear.

  Incorrect

  Finding Information in Help [Heading]

  This is easy to do from the menu bar.

- Use italic type if it would be required in body text. For example, use italic type for placeholder variable names. Follow the capitalization of any case-sensitive terms, even if the capitalization conflicts with normal heading style.

Correct

Dereferencing the *pszIUnknown* Pointer

Incorrect

Dereferencing the pszIUnknown Pointer

Dereferencing the *PszIUnknown* Pointer

- Avoid beginning a heading with an article.

Correct

Parameters Tab

Incorrect

The Parameters Tab

- Use a gerund (-*ing* form) rather than an infinitive (*to* form) in titles of procedural topics, especially in print. After some brief context-setting information to help the reader decide if she has found the right topic, the heading that introduces the procedure itself should be an infinitive phrase.

Correct in topic headings

Running Programs and Managing Files

Modify a file [if authorized by project style sheet]

Incorrect in topic headings

To Run Programs and Manage Files

Correct in procedure headings

To modify a file

Modify a file [if authorized by project style sheet]

Incorrect in procedure headings

Modifying a file

Note: There is considerable variation across product groups in the heading style for procedural topics. If the differences are generally based on valid assessments of user needs, there is nothing wrong with them. In online product documentation, some groups provide only an infinitive heading and the procedure, reasoning that the work the user is doing at the time provides the necessary context. Other groups use "how to" in headings to avoid ambiguity for localization. Still other groups use the imperative form of the verb in topic headings. Consult your project style sheet, and whatever you do, use one form consistently.

2

- For material that does not describe a task, use a noun phrase.

Correct

Error Messages and Their Meanings

Visual Basic Controls

Accessory Programs

Incorrect

Understanding Error Messages and Their Meanings

About Visual Basic Controls

What Accessory Programs Are Included?

- Avoid beginning headings with "Using" or "Working with." Although occasionally useful in very general discussions, these phrases are vague, and they often focus on a product feature in the guise of describing a user task. Consider what the topic is really about, and rewrite the heading to describe either a user task or the concept or feature to be discussed.

Correct

Checking Your Spelling

Defining Control Properties

Incorrect

Using the Spell Checker

Working with Property Sheets

- In printed content, avoid headings of more than one line. If a heading must have two lines, try to make the first line longer than the second. For information about acceptable line breaks in headings, see *Line Breaks* in this chapter.

- Because readers normally act on one thing at a time, headings should normally use singular nouns. It is all right to use plural nouns when the plural is obviously more suitable.

Correct

Formatting a disk

Opening a new document

Managing Folders

- Use *vs.*, not *v.* or *versus*, in headings.

Correct

Daily Backups vs. Weekly Backups

- Do not use ampersands (&) in headings unless you are specifically reflecting the user interface or the application programming interface.

- Use title capitalization or sentence capitalization, depending on the level of heading and the design. Book-level headings in Help generally use title capitalization, but topics use sentence capitalization.

For rules of capitalization in headings, see *Capitalization* in Chapter 9, "Common Style Problems."

Organizational guidelines

Headings help orient users and make content, especially printed material, easier to scan. First-level headings usually apply to the most general material, and subsequent levels deal with more specific topics.

Follow these organizational guidelines for printed content:

- Apply the rules for outlining when organizing headings: When dividing a section, try to make the material fall under at least two subheadings. It is all right to have only one subsection within a section, but only if other methods (such as restructuring the section) will not convey the meaning as well.

- Every heading (except procedure headings) should have text between it and the next heading. However, avoid inserting "filler" text just to adhere to this rule. The intervening text should normally help the reader decide if what follows will be of interest. For example, a description of a user problem that the content will help solve can save the time of readers who have a different problem. Intervening text that seems perfunctory or lacking in content can indicate that restructuring is in order.

- Try to keep headings within a chapter, section, or other unit grammatically parallel, especially those at the same level.

For more information, see *Line Breaks*, *Lists*, *Page Breaks*, and *Tables* in this chapter; and *Capitalization* in Chapter 9, "Common Style Problems."

Line Breaks   Although the right text edge in printed documents is often not aligned, try to avoid very short lines that leave large amounts of white space at the end of a line. An extremely ragged right edge can distract the reader. If necessary, a copyeditor and desktop publisher can break lines manually during the final stages of production.

> **Note:** This section pertains primarily to printed content. Because users of online content can control the screen resolution, the font size, and the size of the browser window, you cannot control the appearance of screen text by explicitly inserting line breaks. You can *prevent* undesired line breaks onscreen by inserting nonbreaking spaces, but the effect on the surrounding text is impossible to predict.

2

Follow these basic rules for line breaks in printed content:

- Do not break a word if it leaves a single letter at the end of the line.
- Do not break a word if it leaves fewer than three letters at the beginning of the next line.

Correct

Be sure there are enough letters at the end of a line. Do
not leave fewer than three
letters at the begin-
ning of a line.

Incorrect

Be sure there are e-
nough letters at the end
of a line. Do not leave fewer than three letters at
the beginning of the next
line.

- Do not end a page with the first part of a hyphenated word.
- Avoid leaving fewer than four characters on the last line of a paragraph, especially if a heading follows.
- Do not hyphenate product names. Avoid breaking product names at the end of a line, especially on first mention.
- Avoid breaking URLs. If you must break them, do so at the end of a section of the address immediately before the next forward slash. Do not include a hyphen.

Correct

For more information, see *http://www.microsoft.com/support*

/products/developer/visualc/content/faq/

Incorrect

For more information, see *http://www.microsoft.com/support-*

/products/developer/visualc/content/faq/

For more information, see *http://www.microsoft.com/support/*

products/developer/visualc/content/faq/

- Try to keep headings on one line. If a two-line heading is unavoidable, break the lines so that the first line is longer. Do not break headings by hyphenating words, and avoid breaking a heading between the parts of a hyphenated word. It does not matter whether the line breaks before or after a conjunction, but avoid breaking between two words that are part of a verb phrase.

Correct

Bookmarks, Cross-References,

and Captions

Incorrect

Bookmarks, Cross-

References, and Captions

- Try not to break formulas, data that should be entered without spaces, or program examples. If a break is unavoidable, break between elements.

Correct

In the cell, type **=Budget!**

AH:C#+1

Incorrect

In the cell, type **=Budget!$A**

$H:$C$#+1

- Try to avoid breaking function names and parameters. If hyphenating is necessary, break these names between the words that make up the function or parameter, not within a word itself.

Correct

WinBroadcast-

Msg

Incorrect

WinBroad-

castMsg

- Do not hyphenate a line of command syntax or code. If you must break a line, break it at a character space, and do not use a hyphen. Indent the run-over when breaking a line of syntax or code. Do not use the line-continuation character unless it is necessary for the code to compile.

Correct

```
void CScribView::OnLButtonDown( UINT nFlags, Cpoint
    point )
```

Incorrect

```
void CScribView::OnLButtonDown( UINT nFlags, C-
point point)
```

For general rules about hyphenation and word division, see *Hyphens*, *Hyphenation* in Chapter 11, "Punctuation"; *The American Heritage Dictionary*; and *The Chicago Manual of Style*.

Lists

Depending on the type of material that you have to present, you can choose among several types of lists: bulleted, numbered, unnumbered single-column, unnumbered multicolumn, or a "term list." A list can incorporate a nested comment, an untitled table, or no more than one nested list.

A *table* is an arrangement of data with two or more columns in which the information in the first column in each row is related to the information in the other column or columns of the same row. A list of similar entries that is arranged in multiple columns is not a table but a multicolumn list—for example, a list of commands. A table usually has column headings and may have a title.

For more information, see *Tables* in this chapter.

Formatting lists

Introduce a list with a sentence or fragment ending with a colon. Begin each entry in a bulleted or numbered list with a capital letter.

If your writing is to be localized, be aware that the grammar and syntax of different languages can make it difficult to match the structure in English of an introductory fragment that is completed by each list element.

Make entries in a list parallel. End each entry with a period if all entries are complete sentences, if they are a mixture of fragments and sentences, or if they all complete the introductory sentence or fragment. An exception is when all entries are short imperative sentences (three words or fewer) or single words. These entries do not need ending punctuation. If all entries are fragments that together with the introductory phrase do not form a complete sentence, do not end them with periods.

If you introduce a list with a fragment, do not treat the list and its introduction like one continuous sentence: Do not use semicolons or commas to end list items, and do not insert *and* before the last list element.

Correct

If you use printer fonts:

- Choose a printer before creating a presentation.
- Install all the fonts and printers that you will use by selecting them in the **Print Setup** dialog box.

The database includes:

- Reports
- Forms
- Tables
- Modules

Incorrect

The database includes:

- Reports,
- Forms,
- Tables, and
- Modules.

Bulleted lists

Use a bulleted list for an unordered series of concepts, items, or options rather than a sequence of events or steps. Capitalize the first word of each bulleted entry.

Correct

The database owner can:

- Create and delete a database.
- Add, delete, or modify a document.
- Add, delete, or modify any information in the database.

Numbered lists

Use a numbered list for procedures or other sequential lists. Introduce a procedure with a heading that uses an infinitive phrase or imperative, depending on your group's style, and avoid explanatory text after the phrase. Capitalize the first word of each entry.

Correct

To log on to a database

1. On the **File** menu, click **Open Database**.
2. In **User Name**, type your name.
3. In **Password**, type your password, and then click OK.

2

Correct

The basic steps for adding scrolling to your application are as follows:

1. Define a size for your documents.
2. Derive your view class from **CScrollView**.
3. Pass the documents' size to the **SetScrollSizes** method of **CScrollView** whenever the size changes.
4. Convert between logical coordinates and device coordinates if you are passing points between GDI and non-GDI functions.

Unnumbered single-column and multicolumn lists

An unnumbered list consists of one or more columns of list entries, all of which are very short, so no bullets or numbers are required to separate one entry from another. Use an unnumbered list to group similar items—for example, a list of keywords. Use a single column for six or fewer items and use balanced multiple columns for seven or more items. You need not capitalize entries. If the list is alphabetical, alphabetize down the columns, not across rows, if possible.

Because there are no page breaks in online content, long multicolumn lists can be difficult to read. In this case, you can alphabetize from left to right (for shorter lists) or sort in labeled alphabetical sections. Alphabetical sections make navigating in long lists of items, such as functions, easier.

Correct

and

or

nor

for

addprocedure

checkpointrule

errorexitsum

nonclusteredtriggerover

A-C

AbsCDbl

AscChoose

AtnChr, Chr$

AvgCIntCLng

CcurCodeDB

D-E

Date, Date$ErrError, Error$

DateAddErl

Environ, Environ$EOF

Term lists

Use term lists, also called *term-def lists*, for a series of terms, parameters, or similar items that are followed by a brief explanation or definition. In the HTML style sheets, the term appears on its own line, usually in bold type, with the definition indented under it. The terms may use additional character formatting if appropriate. In other designs, the term might appear in italics, followed by a period, with the definition immediately following it on the same line.

Correct

Computer name

The name by which the local area network identifies a server or workstation. Each computer name on the network must be unique.

Computer name. The name by which the local area network identifies a server or workstation. Each computer name on the network must be unique.

Incorrect

Computer name—The name by which the local area network identifies a server or workstation. Each computer name on the network must be unique.

For more information, see *Parallelism* in Chapter 7, "Tone and Rhetoric."

Marginal Notes
In printed content, marginal notes, often labeled "Tips," usually accompany procedures to give hints, shortcuts, or background information that the user should know before proceeding. These notes should be easy to read and should help minimize long text or additional steps within the procedure. You can also use marginal notes next to tables and art.

In Help, the equivalent of these notes can be a jump to another step, a pop-up window offering additional information such as a definition, or a tip at the end of a topic.

Begin a marginal note at the first step of the procedure and end it before or at the last step. If possible, place it next to the step it refers to.

You can include a heading to show the subject of the marginal note, as shown in the first example.

Correct

About file names

Some restrictions apply to file names. See Saving and Naming Files.

Tip   If the Formatting toolbar does not appear, click **Toolbars** on the **View** menu, and then click **Formatting**.

The following are some basic guidelines for marginal notes:

- Avoid cluttering a page with too many marginal notes. Even three notes per page should be a rare occurrence.

- Try to limit marginal notes to about three or four lines. They expand when localized.

- Break lines so that they are about the same length.

- Follow the design for a specific project to determine whether or not to apply character formatting in marginal notes.

For more information, see *Notes and Tips* in this chapter and *Cross-References* in this chapter.

Page Breaks   Do not manually break pages in print documents until all art (or art spaces) and textual changes have been added to the manuscript. Page breaks are usually inserted just before the manuscript goes to final production.

The main goal is to keep related material on one page. If this isn't feasible, try to break pages so the user knows that relevant material continues on the next page. Recto (right) page breaks must be handled more carefully than those on a verso (left) page of a spread. Avoid leaving a recto page so short that it looks like the end of a chapter.

- Leave at least two lines of a paragraph at the bottom or top of a page. Do not break a word over a page.

- Avoid separating notes, tips, important notes, cautions, and warnings from the material that they concern.

- Keep material that introduces a procedure or bulleted list with the list. Keep at least two steps or list entries at the bottom or top of a page. A step's explanatory paragraph should accompany the step. Try to keep all steps in a procedure on one verso-recto page spread; avoid continuing a procedure from a recto to a verso page.

- Avoid breaking a table across pages, especially from a recto to a verso page. If breaking is unavoidable, leave the title (if applicable) and at least two rows of the table at the top or bottom of a page. At the top of the next page, repeat the table title—followed by *(continued)*, italic type, all lowercase, in parentheses—and repeat the column headings. If an item is footnoted, the footnote goes at the end of the table. Try to keep a table's introductory sentence with the table.

- Try to keep art on the same page as the material that it illustrates. Always keep an introductory phrase with its art.

- Try to have at least five or six lines on the last page of a chapter.

- In printed indexes, if the main entry is followed by subentries, do not leave the main entry alone at the bottom of the column.

- In printed indexes, if you must break up a list of subentries, at the top of the next column include the main entry followed by *(continued)*, italic type, all lowercase, in parentheses.

Tables   A table is an arrangement of data with two or more rows and two or more columns. Typically, the information in the first column describes something whose attributes are shown in the other columns. A single row shows all the attributes for one item. The format of a table can vary, depending on the project style.

A list of similar entries that is arranged in multiple columns is not a table but a multicolumn list—for example, a list of commands. For more details about lists, see *Lists* in this chapter.

A table usually has column headings, and it can optionally have a title. Introduce tables with a sentence that ends with a period, not a fragment that ends with a colon. If a table is titled, an introductory sentence does not have to immediately precede the table. The title appears above the table.

Tables for onscreen display should follow the same guidelines as tables in other content. Keep in mind these additional points, however:

- Table dimensions must be visible on a minimum screen resolution, typically 800 pixels by 600 pixels.

- Screen readers for the blind can form table text into columns, ignoring the table column format. Providing summary information about the table can help. If possible, arrange the data in the table so that it makes sense when read in a linear fashion.

- Tables can be used to simulate frames. In this case, tables are better because older browsers cannot always process frames correctly.

Capitalization and punctuation

If the table is titled, use title-style capitalization for the title. Capitalize only the first word of each column heading, the first word of each column entry, and proper nouns.

> **Note:** It is all right to use lowercase for the first word in column entries if capitalization might cause confusion—for example, a column of keywords that must be lowercase.

End each entry with a period if all entries are complete sentences or are a mixture of fragments and sentences. An exception is when all entries are short imperative sentences (only a few words); these entries do not need a period. If all entries are fragments, do not end them with periods.

Number tables in printed content if they are not adjacent to their text references or if a list of tables appears in the front matter. Do not number online tables. If you decide to number tables, use numbers consistently throughout the document. The numbers include the chapter number and a sequential table number, such as Table 2.1, Table 2.2, and so on.

Correct

Table 7.4   Formatting Flags

Formatting flag	Action
\a	Anchors text for cross-references
\b, \B	Turns bold on or off

Content

Follow these guidelines for organizing your table:

- Place information that identifies the contents of a row in the leftmost column of the table. For example, in a table that describes commands, put the command names in the left column. Place information about the item identified in the left column in associated columns to the right.

- Make entries in a table parallel—for example, in a description column, be consistent in your use of beginning the entries with a verb or noun.

Correct

Device name	Description
COM1	Serial port 1. This device is the first serial port in your computer.
CON	System console. This device consists of both the keyboard and the screen.
LPT1	Parallel port 1. This device represents a parallel port.

Command	Action
Bold	Turns bold on or off
Italic	Turns italic on or off

To move the insertion point	Press
To the first record	TAB
To a record you specify	ENTER

Incorrect

To	Do This
Close a window	Click **Minimize**.
Size a window	Press CTRL+F8
Copy a picture	The TAB key

- Do not leave a blank column entry. That is, if the information doesn't apply, use *Not applicable* or *None*. Do not use em dashes.

Correct

To	In Windows, press	On the Macintosh, press
Copy a picture	Not applicable	COMMAND+SHIFT+T

Column headings

Make column headings as concise and as precise as possible, but include information that is common to all column entries in the heading, rather than repeating it in each entry. Do not use ellipses.

In tables that list procedures, use active voice in column headings, preferably in phrases that reduce repetition in the entries in the table.

Some tables are organized so that the headings and table entries, read from left to right, form a complete sentence. It is all right to structure a table this way, but be careful if your writing is to be localized. The grammar and syntax of different languages can make it difficult to match the structure in English. For example, infinitives in many languages are only one word, so although the following example is correct, it can be difficult to localize in some languages.

Correct

To	Do this
Open a Web page	Type the address in the **Address** bar, and then press ENTER.
Add a Web page to your favorites list	Click **Favorites**, and then click **Add to Favorites**.

To save a document	Do this
To a folder	Click **Save**.
With a new name	Click **Save As**.
To a network location	Connect to the server location and folder, and then click **Save**.

To	Do this
Close a window	Click **Minimize**.
Size a window	Press CTRL+F8.

Formatting

Most table formatting is done within your design template. These guidelines suggest ways to make tables more readable.

- In printed content, try to limit tables with long entries to two or three columns. Four or more columns can be hard to read unless they contain brief numeric entries. The second column in the following example is approaching maximum readable length.

Addressing Declared with Keywords

Keyword	Data	Code	Arithmetic
_ _near	Data resides in the default data segment; addresses are 16 bits.	Functions reside in the current code segment; addresses are 16 bits.	16 bits
_ _far	Data can be anywhere in memory, not necessarily in the default data segment; addresses are 32 bits.	Functions can be called from anywhere in memory; addresses are 32 bits.	16 bits
_ _ huge	Data can be anywhere in memory, not necessarily in the default data segment. Individual data items (arrays) can exceed 64K in size; addresses are 32 bits.	Not applicable; code cannot be declared _ _huge.	32 bits (data only)

- Try to avoid dividing a table between pages. If a titled table is continued on another page, repeat its title followed by *(continued)* (italic type, all lowercase, in parentheses) and repeat its column headings. For an untitled table, repeat its column headings. If a table is very long, consider breaking the material into logically related subtables.

- Use rules between rows if the column information varies.

Footnotes

Put footnote explanations at the end of the table, not the bottom of the page.

Your choice of footnote designator depends on the material in the table. For example, if the table contains statistical information, use a letter or symbol to designate a footnote. The order of preference for footnote symbols is numbers, letters, and symbols. For a list of symbols, see *The Chicago Manual of Style*.

Notes and Tips   Notes (including cautions, important notes, tips, and warnings—as well as general notes) call the user's attention to information of special importance or information that cannot otherwise be suitably presented in the main text. Use notes sparingly so that they remain effective in drawing the reader's attention.

If your material is cluttered with notes, you probably need to reorganize the information. In general, try to use only one note in a Help topic. For example, if you must have two notes of the same type (for example, tip or caution), combine them into one note with two paragraphs, or integrate one or both of the notes in the main text. Never include two or more paragraphs formatted as notes without intervening text. If you need to put two notes together, format them as an unordered list within the note heading.

You can include lists within notes.

The type of note (distinguished by the heading of the note or its bitmap) depends on the type of information given, the purpose of the information, and its relative urgency. The following sections explain the types of notes possible and their rank, from neutral to most critical.

Notes

A *note* with the heading "Note" indicates neutral or positive information that emphasizes or supplements important points of the main text. A note supplies information that may apply only in special cases—for example, memory limitations, equipment configurations, or details that apply to specific versions of a program.

Correct

Note   If Windows prompts you for a network password at startup, your network is already set up and you can skip this section.

There is no symbol or bitmap to indicate a note.

Tips

A *tip* is a type of note that helps users apply the techniques and procedures described in the text to their specific needs. A tip suggests alternative methods that may not be obvious and helps users understand the benefits and capabilities of the product. A tip is not essential to the basic understanding of the text.

Correct

Tip   You can also use this procedure to copy a file and give it a new name or location.

Important notes

An *important note* provides information that is essential to the completion of a task. Users can disregard information in a note and still complete a task, but they should not disregard an important note.

> **Correct**
>
> **Important**   The device drivers installed automatically during Setup are required by your system. If you remove one of these drivers, your system may not work properly.

There is no symbol or bitmap for an important note.

Cautions

A *caution* is a type of note that advises users that failure to take or avoid a specified action could result in loss of data.

> **Correct**
>
> **Caution**   To avoid damaging files, always shut down your computer before you turn it off.

In online messages, the Warning symbol indicates a caution. There is no symbol in printed content for a caution.

Warnings

A *warning* is a type of note that advises users that failure to take or avoid a specific action could result in physical harm to the user or the hardware.

> **Correct**
>
> **Warning**   Do not let your Microsoft Mouse come in contact with water or other fluids. Excessive moisture can damage the internal circuitry of the mouse.

The warning symbol is used for both printed and online content.

For more information, see *Marginal Notes* in this chapter.

Chapter 3
Global Content

Organizations that deliver products worldwide generally need to provide content suitable for a worldwide audience. This is particularly true of content delivered on the Web, where customers from anywhere in the world may turn to U.S. Web sites for information. Two-thirds of English speakers in the world speak English as a second language. Even in the United States, according to 2000 census data, nearly 47 million people age 5 and over—almost 18 percent of the population—speak English as a second language.

English-language content can be made usable to all readers in two ways: globalization and localization.

Globalization, also known as *internationalization*, is the creation of English-language documents and products that are usable in any country/region or culture. A globalized document communicates clearly and avoids cultural misunderstandings.

Localization is adapting a document or product for use in a locale other than the country/region of origin. Many documents and products are created originally for use in the United States. Localization includes translating the document or product into the language of the intended locale. In addition to translation, localization involves such tasks as converting to local currency, units of measure, and date formats; resolving typographical differences from the U.S. product; and rewriting U.S.-centric scenarios and examples.

In addition to its other benefits, globalized content is usually less expensive to localize. Globalized content requires localizers to do less research and to spend less time on culturally specific issues. If your content is not localized, you should be especially aware of the needs of your worldwide customers. If non-native English speakers cannot read your content, your content cannot help them. The topics in this section will help you assure that your content meets the needs of all your customers.

This chapter contains the following sections:

- Global Art
- Examples and Scenarios
- Global Syntax
- Word Choice
- Technical Terms
- Jargon
- Foreign Words and Phrases
- Time and Place

- Names and Contact Information
- Fonts
- Web, Software, and HTML Issues
- Additional Globalization Resources

Global Art   Art presents many globalization issues. Colors and images that are unexceptionable in one place may be offensive somewhere else. Art that relies on metaphor may not be understood everywhere. In some cases, art can even raise legal problems. To globalize your art, follow these guidelines.

Colors

Choose colors carefully. Many colors have religious or political significance, such as those that are found on flags or used for specific holidays in a country/region. Neutral colors are usually all right. Your international program manager or your localization group can help you with color choice.

Images

Select simple or generic images that are appropriate worldwide. Soccer players and equipment, generic landscapes, pens and pencils, international highway signs, and historic artifacts such as the Egyptian pyramids are examples of worldwide images.

Be especially careful to avoid images that are offensive in some cultures, such as holiday images and situations, whether work or social, involving men and women. Avoid hand signs; nearly every hand sign is offensive somewhere.

Avoid art based on English idioms, such as using a line of cars and a jam jar to indicate a traffic jam.

Limit graphics and animations on the Web. In some countries, users pay for phone calls by the minute, and long page loading times can be prohibitively expensive.

Localization issues

Avoid text in graphics. Some worldwide users use automatic translation software to read English content. This software does not translate text in graphics. Further, it is expensive to localize graphics. Use captions instead, or provide explanation in the main text.

Create descriptive *alt text* for each image, especially for button images. Users who do not understand the image can rely on alt text for an explanation. If you use art to label buttons, include a text description of the button function. Usability studies have shown that text buttons are easier for users to interpret.

Whenever possible, store art in a separate file and link to it from within a document. Subsidiaries or localizers can modify linked art. If a static copy of the art is embedded in the document, the localizers might need to re-create the art at much greater expense.

See Also: alt text

Examples and Scenarios   Fictitious examples that include names of people, places, or organizations are always potentially sensitive, both legally and from a global perspective. Use case scenarios, detailed descriptions of specific user interactions with a product or technology, present similar problems. To globalize examples and use case scenarios, follow these guidelines:

- From example to example, vary the national identity of business and personal names, addresses, phone numbers, e-mail addresses, currency, and URLs.

- Be sensitive to how the cultural aspects of a use case scenario will be interpreted by other cultures. Social situations, politics, religion, events, holidays, sports, traditions, and legal and business practices vary worldwide. For example, greeting cards are uncommon in many parts of the world, and in some cultures men and women do not touch in public, even to shake hands.

- Avoid mentioning real places altogether in examples, or use the names of international cities that are easily recognized. If you must mention real places, vary the countries represented from one example to the next. For example, you might mention Tokyo, Paris, and New York. If there is the potential for confusion, specify where the city is.

- Avoid discussion of technologies and standards that are not used worldwide. Standards for telephone, cellular phone, e-mail, and wireless technologies, as well as electrical and video standards, vary worldwide. For example, the concept of long-distance calls does not exist in some parts of the world, and POP3 mail providers are not common in Europe.

- Do not assume that U.S. standards are familiar to everyone. Keyboard layouts, default paper and envelope sizes, common printers, monitor resolutions, character sets, text direction, and input methods vary worldwide

Global Syntax   For the most part, syntax that is good for the worldwide audience is also good for the native English speaker. These guidelines are helpful to all readers of technical content, but they are especially helpful to those whose native language is not English:

- Keep adjectives and adverbs close to the words they modify, and do not place them too close to other words they might modify instead. Pay particular attention to the placement of *only*.

- Avoid modifier stacks. Long chains of modifying words, whether they are nouns or adjectives, increase the risk of ambiguity and are confusing even to native English speakers.

- Do not overuse abbreviations and acronyms.

- Let active voice and indicative mood predominate. Use *imperative mood* in procedures.

Non-native speakers of English have additional needs:

- Make liberal use of articles to help identify the nouns in a sentence.

- Make liberal use of prepositions and of relative pronouns such as *that* and *who* to eliminate ambiguity and to clarify the sentence structure.

  Correct

  The file that you select is attached to the mail message.

  You can change files by using the Template utility.

  Ambiguous or more difficult

  The file you select is attached to the mail message.

  You can change files using the Template utility.

- Use language that is understandable to English speakers regardless of where they live. Do not use idioms, regionalisms, colloquial expressions, and other culture-specific references. Although these forms add color and interest to your writing for some readers, they are almost always confusing for the non-native reader, and they can be difficult or impossible to translate.

- Be particularly careful with punctuation. Include optional punctuation where it helps clarify the sentence structure.

- Avoid long, convoluted sentences. Even if they are well-written, they are hard for non-native readers to parse.

- Limit your use of compound subjects and predicates. If a clause has more than two subjects or predicates, consider using a list instead.

- Lists and tables can often simplify syntax and aid scanning. Use them instead of complicated sentence and paragraph structures when you can. Be aware, however, that in some languages an introductory sentence fragment that is completed by each list element can be more difficult to translate than an introduction that is a complete sentence.

- Limit your use of sentence fragments.

For more information, see *Lists* and also *Tables* in Chapter 2, "Content Formatting and Layout."

Word Choice   Many aspects of good word choice are the same for native and non-native readers alike:

- Always use the simplest and most specific word possible. Do not *eschew* when it is good enough to *avoid*.

- Spell out geographical names. Abbreviations are often ambiguous. For example, WA is the abbreviation for Washington state and for Western Australia.

- Use one term for one concept and use terms consistently. This guideline is particularly important for technical terms, but it also applies to standard English words. Although the use of synonyms may be more interesting to read, worldwide users—and not only worldwide users—may assume that your choice of a different word indicates a subtle distinction.

- Do not use similar terms to mean subtly different things. For example, do not use *data* to mean computer input and *information* to mean computer output. Such distinctions are easily lost, even on native readers.

- Reserve *accessibility* to refer to features that support users with disabilities.

To globalize your content, also follow these guidelines:

- Avoid noun and verb phrases. Phrases such as *put up with*, *make sure*, *bring to fruition*, and *front-runner* are harder to parse and easier to misinterpret than single words such as *tolerate*, *ensure*, *finish*, and *leader*.

- Avoid participial forms of verbs and also nouns formed from verbs, which are harder to read than the simple verb tenses. For example, replace *be arriving* with *arrive*, and *do some writing* with *write*.

- Avoid idiomatic and colloquial expressions and culturally specific analogies. Idioms can confuse non-native speakers and take extra time to translate. For example, the Italian translation of "kill two birds with one stone" is "catch two pigeons with one bean."

- Avoid surprising or humorous word choices, slang, and sarcasm. Puns and coined phrases can be difficult to interpret. Non-native English speakers might not recognize culturally specific humor or sarcasm, and what is funny to some can be offensive to others.

- Avoid using words for something other than their literal meaning. Be especially careful of slang, idiom, and vogue usage. For example, don't use "what's hot" to label new or fashionable items.

- If your content is to be localized, be aware that abbreviations and acronyms might not be localized along with the phrases they stand for. For example, in German, the abbreviation *DAO*, which stands for *data access object*, is localized as *Datenzugriffsobjekte*, but the abbreviation is still *DAO*.

- Avoid abbreviations and acronyms that include other abbreviations and acronyms, such as *LDIF* for *LDAP directory interchange format*. (*LDAP* stands for *lightweight directory access protocol*.) These nested abbreviations are often very difficult for worldwide readers to decipher. Further, some countries require that abbreviations be fully spelled out at least once, which in this example would result in the impenetrable modifier stack "lightweight directory access protocol directory interchange format."

- Avoid contractions. As basic as contractions are to the native reader, they add unnecessary complexity for the non-native reader. For example, contractions that end in *'s* can be mistaken for possessive nouns, and the *'s* can be read as either *has* or *is*.

- Be careful of words that can be read as both verbs and nouns, such as *file*, *post*, *input*, *screen*, *word*, and *map*. Be careful to ensure that the context and sentence structure make your meaning unambiguous.

- Follow the rules of capitalization for standard written English. In particular, capitalize technical terms and feature names only if they are brand names or if they are based on a proper noun, such as the name of a person or place. With those exceptions, do not capitalize the words that make up an abbreviation, even if the abbreviation is capitalized.

Correct

original equipment manufacturer (OEM)

Boolean algebra

For details about capitalization, see *Capitalization* in Chapter 9, "Common Style Problems."

- Avoid culturally sensitive terms. For example, military terms and analogies, as well as terms that reflect a U.S. worldview, can offend worldwide users. For example, using *international* to refer to countries other than the United States is considered offensive in some parts of the world. *Worldwide* is a better choice. Although the *master/slave relationship* between server and client is in common use, the term is offensive in some cultures. The following table lists some common terms to avoid and suggests alternatives.

Avoid	*Use instead*
master/slave	master/subordinate
collaborator	coworker, colleague
demilitarized zone (DMZ)	perimeter network
hang	stop responding

- Be careful when making generalizations about people, nations, and cultures, especially if the generalizations could be considered derogatory.

- Whenever possible, use the central meaning of a word. Non-native readers are likely to know the most common definition of an English word, but they may not know the others. Most current dictionaries, including the *American Heritage Dictionary, Fourth Edition*, and the *Encarta World English Dictionary* list the central meaning of a word first. Many older dictionaries list definitions in chronological order, with the oldest usage first.

- Avoid verbs with many meanings. Where such verbs are unavoidable, use context to make your meaning unmistakable.

- Include optional hyphens in compound words and following prefixes where ambiguity would otherwise result.

- Include both international and U.S. terminologists in your terminology review process.

Technical Terms   If you are writing for home users or information workers, always minimize your use of technical terms. Non-native English speakers and people who do not think of themselves as computer professionals often consider new technical terms to be a major stumbling block to understanding. Whenever possible, you should get your point across by using common English words. It is all right to use technical terms when they are necessary for precise communication, even with home users, but do not write as if everybody already understands them or will immediately grasp their meaning. Establish meaning in context and provide a glossary.

Using technical terms

Many common technical terms appear in recent editions of the major English language dictionaries. A new word's presence in a dictionary indicates that it is in common usage, but that does not necessarily mean that every reader, especially every worldwide reader, will be familiar with it. Do not assume that readers update their English language dictionaries as often as is typical for professional writers and editors, or that worldwide readers keep current with language and usage trends in the United States.

If you are writing for software developers or information technology professionals, use domain-specific terminology only when your audience, regardless of native language, understands the term in the same sense you are using it and when the terminology is necessary to be clear. Do not rely on unedited Web sites for information about accepted terminology. To verify the industrywide meaning of technical terms, check the *Microsoft Computer Dictionary*, terminology Web sites such as *http://www.webopedia.com* and *http://www.whatis.com*, and industry standard sites such as *http://www.w3.org*. For recent usage citations of words that may be too new for the dictionaries, refer to professionally edited Web sites, such as those for trade and consumer magazines.

Define terms in the text as you introduce them. Provide a glossary with your document, and provide links from the main text to the glossary if you are writing for online Help or for the Web.

Use the same terms in marketing materials as those that are used in the product.

Coining new technical terms

If a term describing a concept already exists, do not coin a new term. If you must create a new term, verify that the term you choose is not already in use to mean something else. Include the U.S. and international terminologists in your process. They can alert you to any reuse, globalization, and localization issues. They can also help you publicize the new term to the rest of the company and ensure that the term is stored in the central glossary and term localization database.

If you create a new term, whatever your audience, avoid giving specific technical meaning to common English words. Even if new terms are well-grounded in the everyday definition of a word, non-native readers may not be attuned to the subtleties of meaning that underlie such terms, and they may try to make sense of the material using the common definition.

Jargon   *Jargon*, as a general reference to the technical language used by some particular profession or other group, is a neutral concept. In the right context, for a particular audience, jargon can serve as verbal shorthand for well-understood concepts. For example, technical terms are normally acceptable in documentation for software developers and information technology professionals, who expect a higher level of technical rigor.

Why, then, does jargon have such a bad reputation? An important reason is that many computer users, especially home users and information workers, do not want to learn a new vocabulary to accomplish their goals. Many such users believe that technical terms make technology harder to understand and therefore harder to use. They prefer that concepts be explained plainly in everyday words or (better yet) that the products they use make such explanations unnecessary.

Additionally, much jargon is little more than technical slang. Many acronyms and abbreviations fall into this category. This category of jargon affects nearly all uninitiated readers at least some of the time, but it causes special problems for worldwide readers. In many cases, jargon is difficult to translate and can cause geopolitical or cultural misunderstandings.

Jargon is not acceptable if:

- A more familiar term could easily be used.

- It obscures rather than clarifies meaning. Be particularly wary of new terms or terms that are familiar only to a small segment of your customers (*glyph*, for example).

- It is not specific to computer software, networks, operating systems, and the like. That is, avoid marketing and journalistic jargon (*leverage*, for example) in documentation.

A technical term that is specific to a product should be defined and then used without apology. In online content, provide a definition or a link to the glossary, or both, where readers might encounter the term for the first time.

Testing for jargon

If you are familiar with a term, how can you tell whether it is jargon that you should avoid? If the term is not listed either in this book or on your project style sheet, consider the following:

- If you are not sure, consider it jargon.

- If an editor or reviewer questions the use of a term, it may be jargon.

- If the term is used in other documentation, it is probably acceptable.

- If the term is used in newspapers such as *The Wall Street Journal* or the *New York Times* or in general interest magazines such as *Time* or *Newsweek*, it is probably acceptable.

- If the term is used in technical periodicals such as *MSDN Magazine*, it is probably acceptable for technical audiences. Be aware, though, that technical magazines often adopt a more idiomatic style than is appropriate for the worldwide audience, and that magazine style can include usages that would be considered slang.

Foreign Words and Phrases   Avoid non-English words and phrases, such as *de facto* or *ad hoc*, even if you think they are generally known and understood. They may not be, or the language may not be understood by a translator. Find a straightforward substitute in English instead.

Do not use Latin abbreviations for common English phrases.

Use these terms	Instead of
for example	e.g.
that is	i.e.
namely	viz.
therefore	ergo

See Also: et al., etc.

Time and Place   To globalize time information, follow these guidelines:

- Avoid A.M. and P.M. notation. Use 24-hour time format.

- To indicate the time for a scheduled event, include the time zone and the corresponding offset from Coordinated Universal Time (UTC).

Correct

13:00 Eastern Time (UTC–5)

3

- Begin calendar weeks on Monday, as is the custom in much of the world, not on Sunday.

- Spell out the names of months. Use the format *month dd, yyyy*.

Correct

January 5, 2003

Do not use numbers to represent months, such as 6/12/2003. This example could be read in different parts of the world as June 12, 2003 or as December 6, 2003.

- Avoid referring to seasons. Remember, summer in the northern hemisphere is winter in the southern hemisphere. Use months or calendar quarters instead. If you must mention a season in other than the most general way, establish which hemisphere you are referring to.

Correct

The product is scheduled for release in July.

The event takes place in northern summer. [Only if necessary.]

Flowers bloom in the spring.

Incorrect

The product is scheduled for release in summer.

To globalize place information, follow these guidelines:

- Include the country/region name in event locations.

- Avoid naming countries, regions, cities, or land features in disputed areas. Errors in names of disputed territory can be highly offensive and even illegal in some countries.

For more information, see *Dates* and also *Time Zones* in Chapter 9, "Common Style Problems."

See Also: A.M., P.M.

Names and Contact Information   If you are creating a form that collects personal information, whether as a Web page or as a documentation example, follow these guidelines to globalize your form:

- Use *first name* or *given name* and *surname* in describing parts of a person's name. *Given name* is preferable to *first name*; in many countries the surname comes first.

Not all cultures use middle names. It is all right to have a middle name field in a form, but do not make it required information.

- Use *title*, not *honorific*, to describe words such as *Mr.* or *Ms.* Not all cultures may have an equivalent to some titles that are common in the United States, such as *Ms.*

- If possible, provide a text field large enough for the user to enter the entire address so that the user can include whatever information is appropriate for the locale. At a minimum, do not require the user to complete fields that do not apply everywhere, such as *state*.

- Use *postal code* instead of *Zip code*. Allow for at least ten characters for a postal code, and allow for a combination of letters and numbers.

- Use *state or province* instead of *state* to accommodate worldwide addresses. Do not require an entry in this field.

- Include a field for *country/region* instead of simply *country* to accommodate disputed territories.

- If you need information for mailing between European countries, include a field for country code.

- Provide enough space for long international telephone numbers. For details on formatting international telephone numbers, see *Telephone Numbers* in Chapter 9, "Common Style Problems."

Many countries/regions strictly control what personal information can be legally collected, stored, and shared. Do not assume that what is permissible in the United States is permissible everywhere.

If you are creating a document that includes information about how to contact you, be aware that toll-free telephone numbers are not generally available worldwide. Provide an alternate way for customers to contact you.

Try to avoid references to specific third-party companies in the United States, even very large ones. In particular, avoid referring users to U.S. resources. If you must provide vendor, supplier, or retailer references, state that they are U.S. companies and suggest where the reader outside the U.S. might look for local resources.

Fonts   Use fonts that are available in browsers and operating systems worldwide. Common fonts are Times New Roman, Arial, Courier New, Verdana, and Symbol. Alternatively, you can design your content so that fonts on the user's system will be substituted if the specified font is not available.

Avoid hand-drawn fonts or fonts that are hard-coded in text or code.

Web, Software, and HTML Issues

If you want to attract a worldwide audience to your content, you cannot do better than publishing on the World Wide Web. Although the Web is the same everywhere, Web users outside North America are less likely to have the newest browsers. Broadband Internet access is far from common outside major cities, and Internet service providers do not always charge a flat monthly rate for access. To accommodate worldwide users, follow these guidelines:

- Use standard HTML tags. Avoid proprietary tags. If you are developing HTML text with scripted code, globalize any text generated by the scripts, too.

- Keep download issues in mind. Charges for Internet service outside the United States are often based on connection time, and the cost in some areas can be considerable. Keep page size under 100 KB whenever possible.

- Include a text-only version of the page.

- Design pages so that text loads first, followed by graphics. This sequence ensures that the page is usable before it is fully loaded.

- Some products and formats are not available worldwide; localized versions of new and updated products and formats may lag behind U.S. availability.

- Decide in advance which browsers to support. If you are supporting old browsers, you might need to:

  - Provide a no-frames version.

  - Avoid certain elements in scripts.

  - Include some design information (such as background color) in the document files instead of in the style sheet.

  - Avoid nested tables.

- A simple design works best.

- Some users read from right to left or from top to bottom. You may not be able to provide an ideal site for these users, but page design can help. You might, for example, provide key information, such as home page links, at both top right and top left to increase your chances of reaching all users.

- If your content is to be localized or might be localized in the future, allow space for text expansion. Some languages require many more words to express an idea that may be expressed compactly in English. Even if text will not be localized, be aware that many worldwide users translate English text using an automated translation engine such as Babelfish.

- Provide support for double-byte text entry in software.

- Follow laws for software restrictions. If software contains code subject to export restrictions in the U.S. or legal requirements in other countries, remove the code from versions that will not meet those requirements.

- Exercise care when providing software for download or on a multiproduct CD. U.S. laws restrict the delivery of certain information and technology internationally. Verify that providing the download will not break U.S. laws.

- Marketing statements; political statements; and names of people, places, and landmarks are restricted by law in some countries. Restrict downloads into these countries unless you are sure that the download is legal.

- If possible, link only to globalized sites and to publications that are available worldwide.

- If possible, link to a site where the user can specify the appropriate country/region.

- Identify links and cross-references that are not globally relevant. If you must link to a site or refer to a publication that is not globalized, inform your users.

- Screen requests for e-mail newsletters to determine user location. E-mail that is sent to customers outside the U.S. must be globalized or customized to meet local requirements.

Additional Globalization Resources   To be more aware of issues of concern to the worldwide audience, become a global consumer of information and media. Subscribe to e-mail newsletters in the countries where your customers live. Do not assume that your customer knows anything about your country or history. Examine the global implications of anything that you say or do instinctively. To better understand strategies for global content, visit these sites on the World Wide Web:

- *http://www.roncheer.com/index.htm*

- *http://www.plainlanguage.gov*

- *http://www.world-ready.com/index.htm*

- *http://www.w3.org/international*

- *http://www.unicode.org*

Chapter 4
Content for Software Developers

Providing content to support software development products requires some special considerations. Such content is highly technical and often complex. It includes everything from technical reference information to code samples and coding tips.

Conventions for presenting and formatting particular kinds of developer information, applying common structures to similar information, and providing descriptions of code are among the devices you can use to make content more helpful to software developers and easier to use.

Although developers are often familiar with technical terminology you would typically avoid for less technical audiences, it is still important to use terminology consistently and correctly.

Accuracy is critical in any technical information, but painstaking attention to detail and accuracy should be your first and foremost consideration for developer software.

This chapter contains the following sections:

- Reference Documentation
- Code Comments
- Code Formatting Conventions
- Coding Style
- Logical Operators
- COM, ActiveX, and OLE Terminology

Reference Documentation
Language reference topics provide developers with factual information about language elements. This information includes:

- Specific information about each element, such as the parameters and return value of a function.
- Details about how to use or call the element in code.

The scope of language reference topics includes:

- Class libraries
- API frameworks
- Object models
- Programming language constructs

Reference topics provide information about how to use a given language element in code. The goal is to help users get the information they must have quickly by standardizing the information and designing the topic so users know what to look for and where to find it on the page.

Reference documentation is not a conceptual exposition of the language elements. Stick to the facts, and use links to appropriate procedural and conceptual topics.

Elements of a reference topic

A reference topic has a title and the body.

Topic title   Language reference topics are titled with the name of the feature they describe. For example, Add Method.

> **Note:** Some topics might digress from the language element + qualifier format. For instance, topics may not use qualifiers. Consult your project style sheet for details.

Body of topic   Because the elements in language reference topics vary depending on the documented language element, the following table lists elements that apply in specific situations. Not all elements will appear in all topics.

Section	*How to use*
Description	Required. No heading. Typically, one sentence describing the element; can be two sentences if there is additional essential information.
	Starts with a verb; for example, "Adds a method to the class."
Declaration/Syntax	Required. No heading. For class libraries, API frameworks, and object models, use declarative syntax instead of calling syntax.
Parameters	Applies if the element defines parameters. For programming language constructs, the heading name is Arguments.
Return Value	Methods and functions only. Required if the element returns a value.
Property Value	Properties only. Required. Describes the value of the property and specifies the default value.
Exceptions/Error Codes	Required if the element can raise exceptions or errors when called.
Remarks	As required to provide additional information about the element and to call out important details or things that are not obvious.
Example	Recommended for most topics. Provides a non-trivial code example of how to use the element.
	Alternatively, the code example can reside in a separate topic. In this case, include a link to the example topic in the Example section.

4

Section	How to use
Requirements	As required to specify language or platform requirements.
See Also	Include at least a parent topic. Include other related language elements. Point to specific tasks and concepts related to the area of the language reference element.

Code Comments

Code comments that describe implementation details and other critical information help users better understand your example. However, you should comment only those lines of code that are significant or difficult to understand. Do not comment the obvious, such as a constructor call. Too many comments impair readability.

Consider using a comment in place of a code step that is not immediately related to the documentation topic. This reduces the length of your example.

When adding code comments to your example, use the following conventions:

- Precede comments with a blank line, and align the comments with the code they apply to. Place comments on the line before the code, not after the code or on the same line as the code. Placing code comments on the same line as the code poses problems for localization. Localized text is, on average, 30–40 percent longer than English text. When endline comments are localized, they often cause lines of code to exceed the recommended 70-character limit.

  Correct

  ```
  // Populate the grid.
  dataGrid1.PopulateColumns();
  ```

  Incorrect

  ```
  dataGrid1.PopulateColumns();   // Populate the grid.
  ```

- Use two forward slashes (//) to denote a comment for C++, C#, and JScript code. Use an apostrophe (') to denote a comment for Visual Basic code.

- Whenever possible, limit each comment to a single line. This makes it easier for localization to translate. If you need more than one line for your comment, consider including the comment information within the body of the topic.

- If you cannot avoid multiline comments, use the // characters rather than the /* */ combination of characters to denote multiline comments for C++, C#, and JScript code. Users who copy and paste our code can run into problems when trying to comment out sections that contain comments denoted with the /* */ combination of characters.

- Insert one space between the comment delimiter (// or ') and the comment text.

- Begin the comment text with an uppercase letter. End the comment with a period. Use complete sentences if possible.

- Use descriptive phrases that explain why the code is important or what the code does.

- For code comments that instruct the developer to perform a task, use the imperative voice. (Example: "Insert code that does <task> here.")

- Follow all casing rules; for example, use Pascal casing and camel casing where appropriate.

- Observe standard rules of punctuation and grammar.

- Avoid slang, jargon, or politically sensitive language.

- Use only approved fictitious names or URLs.

- Use only approved acronyms.

- Do not use "foo," "bar," "fubar," or any other variations of this common, but inappropriate, acronym.

- Do not use first person, such as "we," "our," "I," or "let's." For example, do not say something like "Here we implement our custom control."

- Do not use boldface, italics, or other special formatting.

Code Formatting Conventions

In content for software developers, programming elements must stand out from the text. Most programming elements are formatted according to document conventions: constants, variables, functions, statements, type names, directives, instructions, operators, macros, format specifiers, and any other predefined or user-defined element.

Sometimes, however, document conventions conflict. For example, you might want to refer to something the user must type, in a generic sense, such as "file name." Is that *filename*, **filename**, `file_name`, or some combination thereof? One additional convention for programming elements is monospace text, which can appear within or set off from normal text.

Here are some cases of conflicting conventions; consider how you will treat them in your documentation.

Formatting monospace text

If programming elements consist of less than a logical line, you can format them within normal text as a monospace font, such as Lucida Sans Typewriter. Use a point size that works with your normal text. Format the spaces on either side in the same font as the normal text.

If you choose monospace text, continue to set complete lines or statements of sample code on their own; do not embed them in normal text. Complete the sentence that introduces the sample code.

Sample code

Sample code provided for the user is in monospace text. Continue to use monospace text to refer to a portion of the sample code if the portion is less than a logical line or a full command. If the portion you want to draw attention to can stand on its own as a line or statement, place it on its own line. To show portions of sample code, use horizontal or vertical ellipses.

Correct

In this example, a form named `myForm` contains a command button named `Command1`. The following command changes the Top property of `Command1` to 50.

```
=ChangeTop(myForm.Command1, 50)
```

Keywords in text

For keywords within text, follow document conventions. For keywords in code samples, follow coding conventions.

Correct

This code tries to create a **char** pointer named `ptr` and initialize it with a string:

```
main()
{
    char *ptr;

    // Error!
    strcpy( ptr, "Ashby" );
}
```

However, the declaration `char *ptr` creates a pointer, but does nothing else.

Syntax

Syntax itself follows document conventions, which usually use bold for elements to be typed literally and italic for placeholder variable names. To refer to a part of the syntax, echo the document conventions within the line of normal text.

Correct

```
int _SetObjectProperty(Value FAR *object, char FAR *prop, Value FAR *val,
int fAdd);
```

If *fAdd* is a nonzero value and the property you specify does not exist for the object, the property is added to the object as a user-defined property and contains the property value you specify with *val*.

User output

If code typed at the command prompt produces output, consider how you will distinguish code the user types from text that is displayed as a result. The following example, from Visual FoxPro, uses monospace text for both the input and output and a heading to separate the two sections.

Correct

Because `cFirst` is character data and `nSecond` is numeric data, you get a data type mismatch error if you type the following command:

```
? cFirst + nSecond
```

You can avoid this problem by using conversion functions. These functions enable you to use the following operations:

```
? cFirst + LTRIM(STR(nSecond))
? VAL(cFirst) + nSecond
```

Output

```
12345
168
```

For more information, see *Code Comments* and *Coding Style*, in this chapter; *Command Syntax* in Chapter 1, "Documenting the User Interface"; *Document Conventions* in Chapter 2, "Content Formatting and Layout"; and *HTML Tag, Element, and Attribute Styling* and *XML Tag, Element, and Attribute Styling* in Chapter 5.

Coding Style

Most development tools groups have already developed coding style conventions appropriate to their languages. Acknowledging the inadvisability of recommending a single coding style across groups and languages, these guidelines call attention to the issues each group should consider as it develops conventions for the code listings in the documentation for its product.

General rules

Apply a consistent coding style within a document and across documentation for your development product.

In addition to observing the syntax requirements of your language, use the coding style of the browser that will be used with your product to guide your coding style choices.

Indentation and alignment

Consistent indentation and alignment can make your code easier to read. These are some guidelines to consider for indentation and alignment:

- Use indentation consistently.
- Develop a scheme for positioning the opening and closing braces of a block of code.
- Develop conventions for handling statements that wrap to the next line. You may decide, for instance, to break and indent the line so that elements are aligned for logical parallelism rather than according to the indentation scheme.

- Decide whether you will declare one variable per line even if the variables are of the same type.

- Decide whether variables of the same type that are logically related can be declared on the same line.

- Decide whether you will permit **If-Then** statements to appear on the same line.

- Decide whether you will put the keywords **else** and **do** on their own lines.

Line spacing

Develop line-spacing conventions that help users see the hierarchical relationships in your code and help distinguish between declarations and implementation.

Spacing within lines

These are some places where you will have to decide whether to use spaces within lines:

- Before and after an operator.

- Before and after an array subscript.

- After the commas in an array that has multiple dimensions.

- Between a function name and an initial parenthesis that follows it.

- Between a language keyword and a parenthetical expression that follows it.

- After the initial parenthesis and before the final parenthesis of required parentheses.

- After the initial parenthesis and before the final parenthesis of parentheses that specify or clarify evaluation order ("optional" parentheses).

Naming and capitalization

Establish consistent naming and capitalization schemes for variables, constants, user-defined data types, classes, functions, and user-defined functions. Avoid confusing abbreviations such as *No*, which can mean either "no" or "number."

Also establish consistent naming and capitalization schemes for special programming elements such as character constants, string constants, prefixes, and suffixes. Many groups use variants of Charles Simonyi's Hungarian naming conventions. You can find Simonyi's explanation of Hungarian notation in the MSDN library at *http://msdn.microsoft.com /library/default.asp?url=/library/en-us/dnvsgen/html/hunganotat.asp*.

Finally, establish conventions for octal and hexadecimal notation.

For more information, see *Code Comments* and *Code Formatting Conventions* in this chapter; and McConnell, Steve. *Code Complete*. Redmond, WA: Microsoft Press, 1993.

Logical Operators   Also called *Boolean operators*. The most commonly used are **AND, OR, XOR** (exclusive **OR**), and **NOT.** Use bold all uppercase for logical operators. Do not use them as verbs, and do not use their symbols in text.

Correct

Using **AND** to find *x* and *y* will produce **TRUE** only if both are true.

Incorrect

ANDing *x* and *y* produces **TRUE** only if both are true.

Using **&** to find *x* and *y* will produce **TRUE** only if both are true.

Use parentheses rather than relying on operator precedence. For example:

```
// This is syntactically correct.
if (1 < 2 && 3 < 4)
{
    sum = 1 * 2 + 3 * 4;
}

// This is easier to understand.
if ((1 < 2) && (3 < 4))
{
    sum = (1 * 2) + (3 * 4);
}
```

COM, ActiveX, and OLE Terminology   The Component Object Model (COM) is a collection of services that make it possible for software components to interoperate in a networked environment. COM-based technologies include ActiveX, DCOM, Microsoft Transaction Server (MTS), COM+, and others. For more information about COM, see *http://www.microsoft.com/com*.

ActiveX is a COM-based technology for packaging components for delivery in Web browsers or other COM-based client software. Object Linking and Embedding (OLE), which is also built on COM, is an ActiveX technology. OLE is used primarily in creating compound documents for easier use and integration of desktop programs.

COM terminology constantly evolves, but in general many COM terms have replaced ActiveX terms, which in turn replaced most OLE terms. Some terms specific to ActiveX and OLE do remain in use, however.

Note: The terminology covered in this topic is related in precise ways to the technologies concerned. It should not be used in content for home users or information workers.

Only the most widely accepted guidelines and terms are listed here. For more specific and up-to-date information, see the COM glossary in the Platform SDK documentation on the MSDN Web site: *http://msdn.microsoft.com*.

General guidelines

- Use *ActiveX* only in the context of the specific technologies *ActiveX Controls* and *ActiveX Data Objects*. Otherwise, use *active* and the object under discussion, unless the following table lists an exception.

- Do not make changes that can break existing code (for example, of class names, properties, methods, or events). Do not change any third-party name that includes *OLE* or *OCX*.

- Do not use any OLE-specific terms other than those listed in this table.

- Follow the capitalization in the tables for references to COM and ActiveX technologies.

- The COM-based technology Automation is always capitalized and never preceded by *ActiveX*, *COM* or *OLE*.

Term	Definition	Usage (and Queries)
active content	General term for active objects, active scripts, and active documents.	
active document	A document that contains ActiveX controls, Java applets, HTML pages, or document objects for display in Internet Explorer.	Do not use *ActiveX document*.
active script	A script, regardless of language or file format, that can interact with ActiveX controls.	
active scripting	Technology that uses COM to connect third-party scripts to a browser without regard to language and other elements of implementation.	Do not use *COM scripting*, *ActiveX scripting*, or *OLE scripting*.
Active Server Pages	A feature of Internet Information Services (IIS) that combines HTML and active scripts or components.	Treat the term as a singular (but do not use *Active Server Page*). Use *active server page* (lowercase) or *.asp file* to refer to the file that generates the HTML page. It is all right to use *ASP page* to describe the Web page that appears in the browser. Do not confuse with *ASP.NET* (note there is no space), a .NET technology. ASP.NET files have an extension of .aspx. Do not spell out *ASP* in *ASP.NET*.
ActiveX-based, ActiveX-enabled		Do not use. Use COM-based or write around instead.

Term	Definition	Usage (and Queries)
ActiveX component	See *COM component* in this table.	Do not use. Use *COM component* instead.
ActiveX control	User interface element created using ActiveX technology.	Do not capitalize *control* when referring to programming objects. Do not use *COM control*; there is no such thing. It is all right to use *control* alone if the context is clear.
ActiveX Controls	Technology for creating user interface elements for delivery on the Web.	Capitalize *Controls* when referring to the technology, but not when referring to specific ActiveX controls.
ActiveX Data Objects (ADO)	High-level data access programming interface to the underlying OLE DB data access technology, implemented using COM.	*ActiveX* is correct in this instance. Usually referred to by the acronym, however. Capitalize *Data Objects* when referring to the technology, but not when referring to specific data objects.
Automation	COM-based technology that enables dynamic binding to COM objects at run time.	Automation is always capitalized. Do not use *ActiveX Automation*, *COM Automation*, or *OLE Automation*.
Automation client	An application or programming tool that accesses Automation objects.	
Automation controller		Obsolete term; do not use. Use *Automation client* instead.
Automation object	An object that is exposed to other applications or programming tools through Automation interfaces.	Use instead of *programmable object*.
client	Generic term referring to any program that accesses or uses a service provided by another component.	Do not use *client component*; instead use a phrase such as "is a client of" or "acts as a client." A program is a client in relation to some server object, not in a vacuum. Ensure that the context is clear.
COM class	Definition in source code for creating objects that implement the **IUnknown** interface and expose only their interfaces to clients.	
COM component	Binary file containing code for one or more class factories, COM classes, registry-entry mechanisms, loading code, and so on.	Do not use *ActiveX component*.

4

82

Term	Definition	Usage (and Queries)
COM object	Instance of a COM class.	
component	Code module that serves up objects.	Do not use as a synonym for *object*.
component object		Do not use; use either *component* or *object* instead, whichever is accurate.
compound document (OLE-specific term)	A document that contains linked or embedded objects as well as its own data.	Do not use as a synonym for *compound file*.
compound document object (OLE-specific term)		Obsolete term; do not use. Instead, use *linked object* or *embedded object*, as appropriate.
compound file (OLE)		Avoid; *compound file* is too easily confused with *compound document*. Compound document refers to the default implementation of structured storage. If necessary to refer to the concept, explain it before using the term.
container	An application or object that contains other objects. For example, a *compound document* is a type of container.	A container is a client of the objects it contains.
custom control		Obsolete term. Use ActiveX control.
DCOM	Formerly *distributed COM*. A wire protocol that enables software components to communicate directly over a network.	Do not spell out. Use *DCOM* only to refer specifically to the wire protocol. Use just *COM* in all instances to refer to components that communicate by using DCOM.
docfile (OLE-specific term)	Obsolete synonym for *compound file*.	Do not use. See *compound file (OLE)* in this table.
dynamic COM component	COM component that is created by a run-time environment and that is not explicitly associated with a COM class ID.	
embed (OLE)	To insert an object in its native format into a compound document. Contrast with *linked object*.	

Term	Definition	Usage (and Queries)
embedded object (OLE)	An object whose data is stored along with that of its container, but that runs in the process space of its server.	
expose	To make an object's services available to clients.	
in-place activation	Also called *visual editing*. The process of editing an embedded object within the window of its container, using tools provided by its server. Note that linked objects do not support in-place activation.	Do not use *in-situ editing*. You can also describe the process, for example, "editing embedded objects in place."
in-process component	A component that runs in its client's process space.	It is all right to describe an in-process component as an *in-process server*. Do not, however, use constructions such as *in-process DLL* that refer to the file that contains the server component.
insertable object (OLE)		Avoid except to match the interface in end-user documentation.
invisible object		Avoid; instead, use a phrase such as "an object without a visible user interface."
linked object (OLE)	An object that represents a link source's data in a compound document. The link source is identified by an associated link object.	Differentiate between *link object* and *linked object*.
link object (OLE)		Avoid. Do not use as a synonym for *linked object*.
link source (OLE)	A data object stored in a location separate from the container and whose data is represented in the container by a linked object. When the data in the link source is updated, the corresponding data representation in the linked object can be updated automatically or manually.	

4

Term	Definition	Usage (and Queries)
local component	Obsolete term for a component that runs in a separate process from its client, but on the same computer.	Do not use. Instead, use *out-of-process component* or *out-of-process server*. Refer to computer location only if it is important for a particular discussion.
member function		Avoid; use *method* instead.
object	A combination of code and data created at run time that can be treated as a unit. An instance of a class.	Do not use as a synonym for *component*.
Object Linking and Embedding (OLE)		Capitalize to describe the technology.
object linking and embedding		Use sparingly and only when referring to the act of linking or embedding objects, not to the technology.
object model		Do not use; instead, use *Component Object Model (COM)*. *Object model* is a general term; *COM* is a specific object model.
OCX		Do not use as a synonym for an ActiveX control. Use of .ocx as a file extension is acceptable.
OLE control, OLE Controls		Obsolete terms. In general usage, use *ActiveX control* or *control*. For the technology, use ActiveX Controls. See *ActiveX control* and *ActiveX Controls* in this table.
OLE drag and drop	The technology for dragging and dropping COM objects.	Acceptable term.
OLE object	An object that supports object linking and embedding and that can be linked or embedded, or both.	Do not use as a synonym for *COM object*. OLE objects are a special type of COM object.
out-of-process component	A component compiled as an executable file to provide services. An out-of-process component does not run in the same process as its client.	It is all right to describe an out-of-process component as an *out-of-process server*. Do not, however, use constructions such as *EXE server* that refer to the file that contains the server component.

4

Term	Definition	Usage (and Queries)
remote component	Obsolete term for a component that runs on a different computer from its client.	Do not use. Instead, use *out-of-process component* or *out-of-process server*. Refer to computer location only if it is important for a particular discussion.
server	A synonym for *component*. The term *server* emphasizes a relationship to a client so is useful when this relationship is important.	Do not use without a modifier. In general, avoid *COM server* except in some instances in programmer documentation. Use *COM object* or *COM component* instead. If you use *COM server*, make sure that your usage will not be confused with a server computer.
server application	Obsolete term. See *server* in this table.	Avoid. Instead, use *COM object*, *COM component*, or just *component*, unless you are specifically comparing to a client application.
visual editing	See *in-place activation* in this table.	

4

Chapter 5
Web Content

The World Wide Web is quickly becoming the first place customers go to find information about different products, technologies, and services. Like printed content, the Web is a medium that presents unique issues for writers and editors. It is important that steps are taken to create Web sites that are both effective and accessible so that visitors to the sites can find the content they need easily and successfully.

This chapter contains the following sections:

- Titles of Web Pages
- Descriptions of Web Pages
- HTML Tag, Element, and Attribute Styling
- XML Tag, Element, and Attribute Styling

Titles of Web Pages   When customers visit a Web site and cannot find what they are looking for, they become dissatisfied not only with the Web site, but with the company that publishes it. One of the simplest things you can do to improve your customers' search experience is to write Web page titles that clearly describe what your pages contain. The goal is to attract readers who need your content and to drive away readers who do not.

Clever titles can be eye-catching for the person who happens upon them, but search engines cannot resolve such titles to the real subject of the Web page. Vague titles are just as bad: If a page's title is "Update Information," the reader has no information on what product or version the page covers. To write page titles that help your customers, follow these guidelines:

- Specify the product name. Be as specific as you can within the limits of a title. For example, if the content applies only to certain versions or to certain editions, try not to refer to the product in a general way.

- Be specific in describing what the page is about. Use words people will include in search strings if this document will be useful to them. It is all right to be general if the topic is general, such as in a conceptual overview.

- Titles do not have to be complete sentences or clauses, but they must be clear.

- Do not promise more in the title than the page actually delivers.

- Be concise. Some search sites will display only the first 50 characters of your title, so it is important that the first 50 characters carry as much information as possible.

- Titles must be concise, but they must also be comprehensible. Include whatever articles and prepositions are necessary to make the meaning of the title clear.

- Avoid vague or weak words. They waste space and usually provide little or no information.

- Do not use abbreviations or acronyms in titles unless you are sure that your intended audience will recognize them.

- Avoid the temptation to write a catchy title that will not be clear out of context. Do not make the title a "teaser" to attract clicks from the curious. People who go to your page only to discover that it is irrelevant to them will not be amused.

- Remember that non-native English speakers will read your work. Use global English.

Descriptions of Web Pages

If you do not provide a description of your Web page, most search engines will simply reproduce the beginning of the page. Sometimes this content consists of a first-level heading and the first sentence or two of the content. More often, it consists of words from a navigation bar or other standard text, which offers no information unique to the page. In either case, the content displayed was probably not written with the Web searcher in mind.

And yet most people who read your content probably found it through a search engine. A description that accurately summarizes a page's content greatly improves your customers' odds of finding your content when they need it and not finding it when they do not need it.

A good description should:

- Clearly and accurately describe what the page is about.

- Put the most important information first. Many search engines will display only the first 255 characters of a description.

- Include keywords that users are likely to search for.

- Include relevant product names in as much detail as is appropriate.

- For white papers and other long articles, indicate the length of the document.

- Use short sentences, but do not let the summary become choppy. Given the overall brevity of descriptions, this should not usually be a problem.

- Describe a user action that will motivate people who should read the page and drive away people who shouldn't.

Correct

Find information about a new and improved set of Office services that professional developers can use to build a broad set of business solutions.

Incorrect

The Office XP platform consists of a new and improved set of Office services that professional developers can use to build a broad set of business solutions.

- Where appropriate, indicate what knowledge the reader should have.

Correct

Create top-level folders in various Visual Studio .NET dialog boxes for easy access to Enterprise Template projects. Readers should be familiar with Visual Studio .NET and Enterprise Templates. (5 printed pages)

- Where appropriate, say what the reader will learn from the document.

Correct

After reviewing the types of n-tier applications, you will learn how to create a typed dataset that can return data from a Web service and consume a Web service from a Windows application. (17 printed pages)

- Avoid superfluous words. Do not begin with stock phrases, such as "This article discusses" or "In this technical article, we will ...."

- Do not use the description as a sales pitch for a product or technology. The description should sell only the content, and only to people who need it.

HTML Tag, Element, and Attribute Styling   An "element" includes the tags, the attributes, and the content, if any. For example, consider the following:

```
<h1 align="center">This Is a Heading</h1>
```

In this example, the H1 element consists of the start tag (<h1>), including the **align** attribute, the **"center"** value of the **align** attribute, the content ("This Is a Heading"), and the end tag (</h1>).

Some elements, such as META and IMG (image), do not have start and end tags; they have only a single tag with attributes.

Formatting guidelines

- Use all uppercase for element names, and surround the element name with "the" and "element."

- Use angle brackets and lowercase for tags.

- Use bold and lowercase for attributes and their values.

Correct

The FONT element includes start and end tags, attributes, and any content within the tags. The start <font> tag begins the FONT element, and the end </font> tag ends the FONT element. In the FONT element, you can use attributes such as **face**, **size**, and **color**.

Note: HTML is not case-sensitive.

For more information, see *Document Conventions* in Chapter 2, "Content Formatting and Layout" and *Code Formatting Conventions* in Chapter 4, "Content for Software Developers."

XML Tag, Element, and Attribute Styling

Note: These guidelines also apply to Extensible Hypertext Markup Language (XHTML), Extensible Stylesheet Language (XSL), Extensible Stylesheet Language for Transformation (XSLT), and XML Path Language (XPath).

Elements vs. tags

An element includes the tags, the attributes, and the content, if any. For example, consider the following:

```
<xsl:apply-templates>
   order-by="sort-criteria-list"
   select=expression
   mode=QName>
</xsl:apply-templates>
```

In this example, the <xsl:apply-templates> element consists of the start tag (<xsl:apply-templates>); the **order-by**, **select**, and **mode** attributes; and the end tag (</xsl:apply-templates>).

Note that XML can have empty tags, such as <doctitle/> or `<elementName att1Name="att1Value" att2Name="att2Value"/>`. Empty tags have no textual content, whether or not they have attributes.

Capitalization

XML is a case-sensitive language, so be sure to follow the capitalization of the code, unless otherwise noted. Many items are in lowercase, but not all. When in doubt, check with the author.

Element name formatting

Predefined XSL Transformation (XSLT) element names are always bracketed (for example, the <xsl:attribute> element).

An element name can be presented in brackets if you are specifically referencing an example or code sample (for example, the <schema> element).

When working with document type definitions (DTDs) instead of schemas, some primary element names appear in all caps, and should remain styled as such (for example, the DOCTYPE element).

When working with schemas instead of DTDs, schema element names should appear in bold (for example, the **ElementType** element).

The name of any user-defined element should be left as is (for example, an author element, the bookstore element).

Attribute formatting

Attributes should be bold and capitalized as shown in code (for example, the **xml:space** attribute, the **STYLE** attribute).

Tag and node formatting

Tags and nodes should be bracketed, except when working with DTDs instead of schemas, in which case some tags are all caps, such as DOCTYPE element. For example:

the <first> and </last> tags of the <Schema> node

> **Note:** Capitalization should match what the user must type.

Other formatting

Collections, data types, functions, interfaces, methods, objects, properties, and scopes should be bold.

Parameters should be italic (for example, the *output-stylesheet* parameter).

Namespaces should be enclosed in quotation marks, (for example, the "BookInfo" namespace).

For more information, see *Document Conventions* in Chapter 2, "Content Formatting and Layout"; *Code Formatting Conventions* in Chapter 4, "Content for Software Developers"; and *HTML Tag, Element, and Attribute Styling* in this chapter.

5

Chapter 6
Indexing and Attributing

Technical content is only useful to customers if they can find it. One of the most important things you do as a content professional is index and/or attribute content to ensure that it is discoverable for your target users.

Indexing a printed document is different in some ways from indexing a collection of content that will be delivered online. In this section, you'll find tips and best practices for both.

Because Web search engines behave differently, this style guide does not address attributing content for discoverability on the Web.

This chapter contains the following sections:

- Indexing
- Keywords and Online Index Entries

Indexing   Users of documentation depend on indexes as their primary way to find the information they need, so an index must be complete, thorough, and accurate. Although the number of indexed terms per page will vary depending on the subject and complexity of the book, a rule of thumb is that a two-column index should be about 4 to 8 percent of the total number of pages in the book.

This topic describes some indexing concepts, but it focuses more on mechanical issues such as alphabetizing, style, and cross-references. Many of the points covered pertain primarily to printed indexes.

For information on developing search keywords and online index entries, see *Keywords and Online Index Entries* in this chapter.

Creating entries

When you develop index entries, consider the tasks the user will want to accomplish, previous versions of the product that may have used different terms, and the terminology of similar products the user might be familiar with. These principles are the same for both printed and online indexes.

Try to think like a user. A user who wants to delete paragraphs will probably look for the information under "paragraphs" and "deleting," possibly under "Delete command," but most likely not under "using Delete."

When you create new main entries, place the important word first. Depending on the kind of material, that word should probably be a noun (*commands*, *addresses*, *graphs*), but it can be a gerund (*copying*, *selecting*). Do not use nonessential words as the first in an entry and do not use vague gerunds such as "using" or "creating."

Invert entries whenever possible. For the previous example, you would include an entry for "paragraphs, deleting" and one for "deleting paragraphs." Other examples include items such as "arguments, command line" and "command-line arguments." Page numbers for inverted entries should match exactly.

Likewise, if you use synonyms to help the user find information in more than one place in the index, modifiers, subentries, and page numbers should match.

Creating subentries

For every main entry you create, make a subentry. You might have to delete those subentries later, but that is easier than having to add them.

Consider as subentries these generic terms, especially when a topic is covered in various places in the book: defined (to refer to a term), described (to refer to an action), introduction, and overview.

Avoid the use of prepositions to begin subentries. In some cases, however, prepositions can clarify relationships. Do not use articles to begin subentries.

Do not repeat a main term in the subentry.

Correct

pointers
　far
　function

Incorrect

pointers
　far pointers
　function pointers

Avoid using more than five page references after an entry. Subentries give more direction to the user. Do not, however, use only one subentry; there must be two or more.

Correct

paragraphs, deleting 72

Correct

paragraphs
　deleting 72
　formatting 79, 100

Incorrect

paragraphs
　deleting 72

Incorrect

paragraphs 72, 75, 79, 100, 103, 157

If possible, use only one level of subentries, but never more than two. Localized indexes can become unreadable with two levels of subentries because entry words are often lengthy and must be broken. If you use two levels of subentries, you should consider the impact on localization as early as possible.

Correct (one level of subentries)

paragraph formatting 75
  characters and words 63
  using styles 97
paragraphs, deleting 72

Correct (two levels of subentries)

paragraphs
  deleting 72
  formatting 75
    characters and words 63
    using styles 97

If a main entry is followed by subentries, do not leave the main entry as a widow at the bottom of a column. Also, if a list of subentries is long and will run over to a second column, repeat the main entry, followed by the word *continued*, at the beginning of the second column. If the column break occurs between two second-level subentries, repeat the main entry, followed by *continued*, and the subentry, also followed by *continued*. The word *continued* is lowercase, in parentheses, and italic (including the parentheses). Avoid leaving only one subentry before or after column breaks.

Correct (main entry continued)

paragraphs   paragraphs *(continued)*
  deleting 101   formatting 87–96
                   indenting 98

Correct (subentry continued)

paragraphs   paragraphs *(continued)*
  deleting 101   formatting *(continued)*
  formatting 87–96   characters and words 63
                   using styles 97

Incorrect

paragraphs   formatting 87–96
  deleting 101   indenting 98

Incorrect

paragraphs   paragraphs *(continued)*
                   deleting 101
                   formatting 87–96
                   indenting 98

Page references

Separate multiple page references with commas. Separate page ranges with en dashes. It is all right to use hyphens to indicate page ranges instead if you need to conserve space. Do not abbreviate page references.

If possible, avoid long multiple page references listing consecutive pages. A page range might better represent the topic. Likewise, avoid chapter or section length page ranges if the topic is clearly shown in the table of contents. Users prefer to be able to find more specific information.

Correct

paragraphs 24, 47, 126–130
  deleting 72–76
  formatting 87

Incorrect

paragraphs 24, 47, 126, 127, 128, 129, 130
  deleting 72, 73, 74, 75, 76
  formatting 87

Style and formatting

Use the index style in the same design template you used for your document. The font should be the same as that in the book, but in a smaller point size.

In general, do not use special character formats such as bold, monospace, or italic for entries. Use italic for cross-references (*See* and *See also* references).

Capitalization

If the source is the same for both printed and online documentation, use all lowercase for all index entries except those words that require capitalization and *See* and *See also* references.

Plural vs. singular

Use the plural form of all main entries that are nouns, except where it is awkward or illogical to do so. The following table shows correct use of both plural and singular.

Correct use of plural	Correct use of singular
borders	File command
files	e-mail
headers	ruler
paragraphs	window

Prepositions and articles

Limit the use of prepositions and articles. Use them only when they are necessary for clarity or sense. In general, do not use articles unless required for clarity.

Correct

child windows
    open, list of 128
    opening 132, 137
    reading from 140
    writing to 140
structures, in programming for Windows, 200

Verbs

Use a gerund rather than the infinitive or the present tense form for entries about actions, processes, or procedures.

Correct

selecting
    drawing objects 22
    text 147
shapes
    drawing 37
    fitting around text 140
    fitting text into 131
    substituting text 255

Incorrect

select
    art 255
    text 147
shapes
    to draw 37
    to fit around text 140

Versus vs. vs.

Use the abbreviation vs. (including the period) in index entries.

Correct

voice, active vs. passive 98

97

Cross-references in indexes

An index can have the following types of cross-references:

- *See*

- *See also*

- *See specific [name of item]*

- *See also specific [name of item]*

- *See herein*

Format the cross-reference phrases in italic, and capitalize *See* to avoid confusion with the actual entries. Use lowercase for the name of the entry referred to.

Place *See* cross-references on the same line as the entry, separated by two spaces. Place *See also* references on a separate line and sort them as the first subentry. (Optionally, if the main entry has no other subentries, you can place a *See also* reference on the same line. See the "pontoons" entry in the following example.)

Do not use page numbers with cross-references. Alphabetize multiple topics following one cross-reference and separate them with semicolons.

Correct
airplanes *See* planes
airports *See specific airport*
floatplanes 101–105
planes
  See also specific plane
  rudders
    control 66–67
    types 61
  steering
    See also rudders
    guidelines 45
    taxiing *See herein* takeoff
  takeoff
    control tower 19
    steering 22, 25, 27
pontoons 98 *See also* floatplanes
seaplanes
  See also aeronautics; floatplanes; pontoons
  rudders
    controls 66–67
    types 61
steering *See* rudders
water
  See also seaplanes
  taking off on 18

Order of entries

Special characters appear at the beginning of the index, followed by numeric entries, sorted in ascending order. Alphabetical entries then follow. Separate the categories with headings if there are many of them; if there are only a few headings, no special separation is necessary. Use the heading *Symbols* for special characters if you use a heading.

Alphabetizing indexes

Do alphabetization word by word, not letter by letter. That is, words separated by spaces or commas are treated as two words. Alphabetizing stops at the end of a word unless the first word of two or more entries is the same. Then the first letter of the second word determines alphabetical order, and so on. Letter-by-letter alphabetization ignores spaces, treating each entry as one word. Compare the columns in the following table to see the difference. For more information, see *The Chicago Manual of Style*.

Word by word	*Letter by letter*
D key	Delete command
DEL key	deleting
Delete command	DEL key
deleting	D key

Special characters

Index special characters at least twice. List each character by its symbol, followed by its name in parentheses, as the next example shows. Also list each character by name, followed by its symbol in parentheses. You might also want to index some characters under a general category, such as "operators."

Special characters that are not part of a word are sorted in ASCII sort order. The name of the character follows in parentheses. They appear at the beginning of the index, followed by numeric entries.

Correct

% (percent)

& (ampersand)

((opening parenthesis)

) (closing parenthesis)

* (asterisk)

| (pipe)

~ (tilde)

Special characters followed by letters or within a word are ignored in alphabetizing and are usually included in the alphabetical listing. Sometimes, however, you may want to include such entries in both the alphabetical list and in the list of special characters.

Correct

Error

errors, correcting

^p

paragraphs

#VALUE

values

Sorting numbers as numbers

Numeric entries should be placed in ascending order, with entries containing only numbers falling before those containing both numbers and letters. This requires editing to correct the computer sort. Compare these two lists of sorted numerics:

Computer-sorted	Edited
12-hour clock	80386
2-D chart	80486
24-hour clock	2 macro
80386	2-D chart
80486	3-D chart
1904 date system	12-hour clock
366-day year	24-hour clock
3-D area chart	366-day year
2 macro	1900 date system
1900 date system	1904 date system

Numbers follow the list of special characters and precede alphabetical entries.

Sorting spaces and punctuation

Entries that have the same letters but different spacing or punctuation are governed first by the rules of word-by-word alphabetization and then by the rule for sorting special characters by their ASCII order: Spaces alone come first; then spaces following commas. Next come unusual connecting characters, in ASCII order: periods, colons and double colons, underscores, and so on. Apostrophes, hyphens, and slashes are ignored, so those entries will come last, in that order.

Correct

_name changers

name changers

name, changers

NAME.CHANGERS

name:changers

name_changers

.namechangers

namechangers

namechanger's

name-changers

name/changers

Keywords and Online Index Entries

Online indexes should look similar to print indexes: They have two levels with indented subentries. Many of the same conceptual guidelines for print indexes apply to online indexes.

The *keyword* is the term that a user associates with a specific task or set of information. The user types a keyword in the **Find** or **Index** box to locate specific information in a document. A keyword can lead to a single topic or to many related topics.

When deciding what keywords to list, consider these categories:

- Terms for a novice user of your product
- Terms for an advanced user of your product
- Common synonyms for words in the topics
- Words that describe the topic generally
- Words that describe the topic specifically
- Words commonly used in related products

Look specifically at these elements of your document for potential keywords when you develop your index:

- Headings
- Terms and concepts important to the user
- Overviews
- Procedures and user actions
- Acronyms
- Definitions or new terms
- Commands, functions, methods, and properties

Order of entries

Sort HTMLHelp indexes in the same way as print indexes. You cannot manually sort the search keywords, so the order follows the ASCII sort order. Special characters appear first, then numbers, and then alphabetic entries.

Style of indexed keywords

Follow most of the same general style guidelines as those used for printed indexes:

- Use gerunds (the   form) rather than infinitives (the   form) or the present tense of verbs for task-oriented entries, unless they are unsuitable, as they may be for languages, systems, or localized versions.

- Avoid generic gerunds that users are unlikely to look up: *using, changing, creating, getting, making, doing*, and so on.

- Use plural for nouns unless it is inappropriate. This applies to both single keywords (*bookmarks*, not *bookmark*) and keyword phrases (*copying files*, not *copying a file*).

- Do not use articles (*a*, *an*, *the*) and avoid prepositions at the beginning of a keyword.

- Keep keywords as short as practicable for clarity.

- Use synonyms liberally, especially terms used in competitors' products or terms some users are likely to know: *option* and *radio button*, for example. Provide a cross-reference to the term that you are actually using.

- For acronyms and abbreviations, list both the spelled-out phrase followed by the acronym or abbreviation in parentheses and the acronym or abbreviation followed by the spelled-out version: *terminate-and-stay-resident (TSR)* and *TSR (terminate-and-stay-resident)*. If appropriate, provide a cross-reference at the less-used of the two entries.

- Use all lowercase for all keywords and index terms unless the term is a proper noun or case-sensitive and thus capitalized in the Help topic.

  Correct
  clearing tab stops
  clip art
  Close command
  modems
    dialing a connection manually
    setting up
    troubleshooting

Some content will be shared among products. Single-sourcing—using the same file for both the Help topic about copying and a book chapter about copying, for example—may extend across products instead of just occurring within a single product. Standardizing index entries across such products will simplify content reuse, and it will provide users with a consistent and predictable way of finding such information.

Topics, particularly those for technical support services and accessibility, should have standard keywords. For example, the technical support topic must include these keywords:

- assistance, customer
- customer assistance
- help
- technical support
- phone support
- product support
- support services
- telephone support
- troubleshooting

Merging keywords from multiple files

Help systems today can present a single index for multiple Help files. The keywords from the separate Help files are merged as if the main contents file specifies each Help file. If such a Help system contains an optional component that the user does not install, those keywords will not show up in the index, but will be added to the index if the user installs the component later.

A merged set of keywords can be very helpful for users. However, it is essential that the keywords fit together appropriately. For example, if the main Help file uses the phrase *exiting programs*, all Help files in the project should use this phrase rather than just *exiting*. Otherwise, when the keywords from multiple files are merged, the user will see two entries: "exiting" and "exiting programs."

Cross-references

Avoid cross-references in online indexes. They are more difficult to handle in keyword lists than in print indexes.

Because each keyword must be linked to at least one Help topic, a cross-reference keyword has to jump somewhere, perhaps to an overview, or "main," topic. It is often difficult to determine which topic that should be.

Also, cross-references (*See* and *See also*) are limited to normal keywords that jump directly to the topic containing the K (keyword) footnote with that keyword. The cross-reference does not jump to another location in the index.

Instead of a cross-reference, duplicate all the subentries under both of the main keywords. For example, list all topics for "insertion point" under "cursor (insertion point)" as well.

If you must include a cross-reference to other topics, you will want to force it to the top of the list of subentries. Talk to your indexer about how to do this.

For more information, see *Indexing* in this chapter.

6

Chapter 7
Tone and Rhetoric

An important aspect of style is establishing an authorial voice. Tone helps establish the relationship between the writer and the reader and is a major contributor to the personality of the writing. Being sensitive to the needs of people with disabilities assures them that their potential is important to us. Removing other bias from your content is also essential. This section discusses these issues, along with some rhetorical approaches that can help or hinder the effectiveness of your message.

For more information about writing style, see *Jargon* and *Word Choice* in Chapter 3, "Global Content."

This chapter contains the following sections:

- Tone and the Reader
- Bias-Free Communication
- Parallelism
- Anthropomorphism
- Humor

Tone and the Reader   Tone defines the relationship between the writer and the reader. Because writing represents the company, it is important that we adopt a consistent tone. Certain aspects of writing can vary according to the audience and situation—for example, you would not address an Xbox user who is learning a new game in the same way you would address a system administrator who is deploying Microsoft Exchange Server on a large network—but even at these extremes, our tone in each case should be respectful, reassuring, professional, and friendly.

The tone of writing should convey these values:

- **Empathy.**   We understand our customers' needs, and we see meeting their needs as being in both our interests. We are more focused on solving problems than on describing product features.

  Correct

  To add messaging functionality to your client application, you can use the Simple MAPI functions. The topics in this section cover the major areas of functionality that a Simple MAPI client needs to implement, such as:

  - Initializing your client so that it can use the Simple MAPI functions.
  - Creating messages.
  - Managing attachments.

Incorrect

This overview describes the services available in the audio compression manager (ACM) and explains the programming techniques used to access these services.

- **Responsibility.**   We think through the ways comments will be perceived; we do not dictate in writing.

Correct

Free technical support is available when you register with Microsoft.

- **Passion.**   We strive to make content usable and useful with a minimum of effort on the reader's part. Doing so can be as simple as spelling out common phrases instead of reducing them to an acronym that only initiated readers are really comfortable with.

- **Inspiration.**   We help our customers solve their problems, but we can also help them create opportunities by using our products in ways they had not thought of before.

Most of the writing that we do for our customers can be considered formal writing. *Formal*, in this context, does not mean stiff or academic or overly passive. It simply means that we convey a professional image of competence and helpfulness. There is no contradiction between formal writing and a friendly tone. But a too-casual tone can sound presumptuous, and it will annoy many readers. Knowing who you are writing for and what the goal of your writing is will usually guide you to the appropriate tone for the occasion.

Bias-Free Communication   Documentation and art should show diverse individuals from all walks of life participating fully in various activities. Specifically, avoid terms that may show bias with regard to gender, race, culture, ability, age, sexual orientation, or socioeconomic class.

Use the following sections to evaluate your work and eliminate bias and stereotypes from it.

Avoid racial, cultural, sexual, and other stereotypes

- Use gender-neutral or all-inclusive terms to refer to human beings, rather than terms using *man* and similar masculine terms.

Use these terms	*Instead of*
Chair, moderator	Chairman
Humanity, people, humankind	Man, mankind
Operates, staffs	Mans
Sales representative	Salesman
Synthetic, manufactured	Man-made
Workforce, staff, personnel	Manpower

- Avoid the generic masculine pronoun. Use *the* instead of *his*, or rewrite material in the second person (*you*) or in the plural. If necessary, use a plural pronoun such as *they* or *their* with an indefinite singular antecedent, such as *everyone*, or with multiple antecedents of different or unknown genders, such *John* and *Chris*. Use *his* or *her* for the singular possessive case if you can do so infrequently and if nothing else works.

Correct

A user can change the default settings.

You can change the default settings.

Someone may have the file checked out on his or her computer.

John and Chris each have their own profile.

The message remains there until your friend logs on to the Internet and retrieves his or her messages.

Incorrect

A user can change his default settings.

Each employee can arrive when he wishes.

Each employee can arrive when s/he wishes.

- Use a variety of first names, both male and female, that reflect different cultural backgrounds.
- In art, show men and women of all ages, members of all ethnic groups, and people with disabilities in a wide variety of professions, educational settings, locales, and economic settings.
- Avoid stereotypes relating to family structure, leisure activities, and purchasing power. If you show various family groupings, consider showing nontraditional and extended families.
- Try to avoid topics that reflect primarily a Western, affluent lifestyle.

Avoid stereotypes of people with disabilities

Make products and documentation accessible to all, regardless of disabilities, and portray, positively, people with disabilities in documentation.

Use these terms	*Instead of*
Blind, has low vision, visually impaired (this term encompasses people with blindness, low vision, or color anomalies)	Sight-impaired, vision-impaired, seeing-impaired
People who are deaf or hard of hearing	Hearing-impaired
Has limited dexterity, has motion disabilities, is physically disabled, uses a wheelchair	Crippled, lame, wheelchair-bound, confined to a wheelchair, restricted to a wheelchair
People with disabilities	The disabled, disabled people, people with handicaps, the handicapped
People without disabilities	Able-bodied, normal, regular, healthy
Cognitive disabilities, developmental disabilities	Slow learner, retarded, mentally handicapped
Has multiple sclerosis	Is affected by MS
Has cerebral palsy	CP victim
Has epilepsy or a seizure disorder	Is an epileptic
Has muscular dystrophy	Stricken by MD
Is unable to speak or uses synthetic speech	Dumb, mute
Has mental retardation	Retarded, mentally defective

- Avoid equating people with their disabilities. In general, focus on the person, not the disability. Whenever possible, use terms that refer to physical differences as nouns rather than adjectives. For example, use wording such as "customers who are blind or have low vision" and "users with limited dexterity."

  Note: The phrases "she is blind" and "he is deaf" are acceptable.

- Do not use terms that depersonalize and group people as if they were identical, such as "the blind" and "the deaf."

  Correct

  Customers who are blind can use these features.

  Play-goers who are deaf or hard-of-hearing can attend signed performances.

  Incorrect

  The blind can use these features.

  Theaters now offer signed performances for the deaf.

- Avoid using terms that engender discomfort, pity, or guilt, such as *suffers from, stricken with,* or *afflicted by.*

- Avoid mentioning a disability unless it is pertinent.

- Include people with disabilities in art and illustrations, showing them integrated in an unremarkable way with other members of society. In drawings of buildings and blueprints, show ramps for wheelchair accessibility.

For background reading and in-depth information, see the following sources:

Dumond, Val. *The Elements of Nonsexist Usage: A Guide to Inclusive Spoken and Written English.* New York: Prentice Hall Press, 1990.

Guidelines for Bias-Free Publishing. New York: McGraw-Hill, n.d.

Maggio, Rosalie. *The Bias-Free Word Finder: A Dictionary of Nondiscriminatory Language.* Boston: Beacon Press, 1991.

Schwartz, Marilyn. *Guidelines for Bias-Free Writing.* Bloomington, IN: University Press, 1995.

Parallelism

Parallelism ensures that elements of sentences that are similar in purpose are also similar in structure. Parallel structures emphasize the similarities of the parallel elements, and they enhance readability by making the content more predictable.

Parallelism in lists

Items in lists should be parallel to each other in structure. For example, all the items can complete the introductory fragment with a verb phrase.

Correct

There are several ways to open documents in Windows. You can:

- Open your document from within the program you used to create it.
- Use the **My Recent Documents** command on the **Start** menu to open a document that you have used recently.
- Use the **Search** command on the **Start** menu to locate the document and then open it.
- Double-click a document icon in My Computer.

Incorrect

There are several ways to open documents in Windows:

- You can open your document from within the program you used to create it.
- Use the **My Recent Documents** command on the **Start** menu to open a document that you have used recently.
- The **Search** command on the **Start** menu locates the document, and you can then open it.
- Double-clicking a document icon in My Computer opens a document.

Parallelism in procedures

In procedures, steps should be written in parallel style, typically as sentences with imperative verbs.

Correct

To share your printer

1. Click the **Start** button, point to **Settings**, and then click **Printers**.
2. In the Printers window, click the printer you want to share.
3. On the **File** menu, click **Sharing**.

Incorrect

To share your printer

1. Clicking the **Start** button, you point to **Settings**, and then click **Printers**.
2. In the Printers window, the printer you want to share should be selected.
3. On the **File** menu, click **Sharing**.

Parallelism in sentences

For parallel structure, balance parts of a sentence with their correlating parts (nouns with nouns, prepositional phrases with prepositional phrases, and so on). Sometimes, to make the parallelism clear, you may need to repeat a preposition, an article (*a, an, the*), the *to* in an infinitive, or the introductory word in a clause or phrase.

Correct

The *User's Guide* contains common tasks, visual overviews, a catalog of features, and an illustrated glossary of terms. [parallel objects with the articles added]

With this feature, you can choose which components to install and which ones to file away for later use. [parallel clauses]

Other indicators can appear on the taskbar, such as a printer representing your print job or a battery representing power on your portable computer. [parallel phrases]

Incorrect

The *User's Guide* contains common tasks, visual overviews, a catalog of features, and illustrated glossary of terms.

With this feature, you can choose which components to install and the ones you will file away for later use.

Other indicators can appear on the taskbar, such as a printer to represent your print job or a battery representing power on your portable computer.

Anthropomorphism   Anthropomorphism is attributing human characteristics or behavior to things that are not human. In technical writing, there is an understandable temptation to anthropomorphize to make difficult material easier for the reader to relate to. Do not succumb to this temptation.

Because anthropomorphism is a form of metaphor, it can cause the same readability problems as other forms of metaphor. Not all readers will grasp the limits of the metaphor. Further, anthropomorphic metaphors might be interpreted differently by people from different cultures.

Anthropomorphism in technical writing is often the result of an imprecise or incomplete understanding of the topic at hand. Although anthropomorphism might help you work toward a clearer understanding, your own content should reflect the result, not the process, of your learning.

Correct

If you receive a confirmation message, the engine will store your data in the specified format.

Incorrect

If you receive a confirmation message, the engine will behave as you requested.

Sometimes terminology forces anthropomorphism upon us. For example, in a hierarchical relationship, a *child* object is said to *inherit* attributes from its *parent* or *ancestors*. If, as in this case, the anthropomorphic metaphor is well-established and limited, and its limitations are clear, go ahead and use it—taking care to explain what some readers may not understand about the metaphor. Straining to avoid such usage would introduce more confusion than the metaphor itself, especially among initiated readers.

Be skeptical of established usage, though. If anthropomorphism is not the predominant way a concept is expressed in edited publications or on Web sites, find another way to express the concept.

Sometimes the user interface or application programming interface of a feature is anthropomorphic. In dealing with wizards, assistants, guides, and other characters built into a program, you must let your professional judgment guide you in deciding how much the documentation should reinforce the anthropomorphism of the feature. But do not use

7

words or phrases that convey intention or desire (such as *refuses* or *wants* or *is interested in*), intellect (*thinks, knows, realizes*), or emotion (*likes*).

Correct

The speech recognition engine accepts only the following words.

Documents manage data; views display the data and accept operations on it.

You do not have to use the **sizeof** operator to find the size of a Date object because the **new** operator encapsulates this behavior.

Incorrect

The speech recognition engine is interested only in the following words.

Documents know how to manage data; views know how to display the data and accept operations on it.

You do not have to use the **sizeof** operator to find the size of a Date object because the **new** operator can tell what size the object is.

Words to watch out for

The following words may be acceptable in the right context, but they often signal inappropriate anthropomorphism. Some are appropriate only for programmers or information technology professionals. This list is not exhaustive. When in doubt, check your project style sheet.

answer	demand	realize	think
assume	interested in	recognize	understand
aware	know	refuse	want
behave	like	remember	
decide	own	see	

Humor

Although humor often seems like a good way to liven up a dull topic, in global content it can confuse or even offend people, no matter how straightforward or innocent it seems from the writer's cultural reference point. A jocular tone may sound patronizing to some users, and others may not understand the joke. Humor causes problems in localization, as well. For example, puns can seldom be translated.

In some cultures, certain relationships are customarily handled with deference and respect and should not be the subject of jokes. For example, poking fun at a boss or an older person may be offensive.

Chapter 8
Accessible Content

Products and services—including documentation—should be easy for everyone to use. Content can also be created to maximize accessibility to people with disabilities. For example, printed documentation should be made available in accessible formats for users who have difficulty handling or reading conventionally printed materials. A format most commonly used is XML. HTML is also acceptable if it follows accessible design guidelines.

This chapter contains the following sections:

- Accessibility Appendix
- Accessible Web Pages
- Accessible Writing
- Accessible Graphics and Design
- Acceptable Terminology
- Additional Resources

Accessibility Appendix   In both online and printed documentation, every product should include an appendix describing features and services that can aid persons with disabilities. Each appendix describes accessibility options available in the product or from other sources, such as Recording for the blind. This appendix makes it easier for users with disabilities to use products, raises public awareness of the available options, and demonstrates a company's commitment in this area.

Include this appendix as a Help topic and in the printed book most likely to be the first one opened.

Accessible Web Pages   Keep in mind that not only do people with various kinds of disabilities need information from your Web site, but so do people using various kinds of browsers, who have graphics turned off, or who may not have the latest technical wizardry. The guidelines given here are brief reminders. You can find more details about the rationale for these guidelines and some ways to accomplish them on these Web sites:

- The MSDN Accessibility site at *http://msdn.microsoft.com/default.aspx*
- The Center for Information Technology Accommodation (CITA) of the U.S. General Services Administration at *http://www.gsa.gov/Portal/gsa/ep/home.do?tabId=0*

- Section 508 of the Rehabilitation Act of 1998 at *http://www.section508.gov /index.cfm*

- Trace Research and Development Center at the University of Wisconsin at *http: //trace.wisc.edu*

To enhance the accessibility of Web pages for people who use screen readers, follow these guidelines:

- Always provide *alt text* for nontext elements, including graphics, audio, and video. For simple elements, a brief but accurate description is enough. Use an asterisk (*) or the word "bullet" for bullets, not a description such as "little blue ball." Leave blank information about invisible placeholders. For more complex elements, provide a link to a separate page with more details.

- Provide text links in addition to image maps.

- Write link text that is meaningful but brief. Do not use phrases such as *click here*. Use links that can stand alone in a list. Use the <TITLE> tag to distinguish links and names in image maps from ambiguous or duplicate text.

- Make link text distinct. Use redundant visual cues, such as both color and under-line, so colorblind users can identify link text.

- Plan links and image map links so that navigation with the TAB key moves from left to right and top to bottom, not randomly.

- If you use frames, provide alternate pages without them.

- If you use tables, provide alternate pages without them. Make sure that tables make sense when read from left to right, top to bottom. Note that Internet Explorer versions 3 and 4 have some different and strict requirements.

- Provide closed captions, transcripts, or descriptions of audio content.

- Avoid using scrolling marquees.

Accessible Writing

Many of the following suggestions for maximizing accessibility also help make documentation clearer and more useful for everyone:

- Provide clear, concise descriptions of the product and initial setup, including a section or card that gets the user up and running with the basic features.

- Keep the number of steps in a procedure short. Individuals with cognitive impair-ments may have difficulty following multistep procedures. Keep the steps simple, and keep the reader oriented.

- Keep sentence structure simple. Try to limit most sentences to one clause. Indi-viduals with language difficulties and those who speak English as a second lan-guage, as well as some people who are deaf or hard of hearing, may have difficulty understanding long, complicated sentences.

- Provide descriptions that do not require pictures, or that include both pictures and writing. Using only diagrams causes difficulty transcribing to other media. To test whether the writing is effective, try removing, one at a time, first the words and then the pictures. With only one method, can you still figure out what to do?

- Avoid using directional terms (left, right, up, down) as the only clue to location. Individuals with cognitive impairments might have difficulty interpreting them, as do blind users relying on screen-reading software. A directional term is acceptable if another indication of location, such as *in the **Save As** dialog box*, *on the **Standard** toolbar*, or *in the title bar*, is also included. Directional terms are also acceptable when a sighted user with dyslexia can clearly see a change in the interface as the result of an action, such as a change in the right pane when an option in the left pane is clicked.

- Emphasize key information and put it near the beginning of the text. Use bullets or headings to additionally emphasize important points.

- Keep paragraphs short or otherwise create small sections or text groupings.

- In product documentation, document all keyboard shortcuts. A two-column format, in which the first column describes the user task and the second column describes the shortcut, is best. That way, users with screen readers can hear the task before they hear the keyboard shortcut. Organize keyboard shortcuts in task groupings so related shortcuts appear close together.

Accessible Graphics and Design

It is possible to work within the requirements of standard design templates to make written content as visually accessible as possible. For example, use short paragraphs and break up long passages of text with subheadings.

Follow these guidelines for visually accessible documents:

- Do not use color coding alone. Use additional cues, such as textual annotations or the underlines. Alternatively, use patterns as well as colors to indicate different types of information in charts and graphs.

- Avoid hard-to-read color combinations, such as red and green or light green and white. People with some types of colorblindness may have difficulty seeing the differences between the colors.

- Avoid screened art. Contrasting black and white is easiest to read. Especially avoid text on a screened background, which is difficult to see and for a machine to scan. For the same reason, avoid shaded backgrounds and watermarks or other images behind text.

- Avoid printing text outside a rectangular grid. People with low vision may have difficulty seeing text outside of an established grid. Try to keep text in a uniform space for both visibility and scannability.

8

Acceptable Terminology   In general, refer to "a person with a kind of disability," not "a disabled person." Consider the person first, not the label. Use terms that describe positively people with disabilities and the disabilties themselves.

For more information, see the table of terms in *Bias-Free Communication* in Chapter 7, "Tone and Rhetoric."

Additional Resources   For information about how to make products accessible and for ideas about what you can do to assist in these efforts, see these sources:

- The corporate Accessibility and Disabilities site at *http://www.microsoft.com/enable*

- Accessibility information for software developers on the MSDN Web site at *http://msdn.microsoft.com/default.aspx*

8

Chapter 9
Common Style Problems

Unlike grammatical rules, the formatting style of elements such as dates, numbers, and measurements can be open to interpretation. As a result, customers are faced with inconsistent styles that can lead to confusion and misunderstandings. Providing a consistent style for presenting these elements benefits customers by making your content more readable and easier to understand. This section will discuss some of the most common style problems and provide you with guidelines to address these issues.

This chapter contains the following sections:

- Procedures
- Dates
- Capitalization
- Measurements and Units of Measure
- Numbers
- Protocols
- Names of Special Characters
- Telephone Numbers
- Time Zones
- URLs, Addresses
- Company with Product Names
- Version Identifiers
- Readme Files and Release Notes
- Bibliographies
- Titles of Publications

Procedures   A procedure is a short description of the steps a user takes to complete a specific task. Procedures are set off from the main text by their formatting. In product documentation, a procedure is normally a discrete topic. In Knowledge Base articles or other Web content, a procedure can be part of a how-to article or a white paper.

In most materials, always document the preferred method of performing a procedure if there is more than one way to do something. The preferred method should reflect the needs of the audience as much as possible. For example, the preferred method might be to use menus and commands, or it might be to use toolbar buttons.

The mouse is usually the preferred user input tool for most operations. For the most part, mouse procedures are not a problem for users with disabilities; they know how to translate mouse actions to their preferred style of user input. One way to present alternative methods, however, is by judiciously using tips. For information about documenting an alternative method in addition to the preferred method, see *Branching Within Procedures* later in this section.

Always present a procedure (except a single-step procedure) in a numbered list and, in most cases, include a procedure heading in the form of an infinitive phrase. Do not add punctuation at the end of the heading. This is a typical procedure heading:

To merge subdocuments

Avoid intervening text between the procedure heading and the procedure itself.

Procedure lists

Most procedures consist of a number of sequential steps formatted as a numbered list.

Multiple-step procedures   General rules for numbered lists also apply to procedures, especially the following:

- Set individual steps as separate numbered entries. However, short steps can be combined if they occur in the same place (within one dialog box, for example).

    Both of the following examples are correct, although the first is more commonly used.

    Correct
    1. On the **Tools** menu, click **Options**, and then click the **Edit** tab.
    2. ...

    1. On the **Tools** menu, click **Options**.
    2. Click the **Edit** tab.

- Do not use a period following the step number unless your document design requires it.

- Use complete sentences.

- Use parallel construction.

- Capitalize the first word in each step.

- Use a period after each step. An exception is when you are instructing users to type input that does not include end punctuation. In this case, try to format the text so the user input appears on a new line.

9

- In printed matter, try to keep all steps in a procedure on one page or left-right (verso-recto) page spread, and avoid continuing a procedure across a right-left (recto-verso) break. In online content, try to keep a procedure to one screen.

- Avoid burying procedural information in narrative text; the procedure will be hard to find and follow.

Single-step procedures Most document designs have a single-step bullet to mark a single-step procedure. Each design specifies the type of single-step bullet. Never number a single-step procedure as "1."

Correct

To look at the PERT Chart

- On the **View** menu, click **PERT Chart**.

Incorrect

To look at the PERT Chart

1. On the **View** menu, click **PERT Chart**.

Writing procedure steps

As a general rule, tell the user where the action should take place before describing the action to take. This prevents users from doing the right thing in the wrong place. However, avoid overloading procedures with locators. Assume that the user is looking at the screen and is starting from the position where the procedure begins. For example, the following phrasing is typical: "On the **View** menu, click **Zoom**."

However, if there is a chance that the reader might be confused about where the action should take place or if an introductory phrase is needed, the following wording can be used: "To magnify your document, click **View**, and then click **Zoom**," or "In Control Panel, double-click **Passwords**, and then click **Change Passwords**."

> **Note:** It is not necessary to end a procedure with "Click **OK**" unless there is some possibility of confusion.

The following sections give brief guidelines on how to treat the main elements in the user interface: folders and icons, commands, and dialog box options.

9

Folders and icons   Users *click* or *double-click* a folder or an icon to initiate an action; for example, starting a program or viewing a list of subfolders.

When you want the user to	*Use this syntax*
Switch to a program that is already running on the desktop	On the taskbar, click the **Microsoft Excel** button.
	Switch to Microsoft Excel.
Start a program	Click the **Start** button, and then point to **All Programs**. Point to **Microsoft Office**, and then click **Microsoft Office Word 2003**.
Select an icon before changing its properties, moving it, or taking some other action	Right-click **Microsoft Office PowerPoint 2003**, and then click **Properties**.
Start a Control Panel item	In Control Panel, double-click **Printers**.
Choose any other icon, such as a folder icon or drive icon	Double-click **Recycle Bin**.

Commands   Use the following syntax for commands.

When you want the user to	*Use this syntax*
Run a command on a menu	On the **Tools** menu, click **Address Book**.
Run a command, and then select an option in a dialog box	On the **Tools** menu, point to **Language**, click **Hyphenation**, and then select the **Automatically hyphenate document** check box.
Click a button in a dialog box	Click **Apply**.
Run a command on a submenu	Click the **Start** button, point to **My Recent Documents**, and then click the document you want.
	Click the **Start** button, point to **All Programs**, point to **Accessories**, and then click **Windows Explorer**.

9

Dialog box options Use *click* for selecting dialog box options and tabs and for choosing command buttons.

Tell users to *type* in text boxes or *enter* an element such as a file name that they can either type or select from a list. When you are referring generally to a feature, *turn off* and *turn on* are acceptable, but use *select* and *clear* to refer to check boxes that turn the feature on and off. You can say "click to select" if the action may not be obvious to your audience.

The following table gives a few examples.

When you want the user to	*Use this syntax*
Select an option	In the **Print** dialog box, click **All**.
Open a tabbed section in a dialog box	In the **Font** dialog box, click **Character Spacing**.
Insert text in a combo box	In the **File name** box, enter the name of the file.
Select multiple check boxes	On the **Print** tab, select the **Comments** and **Hidden text** check boxes.
Select items in a group box	Under **Include with document**, select the **Comments** and **Hidden text** check boxes.

Procedure style

Follow standard document conventions in procedures:

- Follow interface capitalization. In most cases, menu and command names use title caps. Capitalization of dialog box options varies. If in doubt, or if necessary for consistency, use sentence-style caps. Use bold type for labels to help the reader parse the sentence correctly.

  Correct

  Click **Date and Time**.

  Select the **Provide feedback with sound** check box.

- If a command name or dialog box option ends with a colon or ellipsis, do not include this punctuation.

  Correct

  Click **Save As**.

  Incorrect

  Click **Save As** ...

9

121

- Limit your use of the descriptors *button* and *option button*, except where the descriptor helps to avoid confusing or awkward phrasing or is necessary to avoid confusion with another element.

- Use bold for user input and italic for placeholders. User input can be on the same line as the procedural step or it can be displayed on a new line. If the input is on the same line, what the user types should be the last word or words of the step and should not be followed by end punctuation (unless the user needs to type the end punctuation).

  Correct

  Type *password*

  In the **Date** box, type:

  April 1

- Use a monospace font for program input and output text.

For more information, see *Dialog Boxes and Property Sheets* and *Menus and Commands* in Chapter 1, "Documenting the User Interface"; *Document Conventions* in Chapter 2, "Content Formatting and Layout"; and *Code Formatting Conventions* in Chapter 4, "Content for Software Developers."

Mouse vs. keyboard procedures

You can document procedures in one of two ways:

- Mouse actions only, using terms such as *click*, *double-click*, and *point to*.

  Note: For pen-computing documentation, use the words *tap* and *double-tap*.

- Separate mouse and keyboard actions, explaining first the mouse method and then the keyboard method. Whenever possible, avoid a page break between the keyboard and the mouse versions of a procedure.

The trend is to document with only mouse actions. Note, however, that this method makes documentation less accessible to people with certain disabilities. When in doubt, consult your project style sheet.

Joystick procedures

Assume that the mouse is the primary input device. Include joystick information in a table along with other alternative input devices.

Branching within procedures

If there are multiple ways to do an entire procedure, and if you must describe each alternative, use a table to detail the alternatives, as in the following example. This approach helps the user know when to use which method.

9

Correct

To	Do this
Save changes to the existing file and continue working	On the **File** menu, click **Save**.
Save changes to the existing file and exit the program	On the **File** menu, click **Exit**. If a dialog box asks if you want to save changes, click **Yes**.

If one step has an alternative, that alternative should be a separate paragraph in the step. In a single-step procedure, an alternative can be separated by the word *or* to make it clearer to the user that an alternative is available.

Correct

Press the key for the underlined letter in the menu name.

You can also use the LEFT ARROW key or the RIGHT ARROW key to move to another menu.

To open a menu

- Press ALT+the key for the underlined letter in the menu name.

  –or–

- Use the LEFT ARROW key or the RIGHT ARROW key to move to another menu.

Incorrect

Press ALT+the key for the underlined letter in the menu name. You can also use the LEFT ARROW key or the RIGHT ARROW key to move to another menu.

1. Press the key for the underlined letter in the menu name; or,

1. Use the LEFT ARROW key or the RIGHT ARROW key to move to another menu.

For several choices within one procedure step, use a bulleted list.

Correct

1. Select the text you want to move or copy.

2. Do one of the following:
   - To move the selection, click the **Cut** button on the toolbar.
   - To copy the selection, click the **Copy** button on the toolbar.

3. Position the insertion point in the new location, and then click **Paste**.

9

Supplementary information and text within procedures

Most of the time, users go to procedures for reference, not for instruction. Avoid putting explanatory or supplementary information, which describes special cases or behaviors that are not essential to completing the procedure, within the procedure itself. If supplementary information is necessary to describe a procedure, put it in a single paragraph after the procedure. If absolutely necessary, put such a paragraph after the step it explains and indent it to align with the procedure text. If the supplementary information includes steps, make it a separate procedure and provide a cross-reference.

Avoid explicit descriptions of system responses. If necessary to orient the reader, include the response in the step or the one immediately following.

Correct

Click **Options**, and then select the **Reverse Print Order** check box.

1. Click **Options** to display more options.

2. Select the **Reverse Print Order** check box.

1. Click **Options**.

2. In the expanded list of options, select the **Reverse Print Order** check box.

Incorrect

1. Click **Options**.

   The dialog box expands to display more options.

2. Select the **Reverse Print Order** check box.

For information about documenting key commands, see *Key Names* in Chapter 1, "Documenting the User Interface."

Dates   Use this format to indicate a date: *month day, year*, as in July 31, 2000. Do not use *day month year* or an all-number method. Do not use ordinal numbers to indicate a date.

Correct

February 23, 2000

June 11, 1999

Incorrect

23 February 2000

6/11/99

11/6/99

April 21st

When a date appears in the middle of a sentence, set off the year with commas.

Correct

The February 23, 2001, issue of the *New York Times* ....

Incorrect

The February 23, 2001 issue of the *New York Times* ....

The February 23 2001 issue of the *New York Times* ....

To indicate a month and year only, do not use commas.

Correct

The February 2001 issue of *MSDN Magazine* ....

Avoid abbreviations of months unless necessary to save space. If you must use abbreviations, use three-letter abbreviations: *Jan.*, *Feb.*, *Mar.*, *Apr.*, *May*, *Jun.*, *Jul.*, *Aug.*, *Sep.*, *Oct.*, *Nov.*, and *Dec.*

Capitalization

In general, capitalize the initial letter of a proper noun but do not capitalize that of a common noun. Follow these general guidelines regarding capitalization:

- Never use all uppercase for emphasis. Use italic type instead.

- Follow the capitalization rules or conventions of software or a specific product as necessary, such as case-sensitive keywords or product names with internal capitalization.

- Do not capitalize the spelled-out form of an acronym unless the spelled-out form is a proper noun. When in doubt, see Chapter 12, "List of Acronyms and Abbreviations," or consult your project style sheet.

- Do not overuse capitalization. Use lowercase unless there is a specific reason for capitalizing.

After consulting your project style sheet and this book, use the *American Heritage Dictionary* as the primary reference for proper capitalization of specific words and *The Chicago Manual of Style* for general guidelines. For capitalization of technical terms, see the *Microsoft Computer Dictionary*.

Capitalization of feature names and technologies

As a general rule, be conservative in capitalizing the names of new features and technologies. To determine whether to capitalize a feature or technology name, follow these guidelines:

- Capitalize the name if there is a marketing or branding campaign around the name.

- Capitalize the name to distinguish a component or product, such as SQL Server, from a general technology with a similar name, such as an SQL database server.

- Capitalize the name for legal reasons.

- Capitalize industry standard terms only if the rest of the industry does so. Search the Internet, the *American Heritage Dictionary*, the *Microsoft Computer Dictionary*, online dictionaries, and other printed industry-specific dictionaries. Do not rely on unedited Web sites.

For new names and terms, consider how capitalizing will affect localization. If possible, check with a localization program manager or your localization vendor.

Work toward consistency in capitalization with other company products, documents, packaging, and marketing.

When in doubt, you can get feedback from the product group and research marketing, localization, and common use.

After your research, make the best decision considering the variables. In some organizations, someone on a centralized team might take on research and compilation responsibility for these questions.

Capitalization in the user interface

The following basic capitalization rules apply to elements of the user interface:

- Menu names, command and command button names, and dialog box titles and tab names: Follow the user interface. Usually, these items use title capitalization. If the user interface is inconsistent, use title capitalization.

- Dialog box and page elements: Follow the user interface. Newer style calls for these items to use sentence-style capitalization. If the interface is inconsistent, use sentence-style capitalization.

- Functional elements: Use title capitalization for the names of functional elements that do not have a label in the user interface, such as toolbars (the Standard toolbar) and toolbar buttons (the **Insert Table** button). Do not capitalize the names of user interface elements, such as *toolbar*, *menu*, *scroll bar*, *button*, and *icon*.

- User input and program output: Do not capitalize unless case is important.

Always consult your project style sheet for terms that require specific capitalization or terms that are traditionally all uppercase or lowercase.

For more information, see *Dialog Boxes and Property Sheets* and *Menus and Commands* in Chapter 1, "Documenting the User Interface" and *Document Conventions* in Chapter 2, "Content Formatting and Layout."

9

Capitalization of titles and headings

Design guidelines today are less formal than they were in the past, so many books and Help topics now use sentence-style capitalization for chapter titles and other headings. The following guidelines represent traditional title capitalization standards. They are especially useful for answering questions about capitalization of adverbs, prepositions, verbal phrases, and the like. If your design does not use title capitalization, follow your design guidelines.

- Capitalize all nouns, verbs (including *is* and other forms of *be*), adverbs (including *than* and *when*), adjectives (including *this* and *that*), and pronouns (including *its*).

- Capitalize the first and last words, regardless of their parts of speech ("The Text to Look For").

- Capitalize prepositions that are part of a verb phrase ("Backing Up Your Disk").

- Do not capitalize articles (*a*, *an*, *the*) unless the article is the first word in the title.

- Do not capitalize coordinate conjunctions (*and*, *but*, *for*, *nor*, *or*) unless the conjunction is the first word in the title.

- Do not capitalize prepositions of four or fewer letters unless the preposition is the first word in the title.

- Do not capitalize *to* in an infinitive phrase ("How to Format Your Hard Disk") unless the phrase is the first word in the title.

- Capitalize the second word in compound words if it is a noun or proper adjective, it is an "e-word," or the words have equal weight (*E-Commerce*, *Cross-Reference*, *Pre-Microsoft Software*, *Read/Write Access*, *Run-Time*). Do not capitalize the second word if it is another part of speech or a participle that modifies the first word (*Add-in*, *How-to*, *Take-off*).

- Capitalize user interface and application programming interface terms that you would not ordinarily capitalize unless they are case-sensitive ("The **fdisk** Command"). Follow the traditional capitalization of keywords and other special terms in programming languages ("The **printf** Function," "Using the EVEN and ALIGN Directives").

- Capitalize only the first word of each column heading.

For more information, see *Lists* and *Tables* in Chapter 2, "Content Formatting and Layout."

9

Capitalization and punctuation

Do not capitalize the word following a colon unless the word is a proper noun or the text following the colon is a complete sentence.

Do not capitalize the word following an em dash unless it is a proper noun, even if the text following the em dash is a complete sentence.

Always capitalize the first word of a new sentence following any end punctuation. Rewrite sentences that start with a case-sensitive lowercase word.

Correct

The **printf** function is the most frequently used C function.

The most frequently used C function is **printf**.

Incorrect

printf is the most frequently used C function.

Measurements and Units of Measure

Avoid using measurements unnecessarily, especially in examples. When you do use measurements, follow these conventions:

- Use numerals for all measurements, even if the number is less than 10, whether the unit of measure is spelled out or abbreviated. For the purposes of this discussion, units of measure include units of distance, temperature, volume, size, weight, points, and picas, but not units of time. Bits and bytes are also considered units of measure.

  Correct

  5 inches

  0.5 inch

  8 bits

  12 points high

- For two or more quantities, repeat the unit of measure.

  Correct

  3.5-inch or 5.25-inch disk

  64 KB and 128 KB

  Incorrect

  3.5- or 5.25-inch disk

  64 and 128 KB

- Connect the number to the unit of measure with a hyphen only if you are using the measurement as an adjective.

Correct

12-point type

3.5-inch disk

8.5-by-11-inch paper

24 KB of memory

- Use the multiplication sign (×), not *by*, to specify screen resolutions. In HTML, the multiplication sign is specified as × or ×. Insert a space on each side of the multiplication sign. If possible, do not use a lowercase or uppercase *x* as a multiplication sign.

Correct

640 × 480 VGA

Abbreviations of measurements

As a general rule, do not abbreviate units of measure except for kilobytes (KB), megabytes (MB), and gigabytes (GB), which can be abbreviated when used with numbers. If space is limited, as it might be in a table, use the abbreviations in the following table.

Term	*Abbreviation*	*Notes*
baud		Do not abbreviate.
bits per second	bps	
centimeters	cm	
days		Do not abbreviate.
degrees	°	Temperature only.
	deg	Angle only.
dots per inch	dpi	
feet	ft	
gigabits		Do not abbreviate.
gigabits per second	Gbps	Spell out as *gigabits*, not *Gb, per second*.
gigabytes	GB	
gigahertz	GHz	
grams	g	
Hertz	Hz	Capitalize both the abbreviation and the word.
hours	hr	

Term	Abbreviation	Notes
inches	in. (or " [inch mark] if necessary for space)	Always include period with *in.* to avoid confusion with the preposition.
kilobits		Do not abbreviate.
kilobits per second	Kbps	Acceptable to use abbreviation Kb in this instance.
kilobytes	KB	
kilobytes per second	KBps	
kilograms	kg	
kilohertz	kHz	Note capitalization of the abbreviation.
kilometers	km	
lines	li	
megabits		Do not abbreviate.
megabits per second	Mbps	Spell out as *megabits*, not *Mb*, per second.
megabytes	MB	
megabytes per second	MBps	
megahertz	MHz	Note capitalization of the abbreviation.
meters	m	
microseconds		Do not abbreviate.
miles	mi	
millimeters	mm	
milliseconds	msec (*or* ms)	
months		Do not abbreviate.
nanoseconds		Do not abbreviate.
picas	pi	
points	pt	
points per inch	ppi	
seconds	sec (*or* s)	
weeks		Do not abbreviate.
years		Do not abbreviate.

9

Abbreviations of units of measure are identical, whether singular or plural—for example, *1 in.* and *2 in.*

When units of measure are not abbreviated, use the singular for quantities of one or less, except with zero, which takes the plural (*0 inches*).

Insert a space between the number and the unit of measure for all abbreviations. Exception: close up *35mm* when used in a photographic context, as in "35mm film."

Do not insert periods after abbreviations of measurements except for *in.* (inch), which always takes a period to distinguish it from the preposition *in*.

Correct

1 point	1 pt
10 points	10 pt
1 centimeter	1 cm
1 inch	1 in.
0.1 inch	0.1 in.
0 inches	0 in.

Numbers   This section discusses when to use numerals and when to spell out numbers, how to treat fractions and ordinal numbers, when to use commas in numbers, and how to treat ranges of numbers.

Numerals vs. words

The use of numerals versus words is primarily a matter of convention. Use the following conventions:

- Use numerals for 10 and greater. Spell out zero through nine if the number does not precede a unit of measure or is not used as input. For round numbers of 1 million or more, use a numeral plus the word, even if the numeral is less than 10.

   Correct

   10 screen savers

   3 centimeters

   Type **5**, and then click **OK**.

   one thousand

   five databases

   zero probability

   7 million

   7,990,000

9

Incorrect

2 disks

0 offset

eighteen books

twelve functions

1 thousand

7 million 990 thousand

- Use numerals for all measurements, even if the number is less than 10. This is true whether the measurement is spelled out, abbreviated, or replaced by a symbol. Measurements include distance, temperature, volume, size, weight, points, picas, and so on; but generally not days, weeks, or other units of time. Bits and bytes are also considered units of measure.

Correct

0 inches

3 feet, 5 inches

3.5-inch disk

0.75 gram

35mm camera

8 bits

1-byte error value

two years

- Use numerals in dimensions. In most general text, spell out *by*, except for screen resolutions. For those, use the multiplication sign × (in HTML, ×).

Correct

8.5-by-11-inch paper

640 × 480

- Use numerals to indicate the time of day. To accommodate the global audience, use a 24-hour clock. Specify midnight as 00:00, not 24:00. It is all right to use *midnight* or *noon*.

Correct

22:00

00:01

Incorrect

nine o'clock

10 P.M.

12:00 A.M.

- To avoid confusion, always spell out the name of the month. The positions of the month and day are different in different countries. For example, 6/12/2000 can be interpreted as either June 12, 2000, or December 6, 2000.

  Correct

  June 12, 2000

  December 6, 1999

  Incorrect

  6/12/00

  12/6/99

- Maintain consistency among categories of information; that is, if one number in a category requires a numeral, use numerals for all numbers in that category. When two numbers that refer to separate categories must appear together, spell out one of them.

  Correct

  One booklet has 16 pages, one has 7 pages, and the third has only 5 pages.

  ten 12-page booklets

- Use numerals for coordinates in tables or worksheets and for numbered sections of documents.

  Correct

  row 3, column 4

  Volume 2

  Chapter 10

  Part 5

  step 1

- Represent numbers taken from examples or the user interface exactly as they appear in the example or the user interface.

- Use an en dash, not a hyphen, to form negative numbers: –79.

- Avoid starting a sentence with a numeral. If necessary, add a modifier before a number. If starting a sentence with a number cannot be avoided, spell out the number.

  Correct

  Lotus 1-2-3 presents options in the menu.

  Microsoft Excel has 144 functions.

  Eleven screen savers are included.

  The value 7 represents the average.

9

Incorrect

1-2-3 presents options in the menu.

144 functions are available in Microsoft Excel.

11 screen savers are included.

7 represents the average.

- Hyphenate compound numbers when they are spelled out.

Correct

Twenty-five fonts are included.

the forty-first user

Fractions as words and decimals

Express fractions in words or as decimals, whichever is most appropriate for the context. Avoid expressing fractions with numerals separated by a slash mark.

- Hyphenate spelled-out fractions used as adjectives or nouns. Connect the numerator and denominator with a hyphen unless either already contains a hyphen.

Correct

one-third of the page

two-thirds completed

three sixty-fourths

- In tables, align decimals on the decimal point.

- Insert a zero before the decimal point for decimal fractions less than one. When representing user input, however, do not include a zero if it is unnecessary for the user to type one.

Correct

0.5 inch

type **.5 inch**

- When units of measure are not abbreviated, use the singular for quantities of one or less, except for zero, which takes the plural.

Correct

0.5 inch

0 inches

5 inches

- If an equation containing fractions occurs in text, you can use the Microsoft Word Equation Editor to format it. Or, to insert a simple fraction, use a slash mark (/) between the numerator and the denominator.

    Correct

    1/2 + 1/2 = 1

Ordinal numbers

Ordinal numbers designate the place of an item in a sequence, such as *first*, *second*, and so on.

Cardinal numbers	Ordinal numbers
One, two	First, second
31, 32	Thirty-first, thirty-second
161	One hundred sixty-first

- Spell out ordinal numbers in text.

    Correct

    The line wraps at the eighty-first column.

    Incorrect

    The line wraps at the 81st column.

- Do not use ordinal numbers for dates.

    Correct

    The meeting is scheduled for April 1.

    Incorrect

    The meeting is scheduled for April 1st.

- Do not add *ly*, as in *firstly* and *secondly*.

Commas in numbers

In general, use commas in numbers that have four or more digits, regardless of how the numbers appear in the interface. When designating years and baud, however, use commas only when the number has five or more digits.

9

Do not use commas in page numbers, addresses, and decimal fractions.

Correct

1,024 bytes

page 1091

1,093 pages

1.06377 units

2500 B.C.

10,000 B.C.

9600 baud

14,400 baud

15601 Northeast 40th Street

Incorrect

1024 bytes

page 1,091

1093 pages

1.063,77 units

2,500 B.C.

10000 B.C.

9,600 baud

15,601 Northeast 40th Street

Ranges of numbers

Use *from* and *through* to describe inclusive ranges of numbers most accurately, except in a range of pages, where an en dash is preferred. Where space is a problem, as in tables and online material, use an en dash to separate ranges of numbers. You can use hyphens to indicate page ranges in an index if you need to conserve space.

Do not use *from* before a range indicated by an en dash. Avoid using *between* and *and* to describe an inclusive range of numbers because it can be ambiguous.

Correct

from 9 through 17

1985–2000

pages 112–120

Incorrect

between 9 and 17

from 1985–2000

For more information, see *Dashes* in Chapter 11, "Punctuation."

See Also: *less vs. fewer vs. under; more than vs. over*

Protocols A protocol is a standard for communication between computers. Most protocols are referred to by their abbreviations. For example, SMTP is an abbreviation for Simple Mail Transfer Protocol.

In URLs, the protocol used by the Web server appears in lowercase before a colon. Protocol abbreviations typically appear in uppercase in text. Typical Web protocols are HTTP, FTP, news, and so on.

Use title capitalization for the spelled-out form of protocol names (except in URLs) unless you know the name is handled differently. If in doubt, check the index to this book, see the *Microsoft Computer Dictionary*, or follow your project style sheet.

Correct

http://www.microsoft.com

Internet Explorer supports Hypertext Transfer Protocol (HTTP).

Names of Special Characters Use the terms in the following table to describe the special characters shown.

Character	Name
´	acute accent (not *accent acute*)
&	ampersand
< >	angle brackets
'	apostrophe (publishing character)
'	apostrophe (user-typed text)
*	asterisk (not *star*)
@	at sign
\	backslash
{ }	braces (not *curly brackets*)
[ ]	brackets
^	caret, circumflex (not *accent circumflex*)
¢	cent sign
« »	chevrons, opening and closing. Also referred to as *merge field characters* in Word.
©	copyright symbol
†	dagger
°	degree symbol
÷	division sign

Character	Name
$	dollar sign
[[ ]]	double brackets
...	ellipsis (s), ellipses (pl). Do not add space between ellipsis points.
—	em dash
–	en dash
=	equal sign (not *equals* sign)
!	exclamation point (not *exclamation mark* or *bang*)
`	grave accent (not *accent grave*)
>	greater than sign. If used in conjunction with the less than sign to enclose a character string such an HTML or XML tag, *right angle bracket* is all right.
≥	greater than or equal to sign
-	hyphen
"	inch mark
<	less than sign. If used in conjunction with the greater than sign to enclose a character string such an HTML or XML tag, *left angle bracket* is all right.
≤	less than or equal to sign
–	minus sign (use en dash)
×	multiplication sign (use * if necessary to match software)
≠	not equal to
#	number sign in most cases, but *pound key* when referring to the telephone
¶	paragraph mark
( )	parentheses (pl), opening or closing parenthesis (s)
%	percent
π	pi
|	pipe, vertical bar, or **OR** logical operator
+	plus sign
±	plus or minus sign
?	question mark
" "	quotation marks (not *quotes* or *quote marks*). *Curly quotation marks* is all right if necessary to distinguish from straight quotation marks.

9

Character	Name
" "	straight quotation marks (not *quotes* or *quote marks*)
' '	single curly quotation marks (not *quotes* or *quote marks*)
' '	single straight quotation marks (not *quotes* or *quote marks*)
®	registered trademark symbol
§	section
/	slash mark (not *virgule*)
~	tilde
™	trademark symbol
_	underscore

Telephone Numbers   For U.S. telephone numbers, use parentheses, not a hyphen, to separate the area code from the seven-digit phone number. In domestic telephone lists, do not precede the area code with 1 to indicate the long distance access code. Do add 1 in international lists to indicate the country code for the United States, as described later in this topic.

Correct

(425) 555-0150

(317) 555-0123

Incorrect

425-555-0150

1-317-555-0123

In North America, some 800 (toll-free) phone numbers are accessible to both U.S. and Canadian callers, and some serve only one country or the other. If a number serves only one country, indicate that the number or the service it provides is not available outside that country.

Correct

(800) 000-0000 (Canada only)

International phone numbers

Precede local phone numbers with country and city codes if your content will be published in more than one country or if you list phone numbers from more than one country. City codes contain one, two, or three digits and are equivalent to U.S. area codes. Separate the country and city codes from the local phone numbers with parentheses, not hyphens or spaces. For local phone numbers, follow the convention of the country that users will call.

In the first example, 44 is the country code for the United Kingdom, 71 is the city code for London, and 0000 000 0000 is the local phone number. In the United Kingdom, the convention for displaying phone numbers is to insert spaces, as shown in the correct example. The second example shows the convention for displaying local phone numbers in Japan.

Correct

(44) (71) 0000 000 0000 [U.K.]

(81) (3) 0000-0000 [Japan]

Incorrect

(44) (71) 0000-000-0000

44-71-0000-000-0000

81-3-0000-0000

In most U.S. cities, you can find a list of international country and major city codes in your local telephone directory.

Do not include the access code for international long distance in phone lists. Access codes vary from one country to the next and they can vary from one phone service provider to the next within countries. Do not put a plus sign (+) in front of a phone number to indicate the need for an access code.

Correct

(81) (3) 000-000

(425) 555-0150 [when only domestic numbers are provided]

(425) 555-0150 [when both domestic and international numbers are provided]

Incorrect

+(81) (3) 000-000

011-81-3-000-000

(1) (425) 555-0150 [when only domestic numbers are provided]

Fictitious phone numbers

For fictitious phone numbers in North America, use the prefix 555 and a four-digit number between 0100 and 0199; for example, 555-0187. These numbers are not assigned to any lines in regional area codes in North America. For fictitious phone numbers outside North America, determine the local phone system's policy regarding phone numbers reserved for examples or for use in works of fiction.

Note: Avoid using fictitious toll-free or direct-bill phone numbers. There are no reserved fictitious phone numbers in area codes used for toll-free calls or direct-billed calls, including but not limited to area codes 800, 877, 888, and 900. Many numbers that would be in the fictitious range for other area codes are assigned to various individuals and organizations in these national and international area codes. Using these phone numbers in examples has been and can be embarrassing.

Time Zones

Time Zones   The names of time zones should be treated as proper nouns. A time zone is a geographical area. Avoid specifying standard time and daylight time, which refer to clock settings within a time zone at specific times of the year, unless you are referring to an event, such as a webcast, for which this information is important.

Correct

Central Time

Eastern Time

Coordinated Universal Time

Pacific Time

Incorrect

Central Daylight Time

eastern time

eastern standard time

Pacific time

It you are referring to a time zone as a geographical area, as opposed to indicating a time within that area, make explicit reference to the time zone as such.

Correct

The event begins at 21:00 Eastern Time. Broadcast times may be different in the Pacific Time zone.

Avoid using *Greenwich Mean Time* or *GMT* alone. The current internationally accepted name for *Greenwich Mean Time* is *Coordinated Universal Time*. Because not everyone might be familiar with this name, it is all right on first mention to refer to *Coordinated Universal Time (Greenwich Mean Time)*. If you must abbreviate Coordinated Universal Time, do not use *CUT*. By international agreement, the universal abbreviation is *UTC*. Do not refer to Coordinated Universal Time as *Universal Time Coordinate* or *Universal Time Coordinated*.

Do not abbreviate the names of time zones, such as *PT*, *ET*, and *UTC*, unless space is severely limited.

If you do not define a context, some time zone names can be ambiguous. For example, North America and Australia both have an Eastern Time zone. Unless you are creating a generic example where geographic location is not important, be sure to resolve such ambiguities. The simplest way to do so is to denote an offset from Coordinated Universal Time that uses standard (not daylight) time. In this case, it is all right to use the abbreviation UTC.

9

Correct

Eastern Time (UTC-5)

Eastern Time (UTC+10)

Not all time zones have names. For time zones without names, refer to the offset from Coordinated Universal Time.

Correct

UTC+7

See Also: *A.M., P.M.*

URLs, Addresses

A uniform (*not* universal) resource locator (URL) is an address, specified in a standard format, which locates a specific resource on the Internet or an intranet. In content that targets home users, knowledge workers, or a general audience, use *address* rather than *URL*. For technical audiences, do not spell out *URL* on first use.

The appropriate indefinite article for URL is *a*, not *an*.

A URL consists of an Internet protocol name; a domain name; and optionally other elements such as a port, directory, and file name. Each of these main elements is in lowercase type, unless case is important.

In a typical URL, separate the protocol name (such as *http:*) from the rest of the destination with two slash marks, and separate the domain name and other main elements from each other with one slash mark.

Typical URLs

http://www.microsoft.com/security/articles/steps_default.asp

http://www.microsoft.com/

http://www.microsoft.com/business/

When you specify a Web address, it is not usually necessary to include *http://*. Most browsers today automatically add this information to the URL if a protocol name is not specified. If the protocol is something other than HTTP, such as File Transfer Protocol (FTP) or Gopher, you must specify the protocol with the URL. When the URL does not specify a file name, a final closing slash mark is optional.

Correct

www.microsoft.com/business

www.microsoft.com/business/

ftp://www.example.com/downloads/myfile.txt

To refer to an entire Web site, as opposed to the home page of the site, it is all right to drop the *www.* at the beginning of the site address. If you do so, capitalize only the initial letter of the address, even if the name associated with the site is capitalized differently.

Correct

The *Gotdotnet.com* Web site is the home of the GotDotNet user community.

If you include *www.* in the site address, with or without the protocol name, the entire address is in lowercase.

Correct

Visit the GotDotNet Web site at *www.gotdotnet.com*.

Visit the GotDotNet Web site at *http://www.gotdotnet.com*.

In conceptual information, use *of* in discussions of the URL of a resource. Use the preposition *at* with the location of an address.

Correct

For each Web page found, the search results include the URL of the page.

You can find information about Microsoft products at *www.microsoft.com*.

URLs often appear at the end of a sentence. If there is a possibility that your readers will interpret the ending period as part of the URL, rewrite the sentence or set the URL off.

Correct

Visit *www.microsoft.com* to find information about Microsoft products.

To find information about Microsoft, visit our Web site:

www.microsoft.com

Although e-mail and newsgroup addresses are structured differently from Web site addresses, they are also considered URLs. Format the entire address in lowercase.

Correct

microsoft.public.dotnet.framework

news.announce.newusers

someone@example.com

mailto:someone@example.com

For more information, see *Protocols* in this chapter.

See Also: HTTP

9

Company with Product Names
On first mention, always precede the name of a product with the company name. On subsequent mention, it is not necessary to precede the product name with the company name.

Correct on first mention

Microsoft Visio

Microsoft Windows XP

Incorrect on first mention

Visio

Windows XP

If you are listing multiple versions of the same product, precede only the name of the first one with the company name:

Correct on first mention

Microsoft Windows XP, Windows Millennium Edition, and Windows 98

OK but not necessary

Microsoft Windows XP, Microsoft Windows Millennium Edition, and Microsoft Windows 98

If you are listing different products, precede each with the company name:

Correct on first mention

Microsoft Office, Microsoft Visio, and Microsoft Encarta Reference Library

Incorrect on first mention

Microsoft Office, Visio, and Encarta Reference Library

Version Identifiers
Product and product component names can include version information by special identifier (for example, Windows XP), by year of release (Windows 2000), or by chronological version number (Windows NT 4.0).

When listing different versions of a product, list the most recent version first.

Correct

Microsoft Windows XP, Windows 2000, and Windows NT 4.0

Incorrect

Microsoft Windows NT 4.0, Windows 2000, and Windows XP

A complete product version number has three components:

- Major release identifier: **X**.x.x

- Minor release identifier: x.**X**.x

- Update identifier: x.x.**X**

Only the major and minor release identifiers are normally significant to the user. Update identifiers appear in the Help About box and in Knowledge Base articles and other content describing the update, but they do not normally appear elsewhere.

Correct

Internet Explorer 4.0

Microsoft Exchange Server 4.0.829

Some products and product components may be identified by major release alone.

Correct

Internet Explorer 5

Windows Media Player 9

In these cases, the version identifier alone also encompasses minor releases of the same version. For example, Internet Explorer 5 identifies both the original release and minor releases such as Internet Explorer 5.1 and Internet Explorer 5.5. To identify only the original release of such a product, append .0 as the minor release identifier.

Correct

Internet Explorer 5 [refers to major release and all minor releases of Internet Explorer 5]

Internet Explorer 5.0 [refers only to major release of Internet Explorer 5]

General guidelines

Avoid specifying a particular version unless it is necessary in context. You might need to specify the version number, for example, when comparing current and previous versions of the same product or for reasons of clarity and technical accuracy. Do not include the update identifier of a product unless it is technically relevant.

If you must mention a version number, specify it on the first mention in a topic or section. Thereafter, refer only to the product name without the version identifier. For products whose original release identifier includes .0, use .x (italicized) to indicate all release numbers of a product (for example, "Windows NT Server version 3.x"), or use *earlier* or *later* (for example, "Windows NT version 3.1 or later"). Do not use *higher* or *lower*.

9

For products with version numbers, on first mention add the word *version* before the version number. It is all right on subsequent mention to use the approved short product name and to drop the word *version*.

It is all right to use *Windows 95/98* when no other solution can be found to list them separately.

Correct

If you are using the Microsoft Windows NT Server operating system version 4.0 or later, ... [first mention]

If you are using Windows NT Server 4.0 or later, ... [subsequent mention]

Readme Files and Release Notes

Readme files and release notes often contain similar types of information and can usually be treated in the same way. The main difference is that readme files provide up-to-the-minute information about a newly released product, and release notes provide information about test and beta releases.

You can use the term *readme file* or *readme* without an extension, but if it is a text file, the extension *.txt* can clarify to the user that it will appear as a text file without character formatting. Capitalize *readme* when you refer to the specific file.

Correct

Look in Readme.txt on Disk A for the most current information.

Look in the Readme file on Disk A for the most current information.

As far as is practicable, the same rules of style and usage pertain to readme files as to all other documentation. Even if they do not follow the same formatting standards as documentation, readme files should not contain jargon and overly technical language and should otherwise conform to house style.

Readme text files

Most readme files are either text files, formatted in Courier, or Help files. Use the following guidelines for organization, content, and formatting of readme text files. See the example following the guidelines.

Front matter   Include these elements at the beginning of the file, following the formatting guidelines listed here and in the example readme file:

- Title of the file centered in the text area, with the date (month and year) centered one line below. Insert a row of hyphens above and below.

- Any necessary copyright notices.

- Introductory paragraph explaining the purpose of the file, flush left.

- Optional section titled "How to Use This Document," flush left, beginning two lines below the introductory paragraph and with one row of hyphens above and below. Use the boilerplate shown in the example readme file.

- Contents listing all the section headings. In general, order the readme file with the most important information or information of the most general interest first. List errata and changes to the documentation last. Section numbers, as shown in the example readme file, are optional.

Sections and topics   This section describes how to format the information in the readme file, including procedures, tables, and errata and corrections. Samples of these are included in the example readme file.

Procedures   Procedures within the text should follow the same general guidelines as all procedures. Begin with an infinitive phrase, preceded by three right angle brackets (>>>), and followed by a colon. Number the steps.

Because the text file will not show character formatting, use all uppercase letters to indicate user input, use title caps for interface elements, and underline words to indicate placeholders.

Tables   You can use tables to list and describe included files and other information. Underline each row of a table heading with one row of hyphens.

Errata and Corrections   If you are listing corrections to documentation, be as specific as possible about the location and the change necessary. For example, for a book, list chapter number and chapter title, section heading, and page number. Tell the user what to replace or add. The words *chapter*, *section*, and so on should be flush left, with two spaces between the longest word and the beginning of the correction text. Align as shown in the example readme file.

Help Files   For Help files, list the specific Help file and the topic or topics.

Example readme file

This document provides late-breaking or other information that supplements the [Product Name] documentation. You can use the following paragraph where there is no other documentation:

9

This document provides information about [Product Name], as well as answers
to questions you might have.

```
       --------------------------------------
                [Product Name] Readme File
                       January 2003
          (c) 2003 by Corporation. All rights reserved.
       --------------------------------------
```

This file provides information that supplements the product documentation.

How to Use This Document

To view the Readme file on-screen in Windows Notepad,
maximize the Notepad window. On the Format menu, click Word
Wrap. To print the Readme file, open it in Notepad
or another word processor, and then use the Print command
on the File menu.


```
---------
CONTENTS
---------
```

1.   WHAT'S NEW IN THIS RELEASE
        1.1 One-Step Installation
        1.2 Windows Control Center

2.   INSTALLATION NOTES
        2.1 Installing over a Previous Version
        2.2 Manually Decompressing Application Files

3.   TROUBLESHOOTING
        3.1 Installation Problems
        3.2 Restoring AUTOEXEC.BAT, CONFIG.SYS, WIN.INI, and
             SYSTEM.INI
        3.3 Renaming the Installed Directory

4.   APPLICATION DISK CONTENTS
        4.1 Driver Files
        4.2 Windows Program Files
        4.3 MS-DOS Program Files
        4.4 Installation Program Files
      .
      .
      .
>>>To change your SmartDrive cache:

1 Open WordPad.
2 On the File menu, click Open.
      .
      .
```
```

```
.
7 On the File menu, click Exit.
When the WordPad dialog box asks if you want to save your changes, click Yes.
.
.

.
Field                    Description
----------               ----------------------------------------------------
Language                 Three-letter language identifier
Welcome String           Text to display when the custom Setup program starts
.

.

.
Chapter:  6, "Using OLE Custom Controls"
Section:  "Using OLE Custom Control Methods"
Page:     173
          Replace "calendar control example" in the first
          sentence on the page with "calendar control example
          described earlier in this chapter" to clarify.

Help:     Scroll Bar Control Help
Topic:    Value Property, Change Event Example
          Replace the Dim statement at the beginning of the
          sbMonth_Change() procedure with the following
          statement:
          Dim Diff As Integer, i As Integer
```

Readme Help files

If you release the readme file as a Help file, follow the same general guidelines for content, but include a general Readme Help contents section on the first screen. The first section should be this boilerplate:

[Product Name] Product Update
Late-breaking information about this release of [Product Name].

Describe briefly the content of each Help section in the contents. Include standard instructions for printing, such as these:

To print a Readme Help topic

1. Display the topic you want in the Help window.

2. On the **File** menu in the Help window, click **Print Topic**.

Vary these instructions according to the setup of the Help file. For example, in programs based on Windows 95 and later, you can organize the readme file as one "book" in Help, which can then be printed in its entirety. Alternatively, you can compile Help readme files as one long topic so that users can print the entire file.

9

Bibliographies

Bibliographies   Scholarly works require documentation of source material in a bibliography. Other works also occasionally require that you cite source material or direct the reader to a publication for further information. If you need to provide a bibliography or provide a formal citation, follow the examples listed here.

Citing books and printed articles

To cite books and printed articles, follow *The Chicago Manual of Style* "Documentation One" format. Exception: Follow the United States Postal Service abbreviations for states.

Bibliographies are usually formatted with a hanging indent. If a design template does not support hanging indents, separate each entry with a line of white space.

Only basic bibliographic entries are listed here. For more information, see "Reference Listings and Bibliographies" in *The Chicago Manual of Style*.

Books, general bibliographic style   The following paragraph lists the order and punctuation for each element in the citation of a book.

Author's name (surname first for the first author, given name first for additional authors). *Title: Subtitle*. Any additional information about the work, including editor's or translator's name and volume number. Edition number, if not the first. Place of publication: publisher, date.

Examples

Dupre, Lyn. *Bugs in Writing: A Guide to Debugging Your Prose*. Reading, MA: Addison-Wesley Publishing Co., 1995.

Li, Xia, and Nancy B. Crane. *Electronic Styles: A Handbook for Citing Electronic Information*. Rev. ed. Medford, NJ: Information Today, 1996.

Printed magazine and journal articles, general bibliographic style   Author's name. "Title of Article." *Title of Periodical*. Volume and issue number (for journals only), date by month, day, year, page numbers.

The order of information and punctuation for the date differs between journals and popular magazines. For more information, see *The Chicago Manual of Style*, Chapter 17.

Examples

Rosenthal, Marshal M. "Digital Cash: The Choices Are Growing." *Websmith*. May 1996, 6–9.

Vijayan, Jaikumar, and Mindy Blodgett. "Train Wreck at DEC." *Computerworld*. July 8, 1996, 1, 15.

Earle, Ralph, Robert Berry, and Michelle Corbin Nichols. "Indexing Online Information." *Technical Communication: Journal of the Society for Technical Communication* 43 (May 1996): 146–56.

Citing electronic information

References to electronic information have the same intent and a format similar to the citations of printed material. That is, they follow the same general order of information such as author and title, but that information is followed by information such as the commercial supplier (if from an information service), the distribution medium (such as CD-ROM) or the Internet address, and the date accessed, if relevant. The important thing is to give enough information so that a user can find the source. Use lowercase for e-mail or other logon names, or follow the protocol of the e-mail service provider.

If the source appears both online and in print, give enough information so it can be found in either format. Rather than indicating page numbers of a magazine article that appears online, give an approximate length indication, usually in number of paragraphs.

This information is adapted from *Electronic Styles*, cited fully in the sample book citations in this topic. *Electronic Styles* itself follows Modern Language Association (MLA) style rather than *The Chicago Manual of Style*, but the kind of information to cite is accurate.

Examples for CD-ROMs and computer programs

"Washington." Encarta Reference Library 2003. 2002. DVD. Microsoft Corporation, Redmond, WA.

Visual Basic 4.0. Microsoft Corporation, Redmond, WA.

Note: You do not need to cite a date of access for CD-ROMs and similar media.

Examples for Internet sites

Buxton, Stephen, and Michael Rys (editors). "XQuery and XPath Full-Text Requirements." World Wide Web Consortium. 2003. *http://www.w3.org/TR/2003 /WD-xmlquery-full-text-requirements-20030214/*

Examples for discussion list messages and e-mail

rrecome. "Top Ten Rules of Film Criticism." Online newsgroup posting. Discussions of All Forms of Cinema. Available e-mail: *listserv@american.edu/Get cinema-l* log9504A. August 1995.

Higa, Sidney (someone@sample.com). "New Terminology." E-mail to Deborah Poe (*someone2@sample.com*).

For more information, see *Cross-References* in Chapter 2, "Content Formatting and Layout."

9

Titles of Publications   The title page of a printed book includes the product name and generally the product descriptor. For example, the title page for the Windows 95 user's guide includes this information:

Introducing Microsoft Windows 95

For the Microsoft Windows 95 Operating System

In the book itself, the title is referred to as *Introducing Microsoft Windows 95*.

As long as the product name is prominently mentioned, it does not necessarily have to be included as part of the actual book title. For example, a book can be titled *Installation Guide* as long as the product name also appears on the cover and title page. For example, the cover and title page could include:

Installation Guide

For Microsoft Exchange Server

> **Note:** Refer to a book as a *book*, not as a *manual*.

Online documentation can use any of the titles listed in this topic.

The following table lists titles of some common publications, the audience for that type of book, and typical content. Users expect to find certain material in certain publications, regardless of what the product is. To maintain consistency across product lines, use the titles precisely and appropriately. The table is not exhaustive; individual projects may need additional unique titles. Do not, however, create a new title when one from this table will serve your purposes.

Table 9.1: Titles of Books

Title	*Audience*	*Content*
Administrator's Guide	Technical support personnel, system and network administrators	Task-oriented information about installing, configuring, and managing a product.
Administrator's Reference	Technical support personnel, system and network administrators	Comprehensive, often encyclopedic information about the product features.
Companion	End users	Overview of product features, often describing projects the user can accomplish with the product, such as publishing a newsletter. Often highly visual and informal.

Table 9.1: Titles of Books

Title	Audience	Content
Conversion Guide	Programmers, administrators	Explanation of how to convert files or programs from one system to another. Not a book that teaches users of one product how to use a similar product.
Design Guide	Programmers, application developers, interface designers	Technical information about designing a program interface.
Developer's Guide	Technical users who may not be programmers, such as database and macro developers	Explanation of development concepts and techniques.
Feature Guide	End users	Overview of product features.
Getting Results with [Product Name]	End users	Task-oriented introduction to the product, possibly including installation. Focuses on helping users accomplish specific kinds of tasks.
Getting Started	End users, often novices	Basic installation and setup information. May include a road map to the product or other documentation, a summary of new features, and tutorial material.
Idea Book	End users	Task-oriented. Highlights certain features of the product. Often includes sample files.
Installation Guide	All users	Information about how to install the product.
Language Reference	Programmers	The complete syntax of a programming language. Usually includes extensive examples and usage notes.

9

Table 9.1: Titles of Books

Title	Audience	Content
Library Reference	Programmers	The functions that ship with a programming language. Includes extensive examples and may include sample files. Often alphabetically organized, sometimes within families of functions.
Network Administrator's Guide	Administrators, technical support personnel	Network setup and maintenance for a product.
Printer Guide	All users	Information about how to use various printers with the product.
Programmer's Guide	Programmers	Programming concepts and techniques.
Programmer's Reference	Programmers	Technical information about writing programs or macros. Includes information about the application programming interface.
Quick Reference	All users	Brief, concise information about commands or features. Avoid using *Guide* or *Pocket Guide* as part of the title.
Resource Kit	Engineers, technicians, support staff, administrators	Overview of a product's technical features and underpinnings.
Road Map	All users	A learning path or a guide to printed or online documentation.
Switching to [Product]	Users of another, similar product	Information for users of a similar product about how to easily learn the product. Often maps features and commands from one product to the other. Do not confuse with *Conversion Guide*.

9

Table 9.1: Titles of Books

Title	Audience	Content
Technical Reference	Product developers and technical end users, not necessarily programmers	Similar to a programmer's reference, but does not include information about the application programming interface. Often covers customizing end-user software.
User's Guide	End users	Information about installing and using the product, possibly including descriptions of new features. Possibly the only printed book that ships with the product.

Chapter 10
Grammatical Elements

Grammatical rules leave little room for opinion. For example, a verb must agree with its subject in person and number. There are times, however, when simply knowing a rule is not enough. Passive voice and subjunctive mood, for example, are well-established elements of English grammar, but overusing them will undermine the effectiveness of your writing. This section describes some basic grammatical elements and explains how they contribute to editorial style.

This chapter contains the following sections:

- Verbs and Verb Forms
- Person
- Noun Plurals
- Possessives
- Prepositions
- Prefixes
- Dangling and Misplaced Modifiers

Verbs and Verb Forms   A sentence can do without almost anything, but no expression is a complete sentence without a verb.

In technical writing, present tense is easier to read than past or future tense. Simple verbs are easier to read and understand than complex verbs, such as verbs in the progressive or perfect tense. One-word verbs, such as *remove*, are easier for worldwide readers than verb phrases, such as *take away*.

Do not vary voice and mood for the sake of variety. Active voice, which is generally more forceful and clear than passive voice, should predominate. Indicative mood should predominate for the same reason, except in procedure steps, where imperative mood should predominate.

Put the action of the sentence in the verb, not the nouns. Do not bury the action in an infinitive phrase. Avoid weak, vague verbs such as *be*, *have*, *make*, and *do*. Such verbs are not always wrong, but use a more specific, descriptive verb whenever you can.

> **Stronger**
>
> By using Windows XP, you can easily organize your digital photos and create slide shows.
>
> You can create a new folder.
>
> If you cannot view the Security log, your user account does not have sufficient user rights.
>
> Back up your files as part of your regular routine.

Weaker

Windows XP enables you to easily organize your digital photos and create slide shows.

You can make a new folder.

If you are not able to view the Security log, your user account does not have sufficient user rights.

Do a backup of your files as part of your regular routine.

Avoid overused verbs that take different meanings in different contexts. Such verbs often result in lifeless prose, and the possibility of different meanings can be a problem for the worldwide audience. Use more specific verbs instead.

Correct

To solve this problem ...

When you speak to an audience, PowerPoint can help make your presentation more effective.

The issue you must resolve is the calling routine's request for additional user rights.

Incorrect

To address this problem ...

When you address an audience, PowerPoint can help make your presentation more effective.

The issue you must address is the calling routine's request for additional user rights.

For information about verbs in procedures and commands, see *Procedures* in Chapter 9, "Common Style Problems."

Verbs, Nouns, and Command Names

Do not use verbs as nouns or nouns as verbs. Rephrase as necessary to make the text clearer and less awkward. If a command name is not a verb, do not use it as a verb.

Correct

You can search the document to find this text and replace it.

You can use the **Paste Link** command to place the data into the worksheet.

Incorrect

You can do a search-and-replace on the document.

You can paste link the data into the worksheet.

Transitive and Intransitive Verbs

A transitive verb is one that takes a direct object to indicate the receiver of the action. Do not use a transitive verb without a direct object. Either supply a direct object or use an intransitive verb instead. If you are not sure if a verb is transitive or intransitive, check the *American Heritage Dictionary*.

The following transitive verbs are often used erroneously without objects: *complete, configure, display, install, print, authenticate,* and *process.*

Correct

The screen displays information. [transitive]

A dialog box appears. [intransitive]

The printer cannot print your document. [transitive]

To complete Setup, restart your computer. [transitive]

Like user accounts, computer accounts provide a way to authenticate requests for access to the network and to domain resources. [transitive]

Incorrect

A dialog box displays. [intransitive]

Your document will not print. [intransitive]

After you restart your computer, Setup completes. [intransitive]

Like user accounts, computer accounts provide a way for the network to authenticate.

For more information, see *Mood, Tense,* and *Voice* in this chapter.

Agreement

It is easy to remember and apply the rule that a verb must agree with its subject in person and number. It is sometimes more difficult to apply the rule that a pronoun must agree with its antecedent, the person or thing the pronoun refers to.

Pronoun-antecedent agreement is particularly difficult with singular personal pronouns. Writers and editors do not want to give offense by using a singular pronoun of a particular gender as a general reference, so they use the gender-neutral but plural *they* to refer to a singular antecedent. Although this usage is gaining acceptance, it remains a problem for localizers and for the worldwide audience. Whenever possible, you should write around this problem.

10

Correct

A user with the appropriate rights can set other users' passwords.

Authentication verifies the identity of the user.

Right-click the name of the person you want to call, click **Make a Phone Call**, and then choose from the list of published numbers.

Incorrect

If the user has the appropriate rights, he can set other users' passwords.

Authentication verifies that a user is who she claims to be.

Right-click the name of the person you want to call, click **Make a Phone Call**, and then choose from the numbers they have published.

If it is impossible to write around the problem, do not alternate between masculine and feminine pronouns to refer to the same individual, and do not use *he/she* or *s/he*. Using the slash mark in this way is confusing for worldwide readers, and even many native English speakers consider it confusing and annoying.

It is all right to use *he or she* occasionally, but doing so excessively may distract the reader. If you need to make third-person references to more than one person in the same topic, use *he* for some individuals and *she* for others. In all cases, leave no doubt about the antecedent for each pronoun.

Voice

Voice refers to the relationship between the grammatical subject of a sentence and the verb. In active voice, the person or thing performing the action of the verb is the grammatical subject. In passive voice, the receiver of the action is the grammatical subject.

In general, active voice should predominate. Passive voice is not a grammatical error, but it has the greatest impact when you use it sparingly.

Passive voice can be a problem for localization. Some languages use passive voice rarely, if at all, so the translation can end up sounding stilted or unnatural.

It is all right to use passive voice:

- To avoid a wordy or awkward construction.

- When the subject is unknown or the emphasis is on the receiver of the action.

- When casting the user as the subject might sound blaming or condescending, especially in error messages and troubleshooting content.

Passive voice is more common and acceptable in programmer documentation, but active voice should still predominate.

Preferred (active voice)

You can divide your documents into as many sections as you want.

Data hiding provides a number of benefits.

Windows XP includes many multimedia features.

Acceptable use of passive voice

The Web site cannot be found. Verify that the page address is spelled correctly in the Address bar.

[In content for software developers] When the user clicks OK, the transaction is committed.

Avoid (passive voice)

Your document can be divided into as many sections as you want.

A number of benefits are provided by data hiding.

Many multimedia features are included in Windows XP.

Use active voice for column headings in tables that list user actions.

Correct

To do this	Press this

For more information, see *Tables* in Chapter 2, "Content Formatting and Layout" and *Verbs and Verb Forms* in this chapter.

Mood

Mood is a way of classifying verbs according to whether the writer intends the verb to express fact, command, or hypothesis. The word *mood* as a grammatical term is an alteration of the word *mode* and is unrelated to *mood* as an emotional state.

Indicative mood expresses statements and questions of fact, *imperative mood* makes requests or commands, and *subjunctive mood* expresses hypothetical information.

Indicative Mood   Indicative mood expresses information such as facts, questions, assertions, or explanations. Simple declarative sentences use indicative verbs.

In any piece of writing except procedural steps, indicative mood should predominate.

Examples

Style sheets are powerful tools for formatting complex documents.

What are the common characteristics of all interactors, including both text windows and scroll bars? They all have a size and relative position.

10

Imperative Mood   Use imperative mood in procedures and other direct instructions. The subject *you* is implied. Imperative mood is always in present tense.

Examples

Type a file name, and then click **OK**.

Insert the disk in the floppy disk drive.

Avoid using imperative mood in marketing tag lines that will be localized. The way imperative mood is used in many languages makes such usage seem more dictatorial than we intend it in English.

Incorrect

Buy it now!

Subjunctive Mood   Subjunctive mood expresses wishes, hypotheses, and conditions contrary to fact. The most common use of subjunctive mood today is in subordinate clauses following a main clause that carry a sense of insisting or recommending.

Example

We recommend that you be careful about opening e-mail attachments.

Like passive voice, subjunctive mood is not a grammatical error, but it has the greatest impact when you use it sparingly and carefully.

Preferred (indicative mood)

You should complete this procedure before taking any other action.

Worth avoiding (subjunctive mood unnecessary)

It is important that you complete this procedure before taking any other action.

Avoid needless shifts between moods.

Correct

Select the text, and then click **Bold**.

Type a file name, and then click **OK**.

Incorrect

Select the text, and then you can click **Bold**.

The first step is to type a file name, and then click **OK**.

10

Tense

Simple present tense, unburdened by helping verbs, should predominate in your writing. Simple present tense is easy to read, especially for the worldwide audience, and it helps readers scan the material quickly.

Correct

Although the Microsoft Mail system is reliable, you should periodically back up important messages.

The next section describes how to write an object-oriented program.

Incorrect

Although the Microsoft Mail system has proven to be reliable, you should periodically back up important messages.

The next section will describe how to write an object-oriented program.

Consider how your use of present tense establishes a sense of time, and use past or future tense only with respect to the present time as you have established it.

Correct

If you are going to use the macro as a demonstration, you will probably play it back at the same speed at which you recorded it.

Gerunds

A gerund is the *-ing* form of a verb used as a noun. Use gerunds to form the titles of procedural Help topics.

Correct

Managing Hardware and Software

Installing New Software

Incorrect

How to Install New Software

Gerunds can sometimes create ambiguity, especially for a worldwide audience. Include whatever words are necessary to make your meaning clear, or rewrite the sentence.

Ambiguous

You can change files using the Template utility.

Clearer

You can change files by using the Template utility.

You can change files that use the Template utility.

Using gerunds to describe general concepts, such as *clustering* and *networking*, can be a problem for localization. Not all grammars allow gerunds to be used in this way, so a single word may be translated as a phrase. In Dutch, for example, *imaging* is translated as

10

image processing, and *licensing* is translated as *the granting of licenses*. Further, not all gerunds are translatable in all languages, so some loss of meaning is inevitable. If you must use gerunds to describe concepts, work with your localization program manager or localization vendor to keep the impact of such words to a minimum.

For more information, see *Headings and Subheadings* in Chapter 2, "Content Formatting and Layout"; *Procedures* in Chapter 9, "Common Style Problems"; and *Verbs and Verb Forms* in this chapter.

Person
Person refers to the relationship between the writer and the grammatical subject of a sentence or clause.

First person singular	Writer is the subject of the sentence.
First person plural	Writer is a member of a group that is the subject of the sentence.
Second person singular	Reader is the subject of the sentence.
Second person plural	In speech, the audience members the speaker is addressing are collectively the subject of the sentence. Not appropriate for writing except in quotations because writing addresses readers one at a time.
Third person singular	Someone or something other than the writer and the reader is the subject of the sentence.
Third person plural	A group of people, places, or things that does not include the writer or the reader is the subject of the sentence.

First Person

Never use *I* except when writing from the point of view of a character. Avoid first person except in marketing or legally oriented sections of books or Help.

Although a second-person statement beginning with *you should* involves the reader more directly, it is all right to say *we recommend* or *we suggest* if you do not want to focus attention on the reader. Do not use the passive *it is recommended*.

Correct

We recommend keeping the product disks, the Certificate of Authenticity, and your purchase receipt.

Second Person

Second person, also known as *direct address*, should predominate in most writing. Using second person focuses the discussion on the reader and helps you avoid passive voice.

Always use second person, imperative mood, in procedural steps.

Correct

In Microsoft Outlook, you can find all your e-mail, appointments, and contact information in one place.

On the **File** menu, click **Open**.

Incorrect

Microsoft Outlook allows you to find all your e-mail, appointments, and contact information in one place.

In Microsoft Outlook, all your e-mail, appointments, and contact information can be found in one place.

Use second person singular, not plural. The verb forms are usually the same, so this guidance is more a matter of sensibility than of grammar. Always keep in mind that even if your writing is seen by millions of readers, you are addressing those readers one at a time.

Correct

If you are creating personalized bulk mail, mail merge will save a lot of time.

Incorrect

If some of you are creating personalized bulk mail, mail merge will save a lot of time.

Third Person

Because conceptual writing describes some concept or thing, third person will inevitably predominate. Even so, remember to involve the reader in the discussion.

Correct

If you are an administrator, you can use the System File Checker to verify the versions of all protected files.

Correct, but remote

Administrators can use the System File Checker to verify the versions of all protected files.

The System File Checker gives an administrator the ability to verify the versions of all protected files.

10

If you are writing for developers or information technology professionals, use second person to refer to your reader, and use third person (commonly *the user*) to refer to the reader's end user.

Clearly distinguish reader actions from program actions. For example, do not refer to a program as *you*.

Correct

You can use Help to present information about your program in a format that users can access easily.

Your program can call this function to allocate memory.

Incorrect

You can use Help topics to present information about your program in a format that can be accessed easily.

You can call this function to allocate memory.

Write most error messages in third person unless you are asking for a response or giving an instruction. By making the user the subject of the error message, it can sound as if you are blaming the user for the error.

Correct

The printer on LPT1 is not responding.

Try restarting your computer.

Text outside the margins might not be printed. Do you want to continue, anyway?

Incorrect

You are unable to print on LPT1.

The computer should now be restarted.

For more information, see *Mood* and *Voice* in this chapter.

See Also: *recommend; should vs. must*

Noun Plurals

In general, form the plural of a noun by adding s. If the noun already ends in s, form the plural by adding *es*. This rule applies to proper nouns as well as common nouns.

Correct

the Johnsons

the Joneses

Form the plural of an abbreviation or acronym by adding an s with no apostrophe.

Correct

ISVs

CPUs

DBMSs

If an abbreviation or acronym already represents a plural, do not add an *s*. For example, the abbreviation for Microsoft Foundation Classes is *MFC*, not *MFCs*.

Form the plural of a single letter by adding an apostrophe and an *s*. The letter itself (but not the apostrophe or the ending *s*) is italic.

Correct

x's

Form the plural of a number by adding an *s* with no apostrophe.

Correct

486s

the 1950s

Avoid adding *(s)* to words so they can be construed as singular or plural. Such words are difficult to translate because not all languages form plurals by adding a suffix to the root word. If a placeholder modifier can result at different times in a singular or a plural noun, use the plural form.

Correct

Wait for *x* minutes.

Incorrect

Wait for *x* minute(s).

There is no fixed rule for forming the plural of words derived from Latin and Greek that retain their Latin or Greek endings. The singular forms typically end in *-a*, *-us*, *-um*, *-on*, *-ix*, or *-ex*. The plural forms often take the Latin or Greek plural endings, but they can also be formed like other English words. To verify the spelling of such plurals, see specific entries in this book, or see the *American Heritage Dictionary*.

For more information, see Chapter 12, "List of Acronyms and Abbreviations" and *Possessives* in this chapter.

Possessives   Form the possessive of singular nouns and abbreviations by adding an apostrophe and an *s*. This rule applies even if the noun or abbreviation ends in *s*.

Form the possessive of plural nouns that end in *s* by adding only an apostrophe. Form the possessive of plural nouns that do not end in *s* by adding an apostrophe and an *s*.

Correct

the encyclopedia's search capabilities

an OEM's products

Brooks's Law

a children's encyclopedia

the articles' links

It is all right to form possessives from acronyms and abbreviations, but avoid doing so unless the abbreviation refers to a person, such as *CEO*, or generically to an organization, such as *ISV*. It is always all right to use alternate expressions, such as an *of* construction.

Avoid forming possessives from company names. Do not use possessive forms of product or feature names. Use the name as an adjective or use an *of* construction instead.

Correct

the Windows interface

Microsoft products and technologies

Word templates

templates in Word

the dictionary in the spelling checker

the **Send** command on the **File** menu

the OEMs' products

the products of OEMs

Incorrect

Windows' interface

Microsoft's products and technologies

Word's templates

the spelling checker's dictionary

the **File** menu's **Send** command

Do not use the possessive form of a property, class, object, or similar programming element.

Correct

the **Color** property of the **Ball** object

Incorrect

the **Ball** object's **Color** property

The possessive form of *it* is *its* (no apostrophe).

Pronouns based on possessives never take apostrophes. Correct forms are *ours*, *yours*, *hers*, *his*, and *theirs*.

For more information, see *Apostrophes* in Chapter 11, "Punctuation."

Prepositions   Avoid making the word or phrase you want to emphasize the object of a preposition. The object of the preposition is generally considered a weak position in a sentence: Readers pay more attention to the main sequence of subject–verb–object.

There is no rule against ending a sentence with a preposition, nor is there a rule requiring it. The preposition should go where it makes the sentence easiest to read. Like other editorial decisions, placement of prepositions depends on the rhetorical situation and requires judgment.

10

Correct

Type the text you want to search for.

More formal, but also correct

Type the text for which you want to search.

Avoid joining more than two prepositional phrases. Long chains of prepositional phrases are difficult to read and easy to misinterpret.

Correct

In the lower-right corner of the **Save As** dialog box, click **Options**.

Incorrect

In the lower part of the right side of the **Save As** dialog box, click **Options**.

For more information about specific prepositions, see the individual entries in Part 2, "Usage Dictionary."

Prefixes   In general, do not use a hyphen between a prefix and a stem word unless a confusing word would result or if the stem word begins with a capital letter. In general, when a prefix results in a double vowel and each vowel is pronounced, the word is not hyphenated.

For more information, see the individual entries in the Usage Dictionary for specific prefixes, the *American Heritage Dictionary*, or *The Chicago Manual of Style*.

Examples

reenter

nonnegative

non-native

cooperate

coworker

un-American

A prefix affects only the word to which it is affixed. Do not use a prefix to affect an entire phrase.

Correct

unrelated to security

Incorrect

non-security related

Avoid coining words by adding prefixes to existing words. Such words can be difficult to translate, especially into languages that are not based on Latin.

10

Dangling and Misplaced Modifiers   A dangling modifier is one that does not modify any element of the sentence in which it appears. A misplaced modifier is one that makes the sentence ambiguous or wrong because it is placed too far from the thing it modifies or too near to something else that it could modify.

The most common error of this type is a participial or infinitive phrase at the beginning of a sentence that does not refer to the subject. If the main clause is in passive voice, it is easy to overlook the lack of connection between modifier and sentence.

To correct a dangling modifier, either change the subject of the sentence or change the modifying phrase into a clause so its referent is clear.

Correct

When you play audio that is written directly, it is difficult to avoid gaps.

By using object-oriented graphics, you can edit each element of the graphic because the structural integrity of the individual elements is maintained.

Even when more data was added, the spreadsheet calculated as quickly as before.

To add original graphics to your document, you need a scanner.

Incorrect (dangling modifiers)

When playing audio that is written directly, it is difficult to avoid gaps.

By using object-oriented graphics, the structural integrity of the individual elements of the graphic is maintained and can be edited.

Even after adding more data, the spreadsheet calculated as quickly as before.

To add original graphics to your document, a scanner is needed.

To correct a misplaced modifier, move the modifier so it clearly, unambiguously modifies the thing you intend. If that is not possible, rewrite the sentence. In this example, the introductory phrase modifies *you*.

Correct

By using object-oriented graphics, you can more easily maintain and edit the structural integrity of the individual elements of the graphic.

Misplaced modifier

By using object-oriented graphics, the structural integrity of the individual elements of the graphic is easier for you to maintain and edit.

For more information, see *Harbrace College Handbook* and *Handbook of Technical Writing*.

10

Chapter 11
Punctuation

Effective writing builds upon the appropriate use of punctuation to clarify meaning. This chapter provides guidelines for using punctuation marks consistently to meet the needs of readers. This chapter contains the following sections:

- Formatting Punctuation
- Periods
- Commas
- Apostrophes
- Colons
- Semicolons
- Quotation Marks
- Parentheses
- Hyphens, Hyphenation
- Dashes
- Ellipses
- Slash Marks

For further information about specific punctuation marks, see the *Harbrace College Handbook* and *The Chicago Manual of Style*, and refer to your project style sheet.

Formatting Punctuation

As a general rule, format punctuation in the same type style as the preceding word. Exception: If the preceding word is a command, option, keyword, placeholder, part of a code sample, or user input that requires special formatting, use roman type for the punctuation to avoid the impression that the punctuation is part of the syntax. This practice may cause inappropriate line breaks online, so try to avoid the problem by rewriting as necessary.

Correct

Type **Balance Due:** in cell A14. [User types the colon.]

Type **Balance Due**: in cell A14. [User does not type the colon.]

On the **Insert** menu, point to **Picture**, and then click **From File**.

Incorrect

On the **Insert** menu, point to **Picture**, and then click **From File**.

In online documentation, use standard paragraph formatting for punctuation marks following a hyperlink or pop-up text.

When parentheses or brackets appear within a sentence, set them in the formatting of the text outside the marks, not the text within the marks. An exception is *(continued)*, which is used for table headings and in indexes. Never use two different styles, such as italic for an opening parenthesis and roman for a closing parenthesis. Use the predominant sentence formatting.

Periods   Use only one space after a period in both printed and online content.

When a colon introduces a bulleted list, use a period after each list element if each element completes the introduction to the list or if at least one element is a complete sentence. Do not end the entries with periods if they are all short phrases (three words or fewer), even if together with the list introduction they form a complete sentence. For more information, see *Lists* in Chapter 2, "Content Formatting and Layout."

Format periods in the same type style as the preceding word. Exception: If the preceding word is a command, option, keyword, placeholder, part of a code sample, or user input that requires special formatting, use roman type for the period to avoid the impression that the period is part of the syntax. This practice may cause inappropriate line breaks online, so try to avoid the problem by rewriting as necessary.

Correct

On the **Insert** menu, point to **Picture**, and then click **From File**.

Incorrect

On the **Insert** menu, point to **Picture**, and then click **From File**.

When referring to a file name extension, precede it with a period, as in ".prd extension" or "an .exe file." For more information, see *File Names and Extensions* in Chapter 1, "Documenting the User Interface."

If a file name appears at the end of a sentence, the sentence ends with a period as usual. If ending punctuation in this case could cause confusion, rewrite the sentence so the file name appears somewhere else.

Correct

To view the answer key for this lab exercise, open Answer_key.doc.

Open Answer_key.doc to view the answer key for this lab exercise.

In numbered procedures, do not put periods after the numbers preceding each step of the procedure unless your document design calls for them.

For more information, see *Key Names* in Chapter 1, "Documenting the User Interface" and *The Chicago Manual of Style*.

11

Commas   Comma usage is governed by both convention and grammar. For more details about comma usage, see *Harbrace College Handbook*.

When to use commas

In a series consisting of three or more elements, separate the elements with commas. When a conjunction joins the last two elements in a series, use a comma before the conjunction.

Correct

Chapter 15 is an alphabetical reference to commands, procedures, and related topics.

You need a hard disk, an EGA or VGA monitor, and a mouse.

Use a comma following an introductory phrase.

Correct

In Microsoft Windows, you can run many programs.

If you specify a full date in midsentence, use a comma on each side of the year.

Correct

The February 4, 2003, issue of the *New York Times* reported that ....

Incorrect

The February 4, 2003 issue of the *New York Times* reported that ....

When not to use commas

Do not join independent clauses with a comma unless you include a conjunction. Online documentation often has space constraints, and it may be difficult to fit in the coordinate conjunction after the comma. In these instances, separate into two sentences or use a semicolon.

Correct

Click **Options**, and then click **Allow Fast Saves**.

Click **Options**; then click **Allow Fast Saves**. [only to save space in online documentation]

Incorrect

Click **Options**, then click **Allow Fast Saves**.

Do not use a comma between the verbs in a compound predicate.

Correct

The Setup program evaluates your computer system and then copies the essential files to your hard disk.

The Setup program evaluates your computer system, and then it copies the essential files to your hard disk.

Incorrect

The Setup program evaluates your computer system, and then copies the essential files to your hard disk.

11

Do not use commas in month-year formats.

Correct

Microsoft introduced Microsoft Windows version 3.0 in May 1990.

Incorrect

Microsoft introduced Microsoft Windows version 3.0 in May, 1990.

Apostrophes   Use apostrophes to form the possessive case of nouns and to indicate a missing letter in a contraction.

Form the possessive case of a singular noun by adding an apostrophe and an s, even if the singular noun ends in *s*, *x*, or *z*. For plural nouns that end in *s*, form the possessive case by adding only an apostrophe.

Correct

insider's guide

the box's contents

Burns's poems

Berlioz's opera

an OEM's product

the Joneses' computer

Note: It is all right to form possessives from acronyms. Avoid forming possessives from company names. Do not use the possessive form of product names or feature names.

Differentiate between the contraction *it's* (it is) and possessive pronoun *its*. Never use an apostrophe with possessive pronouns (*yours*, not *your's*).

Do not use an apostrophe to indicate the plural of a singular noun (*programs*, not *program's*).

For more information, see *Possessives* in Chapter 10, "Grammatical Elements."

Colons   Use colons sparingly. A colon between two statements usually signifies that what follows the colon illuminates or expands on what precedes the colon.

Correct

Treat the unknown risk just like any other risk: Identify the resources available to address it and develop countermeasures to take if it happens.

Use a colon at the end of a sentence or phrase that introduces a list. Do not use a colon following a procedure heading or to introduce art, tables, or sections.

11

Correct

The basic configuration for your computer must include:

- A hard disk with 24 megabytes of free disk space and at least one floppy disk drive.
- A monitor supported by Microsoft Windows.

Do not use a colon to introduce a code example.

Correct

For example, use the following code to open the external FoxPro database on the network share \\FoxPro\Data in the directory \Ap.

```
... code sample
```

Capitalization after a colon

Do not capitalize the word following a colon within a sentence unless the word is a proper noun or the text following the colon is a complete sentence. Always capitalize the first word of each item in a list, however.

Use a colon to separate the title of a book or article from its subtitle.

Correct

The Double Helix: A Personal Account of the Discovery of the Structure of DNA

Use only one space after a colon in both online and printed text.

Semicolons   A semicolon between two independent clauses indicates less of a pause than a period. If the clauses are not joined by a conjunction, use a semicolon. Otherwise, use a comma before the conjunction. Semicolons are useful for joining two contrasting statements.

Correct

A new variable is initialized with a specified value; an existing variable can be assigned a new value.

Use semicolons sparingly. They are hard to see on low-resolution monitors.

Use semicolons within a sentence to separate phrases that contain other internal punctuation, especially commas. This practice is most common in making brief lists. Such sentences, if they include more than three elements, are often easier to read if you break them into separate sentences or use the elements to create an unordered list.

Correct, but hard to read

In this tutorial, you will learn to quickly construct a user interface; easily implement both single-document interface and multiple-document interface applications; implement features that until now were considered difficult, such as printing, toolbars, scrolling, splitter windows, print preview, and context-sensitive help; and take advantage of many built-in components of the class library.

11

Better

In this tutorial, you will learn to do the following:

- Quickly construct a user interface.
- Easily implement both single-document interface and multiple-document interface applications.
- Implement features that until now were considered difficult, such as printing, toolbars, scrolling, splitter windows, print preview, and context-sensitive help.
- Take advantage of many built-in components of the class library.

Formatting semicolons

Format semicolons in the same type style as the preceding word. Exception: If the preceding word is a command, option, keyword, placeholder, part of a code sample, or user input that requires special formatting, use roman type for the punctuation to avoid the impression that the semicolon is part of the syntax. This practice may cause inappropriate line breaks online, so try to avoid the problem by rewriting as necessary.

In online content, do not include a semicolon in a hyperlink.

Quotation Marks

The term *quotation marks*, used without modifiers, refers to double curly quotation marks (" "). In printed content, use quotation marks except in user input and code samples, which call for straight quotation marks ("). If your project style sheet requires straight quotation marks with sans serif fonts, such as in headings, follow the style sheet.

In online content, use straight quotation marks.

Refer to quotation marks as *quotation marks*, not as *quote marks* or *quotes*. Use the terms *opening quotation marks* or *closing quotation marks*; do not use *open quotation marks*, *close quotation marks*, *beginning quotation marks*, or *ending quotation marks*.

Placement of quotation marks

Place closing quotation marks outside commas and periods. For other closing punctuation, placement of the closing quotation mark depends on whether the punctuation is part of the material being quoted.

Quotation marks have specialized uses in many computer languages. Follow the conventions of the language in code examples.

Correct

One Internet dictionary calls an electronic magazine a "hyperzine."

One Internet dictionary calls an electronic magazine a "hyperzine," but webzine is a common synonym.

What is a "smart device"?

A reader asks, "How scalable is .NET?"

```
/*Declare the string to have length of "constant+1".*/
```

11

Incorrect

One Internet dictionary calls an electronic magazine a "hyperzine".

One Internet dictionary calls an electronic magazine a "hyperzine", but webzine is a common synonym.

Parentheses
In general, parentheses should be in the font style of the context of a sentence, not in the format of the text within the parentheses. For example, the text within parentheses might be italic, but the parentheses themselves would be roman if the surrounding text is roman. An exception to this is "*(continued)*," which is used for tables that continue on the next page or index subentries that continue in the next column or on the next page. In this usage, the parentheses and the word "continued" are italic.

Correct

For a single-column array, use INDEX (*array,row_num*).

Hyphens, Hyphenation
Your project style sheet and specific entries in the Usage section of this guide are the primary sources for hyphenation of product and computer-related terms. However, rules of hyphenation are not always easily applied. In general, if there is no possibility of confusion, avoid hyphenation. Note decisions about ambiguous terms on your project style sheet.

For information about hyphenation of common words, see the *American Heritage Dictionary* and *The Chicago Manual of Style*. For information about acceptable hyphenation in line endings, see *Line Breaks* in Chapter 2, "Content Formatting and Layout." For information about hyphenating with prefixes, see *Prefixes* in Chapter 10, "Grammatical Elements."

Observe these rules when hyphenating modifiers:

* Hyphenate two or more words that precede and modify a noun as a unit if confusion might otherwise result.

Correct

built-in drive	lower-left corner
high-level language	high-level-language compiler
read-only memory	floating-point decimal
line-by-line scrolling	memory-resident program
scrolling line by line [adverb]	

* Hyphenate two words that precede and modify a noun as a unit if one of the words is a past or present participle.

Correct

copy-protected disk

free-moving graphics

11

- Hyphenate two words that precede and modify a noun as a unit if the two modifiers are a number or single letter and a noun or participle.

  Correct

  80-column text card

  eight-sided polygon

  8-point font

  16-bit bus

  I-beam insertion point

- Avoid suspended compound adjectives. In a suspended compound adjective, part of the adjective is separated from the rest of the adjective, such as "first-" in "first- and second-generation computers.") If you must use suspended compound adjectives to save space, include a hyphen with both the first and second adjectives of the compound. Avoid forming suspended compound adjectives from one-word adjectives.

  Correct

  Microsoft Project accepts any combination of uppercase and lowercase letters in a password.

  Click the upper-right or lower-right corner.

  Avoid

  Microsoft Project accepts any combination of upper- and lowercase letters in a password.

  Click the upper- or lower-right corner.

- Do not hyphenate predicate adjectives (adjectives that complement the subject of a sentence and follow the verb) unless this guide specifically recommends it.

  Correct

  Microsoft Exchange Server is an enterprise-wide messaging system.

  Microsoft Exchange Server controls complicated messaging enterprise wide.

  Many viruses are memory-resident.

  This type of Help is context-sensitive.

- Hyphenate compound numerals and fractions.

  Correct

  his forty-first birthday

  one-third of the page

  three sixty-fourths

11

- Do not put a hyphen between an adverb ending in *ly* and the verb or adjective it modifies.

  Correct

  Most Internet browsers have a highly graphical interface.

  Incorrect

  Most Internet browsers have a highly-graphical interface.

- Use an en dash (–) instead of a hyphen in a compound adjective in which at least one of the elements is an open compound (such as *Windows NT-based*) or when two or more of the elements are made up of hyphenated compounds (a rare occurrence).

  Correct

  Windows 98–compatible products

  Some programs have dialog box–type options for frequently used operations.

  MS-DOS–compatible products

  Incorrect

  Some programs have dialog box-type options for frequently used operations.

  Some programs have dialog-box–type options for frequently used operations.

  MS-DOS-compatible products

- Do not use a hyphen in key combinations; use a plus sign instead, as in "ALT+O."

For more information, see *Capitalization* and *Numbers* in Chapter 9, "Common Style Problems"; *Line Breaks* in Chapter 2, "Content Formatting and Layout"; and *Dashes* in this chapter.

Dashes   There are two types of dashes, the em dash (—) and the en dash (–).

Em Dash

The em dash (—), based on the width of an uppercase *M*, is used primarily to set off sentence elements.

> **Note:** Do not use word spacing on either side of an em dash. If your style sheet and your publishing process support it, insert a 1/4 en space on each side of an em dash.

Use an em dash:

- To set off within a sentence a parenthetical phrase that deserves more emphasis than parentheses imply. Use one em dash on each side of the phrase.

  Correct

  The information in your spreadsheet—numbers, formulas, and text—is stored in cells.

- To set off a phrase or clause at the end of a sentence for emphasis. Use one em dash.

Correct

Set key names in all caps—for example, CTRL or ALT.

Do not use an em dash in place of a bullet or other typographic symbol to set off items in a list.

Do not use an em dash to indicate an empty cell in a table.

When an independent clause follows an em dash, do not capitalize the first word unless it is a proper noun.

The HTML code for an em dash is —.

En Dash

The en dash (–) is based on the width of an uppercase *N*. It is slightly longer than a hyphen, half the length of an em dash. En dashes are used primarily as connecting elements, especially with numbers.

Use an en dash:

- To indicate a range of numbers such as inclusive values, dates, or pages.

Correct

© 1993–1994

pages 95–110

- To indicate a minus sign.

- To indicate negative numbers: –79.

- Instead of a hyphen in a compound adjective in which at least one of the elements is an open compound (such as "Windows 2000") or to join a hyphenated compound to another word.

Correct

dialog box–type options

Windows NT–based programs

MS-DOS–compatible products

Do not use an en dash to indicate an empty cell in a table.

Do not use spaces on either side of an en dash.

The HTML code for an en dash is –. For more information, see Names of Special Characters in Chapter 9, "Common Style Problems."

Ellipses   In general, avoid using an ellipsis (...) except in syntax lines or to indicate omitted code in technical material. The HTML code for the ellipsis character is **…**. If you are using a font that does not support the ellipsis character, use three periods with no space between them.

In the user interface, an ellipsis is typically used to show truncation, as in a program name, or to indicate on menus and in dialog boxes that a dialog box will appear to obtain more information from the user. Do not use an ellipsis in this context in documentation.

Correct

On the **File** menu, click **Open**.

Incorrect

On the **File** menu, click **Open...**.

In printed material, it is all right to use an ellipsis in multiple-part callouts, especially with a screen shot used in a procedure. Ensure that the reader's path through the callouts is unambiguous as shown in the following illustration.

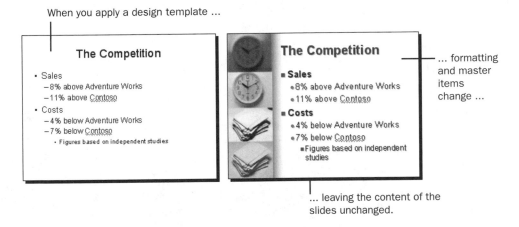

Callouts with ellipses

In callouts, insert one character space before and/or after the entire ellipsis, as shown in the preceding example. If the sentence or phrase ends with additional punctuation such as a period or comma, insert a character space between the punctuation mark and the ellipsis.

In quoted material, an ellipsis indicates omitted material. If the ellipsis replaces the end of a sentence, follow the ellipsis with a closing period, with no intervening space.

Correct

The quick brown fox ....

If the ellipsis indicates omitted material following the end of a sentence, the ellipsis immediately follows the period, again with no intervening space.

Correct

The quick brown fox jumps over the lazy dog....

Slash Marks   Do not use constructions containing a slash mark to indicate a choice, such as *either/or* and *he/she* (*and/or* is acceptable, if necessary).

Do not use a slash mark as a substitute for *or*. If the user interface uses a slash in this way, follow the interface in describing the label, but use *or* in describing the corresponding action.

Correct

Check or clear **Status Bar** to show or hide the status bar.

Incorrect

Check/clear **Status Bar** to show/hide the status bar.

Use a slash mark in constructions that imply a combination.

Correct

client/server

CR/LF, carriage return/line feed

on/off switch

read/write

Use a slash mark to separate parts of an Internet address (use a double slash after the protocol name): *http://mslibrary/catalog/collect.htm*. Use a backslash with server, folder, and file names: *mslibrary**catalog**collect.doc*.

To refer to a slash in documents, it may be useful to differentiate between a "forward slash" for URLs and a "backward slash" for servers and folders.

You can also use a slash mark between the numerator and denominator of fractions in equations that occur in text. The Word Equation Editor includes a format with a slash mark.

Correct

$a/x + b/y = 1$

$x + 2/3(y) = m$

For more information, see *Special Characters* in Chapter 6, "Indexing and Attributing," and *Numbers* in Chapter 9, "Common Style Problems."

11

Chapter 12
List of Acronyms and Abbreviations

Terms are listed alphabetically by acronym or abbreviation, not by meaning. Unless otherwise noted in the "Comments" column, all terms are acceptable to use after spelling out at first mention. Some terms are never acceptable, and some need not be spelled out. Spell out the complete term the first time an abbreviation or acronym appears in the text, reference topic, or Help topic, and then show the abbreviation or acronym within parentheses. When spelling out the term's meaning, follow the capitalization as given in the "Meaning" column unless noted otherwise.

Exclusion of a term does not mean it is not acceptable. Many product-specific terms do not appear here. Follow your project style sheet.

Acronym	Meaning	Comments
ACL	access control list	
ADK	application development kit	
ADO	ActiveX Data Objects	Not *Active Data Objects*.
ADO CE	ActiveX Data Objects for Windows CE	Always spell out at first mention.
ADSI	Active Directory Service Interfaces	Avoid if possible. Always spell out at first mention.
ADSL	asymmetric (*not* asynchronous) digital subscriber line	
ADT	application development toolkit	Avoid; use *ADK* instead, if possible.
AM/FM	amplitude modulation/ frequency modulation	Do not spell out.
ANSI	American National Standards Institute	Spell out only to refer to the organization itself, not to refer to ANSI standards or text format.
API	application programming interface	Not *application program interface*.
APPC	Advanced Program-to-Program Communications	A protocol in Systems Network Architecture.
ASCII	American Standard Code for Information Interchange	Do not spell out.

Acronym	Meaning	Comments
ASP	Active Server Pages *or* application service provider	*Active Server Pages*: A technology for building applications for Internet Information Services. Use the phrase *ASP page*. Do not spell out in the context of ASP.NET.
		application service provider: A provider of application services over the Internet. Always spell out on first mention.
ATM	asynchronous transfer mode	
A/V	audio/video	
AVI	Audio Video Interleaved	A multimedia file format for storing sound and moving pictures in Resource Interchange File Format (RIFF).
BASCOM	Basic Compiler	Do not use acronym.
Basic	Beginners All-purpose Symbolic Instruction Code	Initial cap only. Do not spell out.
BBS	bulletin board system	
BFTP	Broadcast File Transfer Protocol	
BID	board interface driver	
BIFF	Binary Interchange File Format	
BIOS	basic input/output system	
BISYNC	Binary Synchronous Communications Protocol	
BPP	bits per pixel	
bps	bits per second	Lowercase.
BSC	Binary Synchronous Communications Protocol	Use *BISYNC* instead.
BSMS	billing and subscriber management system	
CBT	computer-based training	Avoid; use *tutorial*.
CD	compact disc	Do not spell out. See *CD*.
CDF	Channel Definition Format	Spell out on first use. When referring to the specification, italicize and provide a version number.

12

Acronym	Meaning	Comments
CDS	Circuit Data Services	
CD-ROM	compact disc read-only memory	Do not spell out. See *CD*.
CGA	color/graphics adapter	
CGI	Common Gateway Interface	
CIS	computer information systems	
CISC	complex instruction set computer	Not necessary to spell out in technical documentation.
CMC	1. Continuous Media Controller 2. Common Messaging Calls (MAPI term)	
CMOS	complementary metal oxide semiconductor	
CMS	continuous media server	Do not use; use *MMS* instead.
CMY	cyan-magenta-yellow	
CMYK	cyan-magenta-yellow-black	
COFF	Common Object File Format	Capitalize to refer to the specification. Use lowercase to refer to the file format itself.
COM	Component Object Model	
COM+		Do not spell out.
CPI-C	Common Programming Interface for Communications	
CPU	central processing unit	Do not spell out.
CR/LF	carriage return/line feed	
CRT	cathode-ray tube	Do not spell out.
CSR	customer service representative	
CTI	Computer-Telephony Integration	
DAE	data access engine	
DAO	Data Access Object	
DAT	digital audio tape	
DBCS	double-byte character set	

12

Acronym	Meaning	Comments
DBMS	database management system	
DCE	distributed computing environment	
DCOM	Formerly *distributed COM.*	Do not spell out. Use only to refer to the DCOM wire protocol. For more information, see *COM, ActiveX, and OLE Terminology* in Chapter 4, "Content for Software Developers."
DDBMS	distributed database management system	
DDE	Dynamic Data Exchange	
DDI	Device Driver Interface	
DDL	data definition language	
DDNS	dynamic DNS	Do not use.
DES	Data Encryption Standard	
DFS	Distributed file system	Now all caps.
DHCP	Dynamic Host Configuration Protocol	
DHTML	dynamic Hypertext Markup Language; dynamic HTML	If HTML has already been spelled out, introduce as dynamic *HTML (DHTML).*
DIB	device-independent bitmap	
DIF	Data Interchange Format	
DLC	Data Link Control	
DLL	dynamic-link library	Do not use *dynalink.*
DMOD	dynamic address module	
DNS	Domain Name System (a networking protocol) / The Windows 2000 feature that implements that protocol	Do not use *dynamic DNS* or *DDNS.* Instead, refer to *a DNS server that supports the dynamic update protocol.* Do not use to mean digital nervous system. Do not spell out the Microsoft DNS feature. Say *DNS,* not *DNS Server* or *Microsoft DNS Server.*
DOS	disk operating system	Do not spell out. Avoid except as *MS-DOS.*
DSP	digital signal processor	

12

Acronym	Meaning	Comments
DSS	1. decision support system	
	2. digital satellite system	
DVD	digital versatile disc	Do not spell out. See *DVD*.
DVD-ROM	digital versatile disc, read-only memory	Do not spell out. See *DVD*.
EA	extended attributes	Do not use abbreviation.
ECC	electronic credit card	
EGA	enhanced graphics adapter	
EISA	Extended Industry Standard Architecture	Not necessary to spell out in technical documentation.
EPS	encapsulated PostScript	
FAQ	frequently asked questions	Precede with *a*, not *an*.
FAT	file allocation table	Always spell out *file allocation table* to refer to the table itself. Do not spell out with reference to the file system; always use *FAT file system*.
fax	facsimile	Do not use *FAX*; use *fax* instead. Do not spell out at first mention.
Fortran	Formula Translation	Initial cap only. Do not spell out.
FTP	File Transfer Protocol	All lowercase when used in an Internet address.
FTS	Financial Transaction Services	
GDI	Graphics Device Interface	
GIF	Graphics Interchange Format	
GPI	graphics programming interface	
GUI	graphical user interface	
GUID	globally unique identifier	
HAL	hardware abstraction layer	
HBA	host bus adapter	
HDLC	High-level Data Link Control	An information transfer protocol.
HMA	high-memory area	
H/PC	Handheld PC	
HPFS	high-performance file system	
HROT	host running object table	

12

Acronym	Meaning	Comments
HTML	Hypertext Markup Language	Not *HyperText*.
HTTP	Hypertext Transfer Protocol	Not *HyperText*. All lowercase (http) when used in an Internet address.
IANA	Internet Assigned Numbers Authority	
IBN	interactive broadband network	
ICP	independent content provider	
ICS	Internet Connection Sharing	Do not use acronym.
IDE	1. integrated device electronics 2. integrated development environment	Sometimes seen as *integrated drive electronics*. Spell out at first mention and use one consistently.
IEEE	Institute of Electrical and Electronics Engineers, Inc.	
IFS	installable file system	
IHV	independent hardware vendor	
IISAM	installable indexed sequential access method	
I/O	input/output	
IOCTL	I/O control	
IOS	integrated office system	
IP	Internet Protocol	
IPC	interprocess communication	
IPX/SPX	Internetwork Packet Exchange/Sequenced Packet Exchange	*SPX* also seen as Session Packet Exchange.
IRC	Internet Relay Chat	Service for real-time online conversation.
IS	Information Services	
ISP	Internet service provider	
ISA	Industry Standard Architecture	Not necessary to spell out in technical documentation.
ISAM	indexed sequential access method	

12

Acronym	Meaning	Comments
ISAPI	Internet Server Application Programming Interface (or *Internet Server API*)	
ISDN	Integrated Services Digital Network	
ISO	International Organization for Standardization	
ISV	independent software vendor	
ITV	interactive TV	
JPEG	Joint Photographic Experts Group	Refers both to the standard for storing compressed images and a graphic stored in that format. Also *loss-tolerant JPEG*.
LADDR	layered-architecture device driver	
LAN	local area network	
LCD	liquid crystal display	Not necessary to spell out at first mention.
LCID	locale identifier, locale ID	Do not abbreviate as LCID. Use LCID only as a data type.
LDTR	local descriptor table register	
LED	light-emitting diode	
LISP	List Processor	
LRPC	lightweight remote procedure call	Automation only.
LU	Logical Unit	Endpoint in an SNA network.
MAC	media access control	Spell out on first mention. See *MAC (media access control)*.
MAN	metropolitan area network	
MAPI	Messaging Application Programming Interface	Not necessary to spell out in technical documentation.
MASM	Macro Assembler	
MCA	Micro Channel Architecture	
MCGA	multicolor graphics array	
MCI	Media Control Interface	
MDA	monochrome display adapter	

12

Acronym	Meaning	Comments
MDI	multiple-document interface	
MFC	Microsoft Foundation Classes	
MIDI	Musical Instrument Digital Interface	Not necessary to spell out in technical documentation.
MIDL	Microsoft Interface Definition Language	Do not precede with *the*.
MIF	Management Information Format	
MIME	Multipurpose Internet Mail Extensions	Protocol for defining file attachments for the Web.
MIPS	millions of instructions per second	
MIS	management information systems	Use *IS* instead, unless a specific reference must be to MIS.
MITV	Microsoft Interactive TV	
MMOSA	Microsoft multimedia operating system architecture	Not necessary to spell out in technical documentation.
MMS	Microsoft Media Server	Do not precede with *the*.
MMU	memory management unit	
MOF	Managed Object Format	
MPEG	Moving Picture Experts Group	Sometimes called *Motion Picture(s) Expert(s) Group*, but follow the spelling given.
MS	Microsoft	Do not use as abbreviation.
MSBDN	Microsoft Broadcast Data Network	
MSMQ	Microsoft Message Queuing	For Windows 2000 and later, do not use; use *Message Queuing* instead. On first mention, it is all right to say *Message Queuing (also known as MSMQ)*. For Windows NT 4.0 and earlier, spell out as *Microsoft Message Queuing*.
MSN	The Microsoft Network	
MSO	multiple service operator	
MTA	message transfer agent	
NA	not applicable, not available	Do not use abbreviation, even in tables.

12

Acronym	Meaning	Comments
NAC	network adapter card	Do not use abbreviation.
NAN	not a number	
NCB	network control block	
NCSA	National Center for Super-computing Applications	
NDIS	network driver interface specification	
NDK	network development kit	
NetBEUI	NetBIOS Enhanced User Interface	
NetBIOS	network basic input/output system	
NFS	network file system	
NIC	network interface card	
NIK	network integration kit	
NLS	national language support	
NMI	nonmaskable interrupt	
NOS	network operating system	
NTFS	NTFS file system	The redundant phrase is correct. Do not use *NT file system* or *New Technology file system*.
NTSC	National Television System Committee	
OCR	optical character recognition	
ODBC	Open Database Connectivity	
ODL	Object Description Language	Automation only.
ODS	Open Data Services library	
OEM	original equipment manufacturer	Not necessary to spell out in technical documentation.
OIS	office information system	
OLE	object linking and embedding	Do not spell out.
OOFS	object-oriented file system	
OOM	out of memory	Do not use acronym.
OOP	object-oriented programming	
ORPC	object remote procedure call	

12

Acronym	Meaning	Comments
OS		Do not use as an abbreviation for *operating system*.
OSI	Open Systems Interconnection	
PANS	pretty amazing new stuff (or services)	Refers to telephone services. See also *POTS* in this table.
PAR	Product Assistant Request	Do not use acronym.
PARC	Palo Alto Research Center	
PC	personal computer	Avoid; use *computer* instead.
PCMCIA	Personal Computer Memory Card International Association	
PDC	primary domain controller	
PDF	1. Portable Document Format file 2. Package Definition File	1. File format used by Acrobat. 2. Used in some SDKs.
PERT	program evaluation and review technique	
PFF	Printer File Format	
PIF	program information file	
PIN	personal identification number	
POTS	plain old telephone service	See also *PANS* in this table.
PPV	pay per view	
PROM	programmable read-only memory	
PSU	power supply unit	
QA	quality assurance	
QBE	query by example	
QXGA	quantum XGA	Do not spell out.
RAID	1. redundant array of independent disks 2. retrieval and information database (Microsoft only)	
RAM	random access memory	

12

Acronym	Meaning	Comments
RAS	1. remote access server 2. Remote Access Service	Remote Access Service is Microsoft Windows-based software. The server is a host on a LAN equipped with modems.
RBA	1. relative byte address 2. resource-based approach	
RDBMS	relational database management system	
RFT	revisable form text	
RGB	red-green-blue	Not necessary to spell out in technical documentation.
RIFF	Resource Interchange File Format	
RIP	1. Routing Information Protocol 2. Remote Imaging Protocol 3. Raster Image Processor	Always spell out at first mention to avoid confusion.
RIPL	remote initiation program load	
RISC	reduced instruction set computer	Not necessary to spell out in technical documentation.
ROM	read-only memory	
ROM BIOS	read-only memory basic input/output system	
RPC	remote procedure call	
RTF	Rich Text Format	
SAA	Systems Application Architecture	
SAF	[SQL] Server Administration Facility	
SAMI	Synchronized Accessible Media Interchange	Format used to create a time-synchronized captioning file.
SAP	Service Advertising Protocol	
SAPI	Speech API	
SBCS	single-byte character set	
SCSI	small computer system interface	Precede acronym with *a*, not *an* (pronounced "scuzzy").

12

Acronym	Meaning	Comments
SDK	software development kit	
SDLC	synchronous data link control	
SGML	Standard Generalized Markup Language	
SIC	standard industry classification	
SIG	special interest group	
SIMM	single inline memory module	Not necessary to spell out in technical documentation.
SLIP	Serial Line Internet Protocol	Method of transmitting data over serial lines such as phone lines.
SMB	server message block	
SMP	symmetric multiprocessing	
SMS	system management software	
SMTP	Simple Mail Transfer Protocol	
SNA	Systems Network Architecture	
SNMP	Simple Network Management Protocol	
SPI	service provider interface	
SQL	Structured Query Language	
STB	set-top box	Do not use abbreviation.
SVC	switched virtual circuit	
SVGA	Super VGA	Do not spell out.
SXGA	Super XGA	Do not spell out.
TAPI	Telephony API	
TBD	to be determined	
TCP/IP	Transmission Control Protocol/Internet Protocol	
TIFF	Tagged Image File Format	
TP	transaction processing	
TSPI	Telephony Service Provider Interface	
TSR	terminate-and-stay-resident	
TTY/TDD	teletype/telecommunication device for the deaf	

12

Acronym	Meaning	Comments
TV	television	Okay to use without spelling out.
UDP	User Datagram Protocol	
UI	user interface	
UMB	upper memory block	
UNC	Universal Naming Convention	
UPC	universal product code	
UPS	uninterruptible power supply	
URL	Uniform Resource Locator	Sometimes called Universal Resource Locator, but use *Uniform* in Microsoft documents.
UTC	Coordinated Universal Time	The internationally recognized name for Greenwich Mean Time. Do not spell out as Universal Time Coordinate.
UUID	universally unique identifier	
UXGA	ultra extended graphics array	Do not spell out.
VAR	value-added reseller	
VAT	value-added tax	
VBA	Microsoft Visual Basic for Applications	
VBScript	Microsoft Visual Basic Scripting Edition	
VCPI	virtual control program interface	
VCR	videocassette recorder	Not necessary to spell out at first mention.
VGA	video graphics array	Do not spell out.
VIO	video input/output	
VM	virtual memory	
VRML	Virtual Reality Modeling Language	
VSAM	virtual storage access method (or memory)	
VSD	vendor-specific driver	
VTP	virtual terminal program	

12

Acronym	Meaning	Comments
W3C	World Wide Web Consortium	
WAN	wide area network	
WBEM	Web-based Enterprise Management	
WOSA	Windows Open Services Architecture	
WWW	World Wide Web	All lowercase (www) when used in an Internet address. Okay to use *Web* after first mention.
WYSI-WYG	what you see is what you get	
XGA	extended graphics array	Do not spell out.
XHTML	Extensible Hypertext Markup Language	
XML	Extensible Markup Language	
XMS	extended memory specification	
XSL	Extensible Stylesheet Language	
Y2K	year 2000	Spell out at first mention.
ZAW	Zero Administration for Windows	Spell out at first mention.

12

Part 2

Usage Dictionary

Taking a consistent approach to commonly used language simplifies life for everybody. It gives customers a much more predictable experience with our content. It also reduces the number of decisions that writers and editors are forced to make.

This usage dictionary explains standard usage for technical terms and common words and phrases. The terms in this section are ones that have presented the most common usage problems.

A

-able, -ible   Adjectives ending in *-able* or *-ible* take their meaning from the passive sense of the stem verb from which they are formed. For example, *forgettable* means susceptible to, capable of, or worthy of being forgotten; not of forgetting. The same is true of words whose stem word is derived from a foreign language. For example, *portable* (from the Latin *portare*, to carry) means capable of being carried.

With familiar words, this rule goes without saying; however, people sometimes coin new *-able* words, incorrectly intending them to take the active sense of the stem word. For example, see *bootable disk*, which should not be used.

If you are unsure how to spell a word that ends in *-able* or *-ible*, look it up in the *American Heritage Dictionary*. If you cannot find it, think about writing around the word. Coinages and uncommon word formations can be problems for the worldwide audience.

If you must use a new word with one of these suffixes, follow these guidelines to determine the correct spelling:

- For stem words that end in *-ce* or *-ge*, retain the final *e* to maintain the soft sound: *bridgeable, changeable*.

- For stem words that end in *-e*, drop the final *e* and add *-able*: *scalable*.

- For stem words that end in *-y*, change the *y* to *i* and add *-able*: *reliable*. Exception: When *y* is part of a diphthong, simply add *-able*: *playable, employable*.

- For verbs that end in a consonant, double the final consonant only if the participial form of the verb also takes a double consonant before the suffix: for example, *bidding, biddable*; *forgetting, forgettable*. Exception: Words formed from verbs ending in *-fer* always take a single consonant, such as *transferable*.

The suffix *-able* is much more common than *-ible*. Avoid coining words ending in *-ible*. For a detailed discussion of the use of *-ible*, see *The New Fowler's Modern English Usage* by R. W. Burchfield (Oxford: Oxford University Press, 2000).

abort   Do not use in content written for home users or information workers; instead, use *end* to refer to communications and network connections, *exit* for programs, and *stop* for hardware operations. If *abort* appears in the user interface, it is all right to refer to it, but use the words mentioned in this paragraph to describe the user action.

It is all right to use *abort* in programmer or similar technical documentation if it is part of a function name, parameter name, or some other element of the application programming interface, but avoid it otherwise. In general text, use another appropriate word instead, such as *end* or *stop*.

A

Correct

To end your server connection, click **Disconnect Network Drive** on the **Tools** menu.

If you exit Setup, the program will not be successfully installed.

To stop a print job before it is finished, click **Cancel.**

The PHW_CANCEL_SRB routine is called when the minidriver should cancel a request with STATUS_CANCELLED.

above   Do not use to mean earlier. Use *previous*, *preceding*, or *earlier* instead. You can also use *earlier* to refer to a chapter or section heading. Do not use *above* as an adjective preceding a noun, as in "the above section."

In online content, use a hyperlink to show a cross-reference to another Web page. Even if you refer to a location on the same scrollable Web page, make the reference itself a link; do not use *above*.

Correct

See What Is a Copyright?

See "Connecting to the Network," earlier in this chapter.

Do not use *above* to mean *later*.

Correct

Microsoft Windows 95 and later

Incorrect

Microsoft Windows 95 and above

For more information, see *Cross-References* in Chapter 2, "Content Formatting and Layout."

See Also: *below; earlier*

accelerator key   Obsolete term. Use *keyboard shortcut* instead. In content for software developers, it is all right to use *shortcut key* if it is necessary to distinguish from an access key.

See Also: *access key; shortcut key*

access   It is all right to use *access* as a verb to mean *obtain access to*. Although this usage is grating to many editors, it is well established in the context of computers.

Do not use *access* to mean *start*, *create*, or *open*. Use a more specific verb or phrase instead.

Correct

Start the program from either the **Start** menu or from Windows Explorer.

You can access your personal data from the company intranet.

You can create shortcuts to quickly switch to programs that you use often.

Services that you provide must be configured so that users can access them.

A

Incorrect

Access the program from either the **Start** menu or from Windows Explorer.

You can create shortcuts to quickly access programs that you use often.

See Also: *start, Start (the menu); switch*

accessible   Reserve *accessible* and *accessibility* to refer to things that all people, including those with disabilities, can easily use.

Do not use *accessible* as a synonym for *simple*. Instead, use terms such as *easy to learn, easy to use*, or *intuitive*; or refer to the specific characteristics that make something easy to use, such as *intelligent Help system*.

Correct

A range of enhancements makes multimedia products easier to install and use and provides a great platform for home entertainment.

The availability of high-contrast color schemes enhances the program's accessibility for visually impaired users.

Incorrect

A range of enhancements makes multimedia products more accessible and provides a great platform for home entertainment.

For more information, see Chapter 8, "Accessible Content."

See Also: *assistive*

access key   Do not use in end-user documentation. Use *keyboard shortcut* instead.

Access key is best avoided entirely, but it is permissible in developer documentation or in material about customizing the user interface when you must distinguish between an *access key* and a *shortcut key*. In such cases, use *access key* to denote a *key sequence* used to access a menu item, and provide a definition.

For more information, see *Key Names* in Chapter 1, "Documenting the User Interface."

See Also: *key sequence; keyboard shortcut; shortcut key*

accessory   Use as a general category for programs such as Notepad, Paint, Tablet PC Input Panel, Sticky Notes, or InkBall that appear in the Accessories folder of the Windows Start menu. It is all right to use *program* or *accessory program* to refer to such programs.

Do not refer to accessory programs as *utilities*. Do not make references such as "the Notepad accessory"; use the program name alone.

Correct

Windows includes a number of accessories to help you perform routine tasks.

Notepad is a basic text editor.

A

Incorrect
The Notepad accessory is a basic text editor.

See Also: *tool*

access privileges   Obsolete term. Use *user rights* instead.

See Also: *rights*

access rights   Obsolete term. Use *user rights* instead.

See Also: *rights*

accounts receivable   Not *account receivables*.

acknowledgment   Do not spell with an *e* between the *g* and the *m*. For a section of a book acknowledging the contributions of other people, use the plural *acknowledgments* even if there is only one.

action bar   Do not use. Use *menu bar* instead.

action button   Do not use. Use *button* or *command button* instead.

activate   Use only to indicate the action of verifying that a software product is a legal copy and is installed in compliance with the end-user license agreement.

Correct
If you have not yet activated Windows XP, you can initiate activation at any time by clicking the Windows Activation icon in the system tray.

Do not use *activate* as a synonym for *open*, *start*, or *switch to*.

active vs. current   Use *active* or *open*, not *current*, to refer to open and operating windows, programs, documents, files, devices, or portions of the screen (such as an "open window" or "active cell"). However, use *current* to refer to a drive, directory, folder, or other element that does not change in the context of the discussion.

Note: If *active* causes confusion with ActiveX, try to write around it. For example, be as specific as possible in naming an active element.

Correct
Change the formula in the active cell.

To switch between open documents, on the **Window** menu click the document you want to switch to.

Windows Explorer indicates the current folder.

adapter Not *adaptor*.

Use as a general term to describe hardware that supports connecting a computer to a network or to a peripheral device such as a monitor, speakers, or a camera. An *adapter* can be a printed circuit board, a PC Card or CardBus device, or circuitry that is part of the motherboard itself. Do not use *board* or *card* unless it is important to describe the form of a particular adapter.

Adapter can be used as a noun or as an adjective.

Adapter refers to hardware; it is not the same thing as a *driver*, which is software that controls the behavior of hardware.

See Also: *board; card; graphics adapter*

add-in, add-on Use *add-in* to refer to software that adds functionality to a larger program, such as the Analysis ToolPak in Microsoft Excel. *Add-in* can also refer to a driver or a user-written program that adds functionality to a larger program, such as a wizard, a builder, or a menu add-in.

Use *add-on* to refer to a hardware device, such as an expansion board or external peripheral equipment (such as a CD-ROM player), that is attached to the computer.

In content for home users and information workers, use these terms primarily as modifiers, such as *add-in program* or *add-on modem*.

On menus, the **Add-in** command is capitalized as shown; not *Add-In*.

address Use in content written for home users or information workers to refer to the location of an Internet or intranet site or to an e-mail account name or domain. If necessary for clarity, use a phrase such as *Web address* or *e-mail address*.

In content written for information technology professionals or software developers, use *URL* to refer to a Web address.

Use *path* to refer to the hierarchical structure of a file system from root directory through file name.

Address as a verb is not wrong, but in most cases a stronger, more specific verb is available.

For more information, see *URL, Addresses* in Chapter 9, "Common Style Problems."

See Also: *path*

A

ad hoc   Avoid *ad hoc*, as you would any foreign word or phrase. It means "established only for the specific purpose or case at hand."

adjacent selection   Use instead of *contiguous selection* to refer to a multiple selection (of cells, for example) in which the items touch.

administer   Not *administrate*.

administrator   Use *administrator* or *system administrator* unless you must specify a particular kind of administrator, such as a network administrator or a database administrator.

Do not capitalize *administrator* except in the phrase *Administrator program*. Capitalize *Administrators* only to refer to the Administrators group that is a part of Microsoft Windows security.

Administrator program   Not *Administrator Program*.

affect vs. effect   As nouns and verbs, *affect* and *effect* are often confused. Part of the problem is that the verb *affect* can be defined as "to have an *effect* on."

Correct

Deleting a link on the desktop does not affect the actual program.

Incorrect

Deleting a link on the desktop does not effect the actual program.

The verb *effect* means "to bring about."

Correct

Good software design can effect a change in users' perceptions.

Incorrect

Good software design can affect a change in users' perceptions.

As a noun, *effect* means "result." The noun *affect* is a term in psychology and should not be needed in content about software.

Correct

The effect of the change was minimal.

Incorrect

The affect of the change was minimal.

afterward　Not *afterwards*.

against　Do not use to refer to running or building a program on a particular platform or operating system. Use *on* instead.

Against is acceptable in content for software developers or database administrators in the sense of evaluating a value *against* an expression or running a query *against* a database.

Correct

Show reference queries can be run against the Guide database.

If you want a program built on the newest version of DirectX to run on an older version, define DIRECTDRAW_VERSION to be the earliest version of DirectX you want to run the program on.

Incorrect

If you want a program built against the newest version of DirectX to run against an older version, define DIRECTDRAW_VERSION to be the earliest version of DirectX you want to run the program against.

alarm　Avoid as a general reference to a sound intended to get the user's attention. Use *beep* or a more specific description of the sound instead.

It is all right to use *alarm* in a specific description, such as "the low-battery alarm."

alert　Avoid as a reference to a system message. Use *message* instead. *Error message* is acceptable in content for software developers or information technology professionals when it is necessary to differentiate types of messages.

Use *alerts* (lowercase, plural) to refer to alert messages from .NET or from Internet sites such as MSN or eBay. Capitalize *alerts* in proper names such as MSN Alerts and .NET Alerts, and construe these names as singular.

Do not use *alert* as a synonym for *reminder*.

Correct

You can receive alerts by signing up for MSN Mobile services.

These alerts appear on your desktop or mobile device.

Microsoft .NET Alerts delivers the information you care about to your desktop, mobile device, or e-mail.

A

align, aligned on   Use *align* instead of *justify* to refer to text that is aligned on only one margin. *Right-aligned* and *left-aligned* are correct usage, as are "aligned on the right" and "aligned on the right margin."

Use *justify* only to refer to text that is aligned on both the left and right margins. If you are not sure that your readers will interpret *justify* correctly, define it in place or use another term.

You align text and graphics *on* a margin, but you align one object *with* another. It is all right to use a phrase such as "aligned with each other."

Correct

Align the paragraph on the left.

Left-align the paragraph.

The text is aligned on both the left and the right.

Justified text is aligned on both the left and the right.

Align the text with the headings.

Incorrect

Left-justify the paragraph.

See Also: *justified; left align, left-aligned; right-align, right-aligned*

allow   Use *allow* only to refer to features, such as security, that permit or deny some action. To describe user capabilities that a feature or product makes easy or possible, use *you can*. In content for software developers or system administrators that does not involve permissions or user rights, use *the user can* or *enables the user* when it is necessary to refer to the end user in the third person.

Correct

Windows XP allows a user without an account to log on as a guest.

With Microsoft Word 2000, you can save files in HTML format.

Incorrect

Microsoft Word 2000 allows you to save files in HTML format.

See Also: *can vs. may; enable, enabled; let, lets*

alpha   Refers to the version of a software product that is ready for structured internal testing. Alpha versions are usually not released to external testers.

See Also: *beta*

alphabetical   Not *alphabetic*.

alphanumeric   Use to refer to character sets that include only letters and numerals or to individual characters that can be only letters or numerals.

Do not use *alphanumerical*.

alt text   The common term for the descriptive text that appears as an alternative to a graphic image on Web pages. The text is indicated in the HTML file by the attribute ALT. The code used for the graphic and the alt text looks like this:

```
<IMG SRC="image.gif" ALT="Add the description of the image here.">
```

If you are not sure that your readers understand what *alt text* means, define it on first mention and add it to your glossary.

In HTML content, always provide alt text whenever you use a graphic, and always make the alt text as descriptive as possible: Do not use a word such as "graphic" or "image" alone in alt text. Many users without broadband Internet access, especially those who pay for Internet connection time by the hour, turn off graphics to reduce the time required to display a Web page. Additionally, screen readers for users who are vision-impaired cannot interpret pictures, so they read the alt text instead.

For details on writing alt text for a specific project, consult your project style sheet.

A.M., P.M.   For globalization reasons, avoid in favor of 24-hour time notation. Use *00:00*, not *24:00*, to indicate midnight. If you must use *A.M.* and *P.M.*, use all caps and periods.

Using *12:00 A.M.* or *12:00 P.M.* to refer to noon or midnight is confusing. If you are consistently using 24-hour notation, *00:00* and *12:00* are unambiguous. In any case, simply specifying *noon* or *midnight* is sufficient.

> **Correct**
> The meeting is at noon.
> The show begins at 19:00 Pacific Time (UTC-8).
> The date changes at exactly midnight.

For more information, see *Time Zones* in Chapter 9, "Common Style Problems."

See Also: midnight

among vs. between   Use *among* when referring to three or more persons or things or when the number is unspecified. Use *between* when referring to two persons or things or when referring to relationships between two items at a time, regardless of the total number of items.

A

Correct

Move between the two programs at the top of the list.

Switch between Windows-based programs.

You can share folders and printers among members of your workgroup.

ampersand (&)   Do not use & in text or headings to mean *and* unless you are specifically referring to the symbol on the user interface.

It is, of course, all right to use and refer to the ampersand in appropriate contexts. For example, in HTML, the ampersand precedes the code name or number of a special character, and in C and other programming languages, the ampersand is an operator.

For example, to show less-than (<) and greater-than (>) signs on a Web page, you would use this HTML code:

< >

-or-

< >

and/or   Avoid. Choose either *and* or *or*, or rewrite the sentence. If avoiding *and/or* makes a sentence long or cumbersome, however, it is all right to use *and/or*.

Correct

You can save the document under its current name or under a new name.

Will the new version contain information on how to write object-oriented code and/or use the class libraries?

and so on   Avoid *and so on* except in situations where screen space is too limited for an alternative. This phrase gives no information about the class of items it is meant to represent and so can create ambiguity.

Correct

Body text is most readable in Times New Roman, Palatino, and other serif fonts.

Incorrect

Body text is most readable in Times New Roman, Palatino, and so on.

Do not use *and so on* to end a phrase that begins with *for example* or *such as*. These opening phrases indicate that what follows is not an exhaustive list, so adding *and so on* is superfluous.

Correct

Body text is most readable in serif fonts such as Times New Roman and Palatino.

Incorrect

Body text is most readable in serif fonts such as Times New Roman, Palatino, and so on.

208

It is all right to use *and so on* to indicate a logical progression where at least two items have been named.

Correct

... a, b, c, and so on.

See Also: etc.

antialiasing A technique for making jagged edges look smooth on the screen. Do not hyphenate.

For more information, see the *Microsoft Computer Dictionary*.

antivirus No hyphen.

appears, displays *Displays* requires a direct object; *appears* does not. If necessary in context, you can use the passive *is displayed*.

Correct

If you try to exit the program without saving the file, a message appears.

Windows displays a message if you do not log on correctly.

A message is displayed if you do not log on correctly.

Incorrect

If you try to exit the program without saving the file, a message displays.

appendix, appendixes, appendices Both *appendices* and *appendixes* are acceptable for the plural, but use the same spelling throughout your document or document set. If you share localization tools with other groups, use the same spelling across all products that share the tools.

applet In current usage, *applet* refers to an HTML-based program that a browser downloads temporarily to a user's hard disk. *Applet* is most often associated with Java, but it has also been used to refer to any small program.

Use a more specific term, such as *program*, *add-in*, or the name of the program when referring to a small program in Windows.

Do not refer to the individual programs that make up Control Panel as *applets*. Refer to them by their names. If you must use a generic term, refer to these programs as *items*.

See Also: accessory; add-in, add-on; Control Panel; tool

A

application   Avoid in content for home users and information workers; use *program* instead. *Application* is acceptable in content for software developers or information technology professionals, especially to refer to a grouping of software that includes both executable files and other components.

Do not use *application program*.

See Also: applet; program vs. application

application developer   Avoid. Use *software developer*, *developer*, or *programmer* instead.

Do not use *applications developer*.

application file   Do not use. Use *program file* instead.

application icon   Avoid. Use the specific product name, such as *the Word icon*, whenever possible. If you must use a general term, use *program icon*.

Microsoft
Office Word
2003

Program icon

application window   Avoid. Use the specific product name, such as *the Word window*, instead.

arabic numerals   Use lowercase *a* for the word *arabic* when referring to numbers.

argument vs. parameter   An *argument* typically is a value or expression containing data or code that is used with an operator or passed to a function. For example, in the following expression **x** and **y** are arguments:

```
x = y;
```

A *parameter* is a value given to a variable and treated as a constant until the operation is completed. Parameters are often used to customize a program for a particular purpose. For example, a date could be a parameter that is passed to a scheduling function.

These terms are, however, often used interchangeably. In content for software developers, use the same term consistently to refer to the same kind of element.

In general, use *argument* in content for home users and information workers. The difference between an argument and a parameter is unimportant for such users because it appears so infrequently. Differentiate between the two only if necessary.

For more information, see *Command Syntax* in Chapter 1, "Documenting the User Interface," and *Document Conventions* in Chapter 2, "Content Formatting and Layout."

A

arrow   In documentation for inexperienced computer users, you may want to use *arrow* to identify the arrow next to a list box label. Do not use *up arrow* or *down arrow*, which refer to the *arrow keys* on the keyboard.

> **Correct**
>
> Click the **Font** arrow to display the list.

arrow keys   The arrow keys are the keys that are labeled only with an arrow. If you need to make special mention of the similar keys on the numeric keypad, refer to the *arrow keys on the numeric keypad.*

Refer to a specific arrow key as the LEFT ARROW, RIGHT ARROW, UP ARROW, or DOWN ARROW key. It is all right to use *arrow key* as a general term for any single arrow key.

Do not use *direction keys, directional keys,* or *movement keys.*

Use specific names to refer to other navigational keys, such as PAGE UP, PAGE DOWN, HOME, and END.

> **Correct**
>
> To move the cursor one character, press the appropriate arrow key.

For more information, see *Key Names* in Chapter 1, "Documenting the User Interface."

arrow pointer   Do not use; use *pointer* instead.

> *See Also:* *pointer*

article   Use *article* to refer to a topic in an encyclopedia (such as the Microsoft Encarta Reference Library) or similar reference program and to the contents of magazines, journals, newspapers, and newscasts, whether online or in print. For example, you can refer to an opinion column on MSNBC or a product-related white paper as an article. It is, of course, all right to use a more specific name for such articles.

Do not use *article* to refer to Help topics or sections or chapters of printed or online books.

as   Do not use as a synonym for *because* or *while* in subordinate clauses. Both uses are grammatically correct, but they make reading more difficult for the worldwide audience.

> **Correct**
>
> You can use the Forms Designer as a complete development environment.
>
> Use the active voice whenever possible, because it is easier to translate.
>
> Fill out your registration card while you wait for Setup to finish.
>
> **Incorrect**
>
> Use the active voice whenever possible, as it is easier to translate.
>
> Fill out your registration card as you wait for Setup to finish.

A

assembly language   Not *assembler* and not *machine language*. *Assembly language* is a low-level language that uses an assembler rather than a compiler to translate the source code into machine code.

Hyphenate *assembly language* as an adjective.

assistive   Use *assistive* to refer to devices and organizations that help people with disabilities.

For more information, see Chapter 8, "Accessible Content."

asterisk (*)   Not *star*, except when referring to the key on a telephone keypad. Indicates multiplication in programming languages and also serves as a *wildcard character* representing one or more characters.

See Also: wildcard character

as well as   *As well as* is often misused and is worth avoiding. Although *as well as* can be used as a synonym for *and*, it is used more often as a prepositional phrase. *As well as* can be a globalization problem because it is also used an adverb phrase. ("She can play the piano as well as he.")

If it is not important to use *as well as*, use *in addition to* instead, or rewrite the sentence so that you can use *and*.

> **Correct**
>
> With Word, you can format whole documents, insert headers and footers, and develop an index in addition to writing a simple letter.
>
> With Word, you can write a simple letter. In addition, you can format whole documents, insert headers and footers, and develop an index.
>
> **Avoid**
>
> With Word, you can format whole documents, insert headers and footers, and develop an index as well as write a simple letter.

at sign (@)   In Internet e-mail addresses, @ separates the user name from the domain name, as in username@sample.com. In addresses, it is pronounced *at*.

attribute   Do not use as a synonym for *property*.

In the .NET Framework, an attribute is a descriptive declaration that annotates programming elements such as types, fields, methods, and properties.

In HTML and XML, an attribute is a named value within a tagged element that can change default characteristics of the tag. For example, in a table, the attributes WIDTH and HEIGHT specify the size of a table or table cells. The code for an HTML attribute looks like this:

```
<TABLE WIDTH=50% HEIGHT=50%>
```

Files can have attributes such as hidden and read-only.

See Also: properties

audit trail   Not audit *log*.

author   Avoid as a verb to mean *write*, especially in content written for home users and information workers. It is all right in content for information technology professionals and software developers to mention *authoring tools* or *authoring environments*.

It is all right to use *author* to refer to *authoring* in language-specific or tool-specific contexts—for example, "authoring in XML." It is better to write around such constructions for home users and for many information workers. A phrase such as "writing in XML" or "creating content in XML" is more suitable.

auto-   In general, do not hyphenate words beginning with *auto-*, such as *autoanswer*, *autodemo*, and *autodial*, unless it is necessary to avoid confusion. If in doubt, check the latest edition of the *American Heritage Dictionary* or the *Microsoft Computer Dictionary*, or consult your project style sheet.

Avoid coining words beginning with *auto-*. Coinages are often globalization problems.

B

backbone   Usually, a large, fast network that connects other networks. For more information, see the *Microsoft Computer Dictionary*.

You do not need to define *backbone* in content written for information technology professionals. Avoid in content written for home users or information workers.

back end   Avoid. Use a more specific term instead, such as *server*, *operating system*, *database*, or *network*.

backlight   One word. Refers to the lighting that makes a flat panel display, such as that on a laptop computer, easier to read.

backspace   Okay to use as a verb.

backtab   Do not use. If necessary to explain the procedure, refer to the SHIFT+TAB key combination.

back up, backup   Two words as a verb; one word as an adjective or a noun.

> **Correct**
> Back up the files before you turn off the computer.
> Save the backup copies on a floppy disk.

backward   Not *backwards*.

base line vs. baseline   Use *baseline* (one word) to refer to an established standard, as in "baseline data." Use *base line* (two words) only to refer to the bottom alignment of uppercase letters in print (a typographic term).

baud   Refers to the rate of signals transmitted per second. Because baud is a rate, the phrase *baud rate* is redundant.

Do not use *bits per second* or *BPS* as a synonym for baud. Modems are conventionally designated by bits per second or kilobits per second, not baud. A 28.8 Kbps modem runs at a different baud, depending on how events are coded for transmission.

When designating baud, use commas when the number has five (not four) or more digits.

B

because vs. since   Avoid using *since* to mean *because*. It is a globalization problem and in some cases it can result in ambiguity.

Use *because* to refer to a reason and *since* to refer to a passage of time. If it is possible to misinterpret the meaning of *since* as referring to a reason, rewrite the sentence.

Correct

Because I installed the fast modem, I can download messages very quickly.

Since installing the fast modem, I can download messages very quickly.

Ambiguous

Since I installed the fast modem, I can download messages very quickly.

beep   Use as a noun instead of *alarm* or *tone* to refer specifically to a beeping sound.

Correct

When you hear the beep, insert the floppy disk in the drive.

below   Do not use to mean *later* in a book or online document; use *later* instead. You can also use *later* to refer to a chapter or section heading. Do not use *below* as an adjective preceding a noun, as in "the below figure."

In online content, do not use *below* or *later*. Use a hyperlink instead. *Later* in this context makes an unverifiable assumption about the user's path through a site. It is all right to use *later* to refer to content on the same Web page, but provide a hyperlink if the reader must scroll to find the material referred to.

For more information, see *Cross-References* in Chapter 2, "Content Formatting and Layout."

See Also: above; later

beta   A software product that is ready for unstructured testing by customers.

Avoid referring to a beta release as a *preview*. *Preview* is often used to denote a version of a released product that will run only long enough for the user to make a purchasing decision.

See Also: alpha

bi-   In general, do not hyphenate words beginning with *bi-*, such as *bidirectional*, *bimodal*, and *bimonthly*, unless it is necessary to avoid confusion. If in doubt, check the *American Heritage Dictionary* or refer to your project style sheet.

big-endian, little-endian   *Big-endian* refers to the method of physically storing numbers so that the most significant byte is placed first. *Little-endian* is the opposite. For more information, see the *Microsoft Computer Dictionary*. These are acceptable terms in content for software developers.

bitmap   One word. Refers to a specific file format for online art.

Do not use generically to refer to any graphic. Use *figure*, *picture*, or a similar term as a general reference.

bitmask   One word.

bitplane   One word. Refers to one of a set of bitmaps that together make up a color image. For more information, see the *Microsoft Computer Dictionary*.

bits per second (BPS)   In general, spell out at first mention; then use the abbreviation *BPS*. If you are sure your audience is familiar with the term, you do not need to spell it out.

Do not use as a synonym for *baud*.

See Also: baud

bitwise   One word. Refers to a programming operation that determines the settings of individual bits in a variable. Use only in content written for software developers, and do not define it.

black box   Jargon. Do not use. A black box is a unit of hardware or software whose internal structure is unknown but whose function is documented.

black hole   Jargon. Do not use. A black hole is a condition of an internetwork where packets are lost without an indication of the error.

blank   Do not use as a verb.

blog, weblog   Acceptable in content that either introduces the concept of blogs or addresses an audience that understands and expects these terms. *Blog* is the preferred term.

Always define on first use in introductory content, and consider defining on first use elsewhere if the content may reach a broader audience. In introductory content and glossary entries, make clear that *blog* and *weblog* are synonymous.

Blog is also acceptable as a verb meaning "to publish or write entries for a blog." *Blogger* is acceptable to refer to a person who publishes or writes entries for a blog.

blue screen, bluescreen   Do not use *blue screen* or *bluescreen*, either as a verb or as a noun, to refer to an operating system that is not responding. The correct verb is *stop*; the correct noun phrase is *stop error*.

It is all right to use *blue screen* (two words) to refer to the screen display itself.

Correct
The operating system stops unexpectedly and an error message appears on a blue screen.

board   Use as part of *motherboard* (not *system board*). Otherwise, avoid. As a general term for hardware that provides a connection between a peripheral device and the motherboard, use *adapter*.

See Also: *adapter; card*

bold   Not *bolded*, *boldface*, or *boldfaced*. Use *bold type* as a noun. Do not use *bold* as a verb or a noun.

Correct

To make the selected characters bold, press CTRL+B.

Incorrect

To bold the selected characters, press CTRL+B.

Note: Use *roman type* to describe type that is neither bold nor italic. Do not confuse *roman type* with the *Times Roman* or *Times New Roman* font.

For more information, see *Document Conventions* in Chapter 2, "Content Formatting and Layout."

See Also: *font and font style*

bookmark   In general Internet usage, a saved reference in the form of a URL or link that helps users return to a particular location, page, or site. Use *favorite* to refer to a bookmark in Internet Explorer.

See Also: *favorite*

Boolean   Always capitalize.

boot   Do not use *boot* as a verb; use *start* or *restart* instead, and make clear that *start* refers to the computer, not to a program. Use *turn on* to refer to turning on the computer.

It is all right to use *boot* as an adjective, as in *boot sector* and *boot sequence*, in content for software developers or information technology professionals. Where possible, though, use *startup* instead.

If the user interface or application programming interface uses *boot* in a label or element name, it is all right to reproduce the label or element name, but use *start* or *startup* to refer to the action or event described.

Correct

The Boot.ini file is a text file that stores startup options.

See Also: *turn on, turn off*

bootable disk   Avoid. Use *system disk* or *startup disk* instead. It is acceptable to use *boot disk* in content for software developers.

bot   Short for *robot*. Technical jargon, but a commonly used term on the Internet to refer to a program that performs a repetitive task, particularly posting messages to newsgroups and keeping Internet Relay Chat (IRC) channels open.

Avoid in most instances except in material about IRC, chat rooms, and multiuser dungeons (MUDs), where it may be appropriate. If you have any doubts that your readers will be familiar with *bot*, substitute a clearer and more descriptive term.

See Also: spider

bottom left, bottom right   Avoid; use *lower left* and *lower right* instead, which are hyphenated as adjectives.

bounding outline   Technical term for the visible element, usually a dotted rectangle, that appears when a user selects a range of items.

Do not use *marquee* as a synonym for *bounding outline*. It is all right to use *dotted rectangle* or *dotted box* if necessary to describe the bounding outline, especially in content that is primarily for home users or information workers, but establish the term *bounding outline* and use it.

box   In content about a dialog box, use *box* instead of *field* to refer to any box except a check box or a list box. For a check box, use the complete term: *check box*. For a dialog box element that displays a list, such as a drop-down list box, use *list* rather than *box* for clarity.

> **Correct**
> the **Read-Only** box
> the **File Name** box
> the **Hidden Text** check box
> the **Wallpaper** list
>
> **Incorrect**
> the **User Name** field

For more information, see *Dialog Boxes and Property Sheets* in Chapter 1, "Documenting the User Interface."

breakpoint   One word. Technical term related to testing and debugging.

broadcast   *Broadcast* can be a noun, an adjective, or a verb. The past tense of the verb *broadcast* is *broadcast*, not *broadcasted*.

To refer to a broadcast over the World Wide Web or over an intranet, use *webcast*.

browse   Use to refer to scanning Internet sites or other files, whether in search of a particular item or only in search of something that might be interesting.

If your product refers to the ellipsis button as the Browse button, use *browse* to describe the user action associated with the button. Consult your project style sheet for details.

It is all right to use *browse* the Internet, but use *browse through* (not *browse*) a list, database, document, or similar item.

Browsing is a manual activity. To describe using a product's search feature or using an Internet search engine, use *find* or *search*.

See Also: *ellipsis button; find and replace; search and replace; surf*

browser   Use *browser* or *Web browser*, not *Web viewer*, to refer to a program that downloads and displays HTML pages.

browse vs. find   *Browse* is when the user manually looks for something in a folder, tree structure, or Internet site.

Find is when the user instructs the computer to search for something, such as a specific file, object, computer, Web site, server, term, or phrase.

bug   Use without definition or apology to refer to a software or hardware error.

build   Avoid in content written for home users and information workers. Use *create* for such items as documents, charts, and worksheets.

It is all right to use *build* as a verb in content written for software developers to mean to compile and link code. If necessary, it is all right in such content to use *build* as a noun.

bulleted   Use *bulleted list*, not *bullet list*. *Bullet* is correct, however, in referring to the graphical symbol for a bullet (•) or to a single item, as in a *bullet point*.

burn   Acceptable term to refer to recording data on a CD or a DVD.

button   Use as the shortened form of *command button* or *option button*. Do not use *action button*.

In general, refer to a button only by its label. If you need to incorporate *button* in the name for clarity—for example, if the button label is an image rather than text—button is lowercase.

Correct

Select the file you want to open and then click **OK**.

To enlarge a window to fill the entire screen, click the **Maximize** button.

For more information, see *Dialog Boxes and Property Sheets* in Chapter 1, "Documenting the User Interface."

See Also: *command button; option, option button*

B

C

C, C++, C#   *C*, *C++*, and *C#* are programming languages. It is all right to use these names as adjectives—for instance, *a C program*—but avoid forming hyphenated adjective phrases with them.

C# is pronounced "c-sharp." Because not all fonts include the musical sharp sign, use the *number sign (#)* to form *C#*.

See Also: number sign (#)

cable   Use as a noun; do not use as a verb.

> **Correct**
>
> The cable is connected to the computer.
>
> **Incorrect**
>
> The printer is cabled to the computer.

cabling   Avoid. Use *cable* or *cables* instead. If necessary in a discussion of network connections, it is all right to use *cabling* to refer to a combination of cables, connectors, and terminators.

cache vs. disk cache   Differentiate between *cache* and *disk cache*. A *cache* generally refers to a special memory subsystem in which data values are duplicated for quick access. A *disk cache* refers to a portion of RAM that temporarily stores information read from disk. For details, see the *Microsoft Computer Dictionary*.

Do not use *cache* or *file cache* to refer to the storage location of Internet files that are downloaded as you browse the Web. The Internet Explorer term is *Temporary Internet Files folder*.

calendar   Do not use as a verb. Use *schedule*, *list*, or another appropriate verb instead.

call back, callback   Use *call back* (two words) as a verb and *callback* (one word) as a noun or adjective.

In content for software developers, do not use *callback* when you mean *callback function*.

call out, callout   Two words as a verb; one word as a noun or adjective.

> **Correct**
>
> You should call out special features in the interface.
>
> Add callouts to the art. The callout wording should be brief.

For more information, see *Art, Captions, and Callouts* in Chapter 2, "Content Formatting and Layout."

caller ID   Do not spell out *ID*.

can vs. may   Use the verb *can* to describe actions or tasks that the user or program is able to do. Use *may* to express possibility, not to imply that the user has permission to do something. Use *might* to connote greater doubt than *may* or to eliminate ambiguity when *may* could be interpreted to imply permission.

Correct

You can use the **/b** option to force a black-and-white screen display.

If you use the **/b** option, your code might not be portable.

If the table overlaps the text or the margin, you may need to resize the table and wrap text around it.

If the table overlaps the text or the margin, you can resize the table and wrap text around it.

Many new programs may run very slowly on less powerful computers.

You may want to change your settings.

Incorrect

You may use the **/b** option to force a black-and-white screen display.

The random password that is generated when an account is created may not meet the strong password requirements.

The spelling or format of the server name you specified may be incorrect.

If a language does not appear in the **Input language** list, the fonts for that language may not be installed.

Do not use *could* when you mean *can*. Like *might*, *could* conveys a tone of doubt that is best avoided in technical writing. It is all right to use *could* as the past tense of *can* when users cannot mistake its meaning.

See Also: *should vs. must*

cancel the selection   Not *deselect* or *unmark*. Use *clear* to refer to check boxes.

canceled, canceling   One *l*, but use two *l*'s in the noun *cancellation*.

card   Avoid in a hardware context unless making specific reference to a device that has *card* in the name, such as *smart card*. In general, use *adapter* to describe hardware that connects a network or a device to a computer.

Correct

graphics adapter

sound adapter

network adapter

Incorrect

graphics card

sound card

network card

It is, of course, all right to use *card* in nontechnical ways, such as *credit card* or *business card*.

See Also: *adapter; board*

carriage return/line feed (CR/LF)   Follow conventional practice and use a slash mark, not a hyphen, when referring to this ASCII character combination. Abbreviate as CR/LF for subsequent references.

cascade   Avoid except to refer to the **Cascade** command or to describe cascading style sheets.

See Also: *cascading style sheets*

cascading menu   Do not use except in content for software developers where *cascading menu* appears in the user interface or the application programming interface. Use *submenu* instead when you must identify such a menu.

For more information, see *Menus and Commands* in Chapter 1, "Documenting the User Interface"

See Also: *submenu*

cascading style sheets   *Cascading style sheets* (note that the phrase is lowercase) is an accepted industry term in the context of HTML and XML. Do not abbreviate as *CSS*.

See Also: *style sheet*

catalog   Not *catalogue*.

category axis   In spreadsheet programs, refers to the (usually) horizontal axis in charts and graphs that shows the categories being measured or compared. For clarity, refer to it as the *category (x) axis* at first mention; *x-axis* is acceptable for subsequent mentions. You can also use *horizontal (x) axis* in documentation for inexperienced computer users.

See Also: *value axis*

caution   Advises users that failure to take or avoid a specified action could result in loss of data.

In online documentation and messages, precede a caution with the warning symbol.

Warning Symbol

For more information, see *Notes and Tips* in Chapter 2, "Content Formatting and Layout."

CBT   Avoid *CBT* and its spelled-out form, *computer-based training*. Use *tutorial* instead. Use *online tutorial* only to distinguish from a printed tutorial.

CD   Do not spell out. If you refer to a CD as a *disc*, use the correct spelling.

It is all right to use *CD* alone as long as either the reference is general or there is no possibility of confusion as to what type of CD is under discussion: audio CD, CD-ROM, CD-R, or CD-RW. When it is necessary to be specific, be specific.

Refer to the drive for a CD as the *CD drive*, not the *CD player*. If you are referring to a specific type of drive, such as a CD-RW drive, use the appropriate name.

Do not use *CD disc, CD-ROM disc*, or similarly redundant constructions.

CD case   Use instead of *jewel case*.

CD key   A combination of letters and numbers that identify an individual product license. The CD key is normally found on the back of the product CD case.

Use only when necessary to refer to a key that is specific to a CD. In general, use *product key* instead.

CD Plus   Refers to a method of combining audio and data on one compact disc. In general, use the term as an adjective, as in "CD Plus format" or "CD Plus technology." Note spelling and capitalization—not *CD+, CD-plus*, or other variations.

center around   Do not use; use *center on* instead.

certificate   A digital certificate binds a client's or server's identity to a pair of electronic keys that can be used to encrypt and sign digital information. Certificates help ensure secure, tamper-proof communication on the Internet. A certificate is obtained by a process called code signing.

The certificate identifies the author and software publisher, so the user can contact them if the code is not satisfactory.

For more information about security, see the Microsoft Security Web site at *http://www.microsoft.com/security*.

channel   Use lowercase to refer to the channels on MSN or Internet Explorer 4.0. Use uppercase when necessary to match the user interface.

Correct

the Arts & Entertainment channel

the Channel bar

chapter   Use only in reference to printed documents. For online documents, use *section, topic, site*, or other appropriate term.

See Also: article

226

character set   Do not use as a synonym for *code page*. A character set appears on a code page.

For more information, see the *Microsoft Computer Dictionary*.

chart   Do not use as a verb when referring to entering data for a graphic; use *plot* instead.

Use the noun *chart* instead of *graph* to refer to graphic representations of data—for example, *bar chart*, *pie chart*, and *scatter chart*.

chat   Use as noun, adjective, and verb in the context of Internet or intranet chat.

check   Use *check* or *checked* as an adjective in phrases such as *check mark* or *checked command*.

Do not use *check* and *uncheck* as verbs meaning to add and remove a check in a check box; use *select* and *clear* instead. Do not use *check* as a noun to mean *check mark*.

See Also: checked command

check box   Use the identifier *check box*, not just *box*, to refer to this option. *Box* alone is ambiguous, especially for worldwide readers.

You *select* and *clear* a check box (not *turn on* and *turn off, mark* and *unmark, check* and *uncheck*, or *select* and *deselect*).

Check boxes

For more information, see *Dialog Boxes and Property Sheets* in Chapter 1, "Documenting the User Interface."

check mark   Two words.

checked command   A command name on a menu that follows a check mark or a bullet that appears or disappears each time the user clicks the command or a related command. Checked commands can be either mutually exclusive (document views in Microsoft Word, for example) or independent of each other (settings on the **View** menu in Microsoft Excel). In the latter case, it is all right to call them *marked commands*.

Use *turn on* or *turn off* in procedures to refer to activating or deactivating the command, but use *click* as the means of turning it on or off.

> **Correct**
>
> To turn on Outline view
>
> On the **View** menu, click **Outline**.
>
> If the **Outline** command is checked, the document is in Outline view.

child folder   Avoid. Use *subfolder* or *subdirectory* instead.

choose   Use *choose* when the user must make a decision, as opposed to selecting (not *picking*) an item from a list to carry out a decision already made.

> **Correct**
>
> If you do not have an Internet account, click **Choose from a list of Internet service providers (ISPs)** and then click **Next**.
>
> If you choose to encrypt only the folder, no files or subfolders contained in the folder are encrypted.

Do not use *choose* as an alternative to *click* or *double-click*. *Choose* does not convey any additional information to those who do not use a mouse, and such users normally understand the equivalent action that they must take when a procedure step says to click.

> **Correct**
>
> On the **File** menu, click **Open**.

> **Incorrect**
>
> On the **File** menu, choose **Open**.

See Also: click; select

clear   Use *clear* as a verb to describe the act of removing a check from a check box or removing a tab stop. Do not use *turn off*, *unmark*, *uncheck*, or *deselect*.

The antonym of *clear* is *select*.

> **Correct**
>
> Clear the **Mirror margins** check box.
>
> To clear a tab stop, click **Clear**.

For more information, see *Dialog Boxes and Property Sheets* in Chapter 1, "Documenting the User Interface."

See Also: select

click   Use *click*, rather than *choose* or *select*, to refer to the user action of issuing a command or setting an option.

If a user can set an option to use either a single click or a double click to perform some action, use the default mode when documenting a feature. Explain the various options in the product documentation.

Do not use *click on* or *click at*; "*click in* the window" is acceptable, however. With this exception, *click* should always be a transitive verb.

Note: It is all right to omit "Click **OK**" at the end of a procedure if the user interface makes it clear that clicking the **OK** button is necessary to complete the procedure.

Correct

To open Add or Remove Programs, click **Start**, click **Control Panel**, and then double-click **Add or Remove Programs**.

See Also: *choose; pen; point to; select*

For more information, see *Dialog Boxes and Property Sheets* in Chapter 1, "Documenting the User Interface."

clickstream   One word. Refers to the path that users take when they browse the Internet. Each click adds to the stream.

Clickstream is primarily a marketing term. Avoid in content for home users and information workers.

clickthrough   Do not hyphenate. Do not use in content for home users or information workers.

client   Use *client* as an adjective to refer only to a computer, object, or program that obtains data or services from a server.

Correct

client workstation

client computer

Do not use *client* to refer to a person. Use *customer* instead.

client area   Do not use unless necessary—and then only in content for software developers or information technology professionals. Use *desktop* or *workspace* instead.

See Also: *workspace*

client side   Avoid, especially as an adjective. Use *client* instead.

Client side is acceptable when it refers specifically to the client part ("side") of a program or protocol that acts on both a server and a client computer. In general, such usage should be necessary only in content written for software developers or information technology professionals.

If you must use *client-side* as an adjective, hyphenate it.

See Also: *client*

client/server   Use the slash mark in all instances.

clip art   Two words.

C

Clipboard Capitalize when referring to the component, in Windows documentation. Do not precede with *Windows*. Material is moved or copied *to* the Clipboard, not *onto* it.

close Use *close* for windows, documents, and dialog boxes. For programs, use *exit*. For network connections, use *end*.

Use *close* to refer to the action a program takes when it has encountered a problem and cannot continue. Do not confuse with *stop responding*, which indicates that the program cannot close itself.

See Also: exit

Close button In Windows-based programs, the box with × at the upper right of the screen that, when clicked, closes the window.

Close button

It is all right in procedures to use a graphic instead of the name **Close** button. If you spell out *Close* in reference to the button, capitalize *Close* and use the word *button*. *Close* as part of *the* **Close** button should always appear in bold type.

Correct

... and then click .

... and then click the **Close** button.

co- In general, do not hyphenate words beginning with the prefix *co-*, such as *coauthor* and *coordinate*, unless it is necessary to avoid confusion. If in doubt, check the *American Heritage Dictionary* or consult your project style sheet.

code example, code sample Not *code snippet.*

Use *code example* to refer to an illustrative fragment of source code. Introduce a code example with a complete sentence that ends with a period, not a colon.

Correct

A nested class is a class that is fully enclosed within another class declaration, as in the following example.

Use *code sample* to refer to a complete sample program that can be compiled and run.

code page Do not use as a synonym for *character set*. A character set appears on a code page. For more information, see the *Microsoft Computer Dictionary*.

code point Two words, lowercase.

code signing Use to refer to the act of providing a digital certificate that ensures that the software to be downloaded over the Internet has not been tampered with.

codec Lowercase. Do not spell out as *compressor/decompressor* or *coder/decoder*. Use only in content for software developers or when *codec* appears in the user interface.

collaborate, collaboration, collaborator It is all right to use *collaborate* and *collaboration* to refer to two or more people who are working on a shared document.

Avoid *collaborator* to describe a worker in such an environment. *Collaborator* is a sensitive term in some regions. Use a synonym, such as *colleague* or *coworker*, instead.

color map Two words. Refers to the color lookup table in a graphics adapter.

column format Not *columnar* or *columnlike*.

COM, .com As the name of a communications port (also known as serial port), use all uppercase followed by a number, as in *COM1*. As an extension and the indicator of a commercial organization in a URL, use all lowercase preceded with a period, as in *.com file* and *Microsoft.com*.

COM is also an abbreviation for *Component Object Model*. Be sure that the user cannot be confused about what *COM* means in your content.

For more information, see *COM, ActiveX, and OLE Terminology* in Chapter 4, "Content for Software Developers."

See Also: communications port

combo box Use in content for software developers to describe a box in which the user can select an item from a list or type a value directly in the box. Do not use *combo box* in content for home users or information workers. Refer to as a *box* instead, using the label provided in the user interface.

Combo box

Use *enter* to refer to either selecting or typing a value in a combo box.

Correct

In the **Size** box, enter the font size, in points, that you want.

For more information, see *Dialog Boxes and Property Sheets* in Chapter 1, "Documenting the User Interface."

command Use *command* to describe a command on a menu, not *menu item*, *choice*, or *option*. In content for software developers, it is all right to use *menu item* if it is necessary to distinguish a command on a menu from a command issued at a command prompt.

For more information, see *Menus and Commands* in Chapter 1, "Documenting the User Interface."

command button Use in content for software developers to refer to a usually rectangular button in a dialog box that carries out a command.

To describe a specific command button in the user interface, use the button label without the word *button*, especially in procedures. Follow the user interface for capitalization and spelling. When it is important to identify a command button as a type of user interface element, it is all right to refer to the label and just the word *button*.

Correct

For information about the dialog box, click the **Help** button.

Better

For information about the dialog box, click **Help**.

Incorrect

For information about the dialog box, click the **Help** command button.

Do not refer to a command button as an *action button* or *push button*. In content for software developers, it is all right to say something like "a command button, also known as a push button" if a segment of your readers will be more familiar with that term.

Command button

For more information, see *Dialog Boxes and Property Sheets* in Chapter 1, "Documenting the User Interface."

command prompt Not *C prompt*, *command-line prompt*, or *system prompt*. If necessary, use a specific reference, such as *MS-DOS prompt*.

The command prompt refers only to the prompt itself, for example, `c:>`. Refer to the window in which the command prompt appears as the *Command Prompt window*. Note the capitalization.

Avoid referring to the Command Prompt window as a *console window* except in content for software developers.

Users type commands *at* a command prompt, not *on* a command line.

Correct

At the command prompt, type **certutil -setreg ca**.

Incorrect

On the command line, type **certutil -setreg ca**.

See Also: *console*

communications port　Use to refer to a computer port that supports asynchronous communication one byte at a time. It is all right to abbreviate as *COM port* after first mention if you are referring specifically to the ports on a computer numbered COM1, COM2, and so on. Be sure that the context does not allow the reader to confuse the *COM* in *COM port* with the abbreviation for *Component Object Model*.

It is all right to refer to a communications port as a *serial port*. If you are referring specifically to the COM ports, it is useful, especially for home users and information workers, to be explicit about the reference.

Correct

Connect the infrared device to a serial port on your computer, and note the serial port number (typically COM1 or COM2).

compact disc (CD)　Do not spell out. Use *CD* instead. If you must spell out *compact disc*, it is *disc*, not *disk*.

See Also: *CD*

compare to vs. compare with　Use *compare to* to point out similarities between dissimilar items. Use *compare with* to comment on the similarities or differences between similar items. The use of *compare to*, which is often metaphorical, is generally unnecessary in technical content.

Correct

People have compared a computer to a human brain.

Compared with a Pentium 4 processor, a 386 processor is extremely slow.

compile　Acceptable as a verb or as an adjective, as in "compile time." Do not use as a noun.

Correct

After you save the file, compile your program.

Incorrect

After you save the file, do a compile.

comprise   Avoid. *Comprise* has a history of misuse and is misunderstood even by many native English speakers. It means "to include" or "to (metaphorically) embrace." The whole *comprises* or is *composed of* its parts; the parts *compose* or are *comprised in* the whole. *Comprised of* is always incorrect.

The forms of *compose* are generally better understood than those of *comprise*, but clearer synonyms, such as *include* and *contain*, are clearer to most readers.

computer   Not *PC* or *machine* or *box*, regardless of audience. Do not use *client* or *server* as a synonym for computer. Use *client computer* or *server computer* instead.

connect   In general, use *connect*, *make a connection*, and similar phrases only to refer to the act of physically attaching a computer to peripheral hardware, a network, or the Internet.

Exceptions are:

- Connector applications and connector queues in Message Queuing.

- Connecting graphical objects in programs such as Microsoft Visio.

- Connecting a computer to a shared network folder.

- Establishing a user session with Remote Access Server.

- In the context of Windows Server, creating a connection profile.

Do not use *connect* as a synonym for *sign in* or *log on*. Do not use *connect* as a synonym for *map*, as in mapping a drive letter to a shared network folder, even if *disconnect* is the correct term for removing a mapped network drive.

See Also: *log on, log off, logon, logoff; sign in, sign out, sign on, sign up*

console   Avoid *console window* and *console application* except in content for software developers. Use *Command Prompt window* and *command-line program* instead.

Avoid *console* to describe a configuration of snap-ins. It is all right to refer to *console trees* and *console panes*.

Do not use *console* as a synonym for *snap-in*.

See Also: *command prompt; snap-in*

context menu   Do not use *context menu* or *right-click menu* to refer to the menu that appears when a user clicks the right mouse button in certain areas (or "contexts"), such as in a toolbar region. If you must refer to this menu by name, use *shortcut menu* instead.

It should be necessary to use *shortcut menu* only in content for software developers. In other content, avoid making specific reference to the menu.

Correct

Right-click the selected text, and then click **Copy**.

Incorrect

Right-click the selected text, and then click **Copy** on the shortcut menu.

If the application programming interface uses *context menu* (or *ContextMenu* or similar constructions), follow the interface, but make clear that it refers to the shortcut menu.

Correct

The **Control.ContextMenu** property gets or sets the shortcut menu associated with the control.

See Also: *pop-up*

context-sensitive   Always hyphenate when used as an adjective.

contiguous selection   Avoid. This term may be unfamiliar to many users. Use *adjacent selection* instead.

See Also: *adjacent selection*

control   In content for software developers, *control* is a generic term for most dialog box elements. Do not use with this meaning in content for home users or information workers.

In some hardware products, particularly joysticks, use *control* to refer to buttons, switches, and other elements with which the user "controls" various actions, especially moving around the screen.

Control Panel   Do not use *the* when referring to Control Panel.

When referring to Control Panel itself, use roman type except when you are referring to the command on the Start menu. In that case, use bold type.

Correct

In Control Panel, open Network Connections.

To open Network Connections, click **Start**, click **Control Panel**, and then double-click **Network Connections**.

For more information, see *Control Panel* in Chapter 1, "Documenting the User Interface."

control-menu box   Use to describe the button at the far left on the title bar in Windows-based programs. This box displays the program icon in the main window and the generic window icon in secondary windows other than message boxes and dialog boxes. Avoid referring to this icon and the menu it opens by name. If such a reference is necessary, refer to the *[Program Name] icon* or the *[title bar] shortcut menu*.

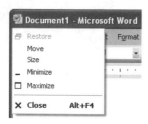

Control-menu box

For more information, see *Screen Terminology* in Chapter 1, "Documenting the User Interface."

copy   Do not use to mean photocopy.

corrupted   Use to describe a file or data that has been damaged. Do not use *corrupt* to describe this condition.

Correct

The file may be corrupted.

Incorrect

The file may be corrupt.

country/region   Use instead of *country* in list headings and forms and in other contexts where specific reference may include named disputed territories.

It is not necessary to replace *country* with *country/region* in general discussion.

Correct

This product is not available in all countries.

In the **Country/Region** box, enter your country/region.

crash   Jargon. Do not use in content for home users and information workers, and avoid in content for software developers and information technology professionals.

Use *fail* for disks or *stop responding* for programs or the operating system. In content for software developers or information technology professionals, *crash* may be the best word in certain circumstances, but it is well worth avoiding whenever possible.

See Also: *blue screen, bluescreen; fail*

criteria   Plural of *criterion*. It is acceptable to use *criteria* in database documentation to refer to one or more instructions about records.

critical process monitor   Do not abbreviate.

critical section object   Do not hyphenate.

current drive   Not *current disk drive*.

current folder   Use to refer to the folder that you are currently looking at (for example, in My Computer) or saving something to (for example, the folder that appears in the **Save in** box in the **Save As** dialog box). Do not use *active* or *open* in this context.

See Also: *active vs. current*

current window   Do not use. Use *active window* or *open window* instead.

See Also: *active vs. current*

cursor   Do not use except in specific situations in content for software developers and in references to MS-DOS-based programs. See your project style sheet for these correct uses. In all other content, use *pointer*. Do not use *mouse cursor* or *mouse pointer*, because other input devices can also control the pointer.

See Also: *insertion point; pointer*

cut   Do not use *cut* as a verb, even when referring to the **Cut** command. Use *delete* instead.

Do not use *cut* as a noun to refer to the action of the **Delete** command (use *deletion*) or as an imperative in procedures involving either the **Cut** or **Delete** command. Use *delete* instead.

Do not use *cut-and-replace* or *cut-and-paste* as a verb or a noun.

Correct
Use the **Cut** command to delete the selected text.
Select the text you want to delete, and then click **Cut**.

Incorrect
Cut the selected text.
Cut-and-paste the selected text.
Do a cut-and-paste on the second paragraph.

Do not use the verb *cut* to describe temporarily moving text to the Clipboard.

Correct

Use the **Cut** command to move the selected text to the Clipboard.

Incorrect

Cut the selected text to the Clipboard.

See Also: delete

cut-and-paste   Acceptable only as an adjective. Do not use as a noun phrase, with or without hyphens.

Do not use *cut and paste* as a verb phrase. The correct verb for the action of the **Cut** command is *delete*. Deleting is one act and pasting another, so *cut and paste* or *delete and paste* can be confusing.

Correct

Perform a cut-and-paste operation.

In Notepad, you can delete text from one place and paste it somewhere else.

Incorrect

Do a cut-and-paste.

In Notepad, you can cut and paste text.

In Notepad, you can delete and paste text.

D

data   Use as either singular or plural in meaning, but always with a singular verb. That is, always use "the data is" (or another appropriate verb) whether you mean a collection of facts (plural) or information (singular). If you want to emphasize that something is plural, rewrite to use a term such as *facts* or *numbers*.

Do not use *datum* or *data are*. They are etymologically correct, but many readers will fail to recognize *datum* and will see both *datum* and *data are* as pretentious.

> **Correct**
>
> The data shows that 95% of the users prefer a graphical interface.
>
> The data gathered so far is incomplete.
>
> These facts contradict the earlier data.

data binding   Two words.

data center   Two words.

data modem   Two words. A modem that can both send and receive serial data. A data/fax modem can also send and receive faxes.

data record   *Data* in this phrase is superfluous. Use *record* instead.

database   One word as a noun or an adjective.

datagram   One word. Refers to one packet, or unit, of information sent through a packet-switching network.

datum   Do not use; use *data* instead.

> *See Also: data*

deaf or hard of hearing   Use this phrase in its entirety in accessibility information or to refer to people who are deaf. Hyphenate *hard-of-hearing* only if it precedes the noun it modifies. If space is limited, use *deaf* alone.

Do not use *hearing-impaired*.

For more information, see *Bias-Free Communication* in Chapter 7, "Tone and Rhetoric."

debug   *Debug* is a valid technical term in content for software developers. Do not use *debug* in any context as a synonym for *troubleshoot*. Use *troubleshoot* or a more accurate word or phrase instead.

decrement   Use as a verb only in content for software developers or information technology professionals to refer specifically to decreasing an integer count by one. Do not use as a synonym for *decrease*.

default   Many home users and information workers do not understand that *default* refers to something that happens if the user does not take an action or does not supply a required value. Consider whether you need to explain the meaning of *default* in your content or even whether your content can dispense with *default* altogether.

> **Correct**
>
> If you do not select a template, Word uses Normal.dot.
>
> This value specifies the number of sheets to add. If you omit a value, the program adds one sheet.

Avoid *default* as a verb. It is jargon. *Default* is acceptable as a noun or as an adjective.

> **Correct (adjective)**
>
> If you do not select a template, Word uses Normal.dot, the default template.
>
> This value is the context ID for the custom Help topic of the command. If it is omitted, the default Help context ID assigned to the macro is used.
>
> **Correct (noun)**
>
> If you do not select a template, Word uses Normal.dot by default.
>
> This value specifies the number of sheets to add. The default is one sheet.
>
> **Incorrect (verb)**
>
> If you do not select a template, Word defaults to Normal.dot.
>
> This value specifies the number of sheets to add. If you omit a value, the program defaults to one sheet.

defragment   Use as a verb to refer to the action of the Disk Defragmenter program or similar programs. Do not use *defrag*.

> **Correct**
>
> To defragment your files and speed up performance, use Disk Defragmenter frequently.

deinstall   Do not use unless *deinstall* appears in the user interface or the application programming interface. If *deinstall* does appear in the product interface, refer to the user action as *removing*.

See Also: *uninstall*

delete   Use *delete* to refer to actions that the **Delete** command takes, such as moving files to the Recycle Bin and moving items in Microsoft Outlook to the Deleted Items folder. You can use *delete* to describe these actions even if the user arrives at them by some other way, such as by dragging a file to the Recycle Bin.

Use *delete* to refer to actions that result from pressing the Delete or Backspace key on the computer, such as deleting selected text.

Do not use *delete* as a synonym for *remove*. Do not use *cut* or *erase* as a synonym for *delete*.

> **Correct**
> Delete the second paragraph.
> Delete MyFile.txt from the Windows folder.
> Remove the Size field from the Inbox.

See Also: *cut; erase; remove*

demilitarized zone (DMZ)   Do not use as a technical term except on first mention, in which case use *perimeter network* (also known as *DMZ, demilitarized zone,* and *screened subnet*). On subsequent mention, use *perimeter network*.

See Also: *perimeter network*

deprecated   Refers to a program or feature that is obsolete and in the process of being phased out, usually in favor of a specific replacement. Deprecated features can linger on for many years to support compatibility across product versions.

It is all right to use *deprecated* in content for software developers and information technology professionals. In content for home users and information workers, use *obsolete, obsolescent,* or another more appropriate word.

depress   Do not use; instead, use *press* for the action of pushing down a key. Write around or otherwise avoid using *depressed* as a description for an indented toolbar button.

For more information, see *Key Names* in Chapter 1, "Documenting the User Interface."

deselect   Do not use. Use *cancel the selection* instead, or use *clear* in the case of check boxes.

Designer   Naming convention for a window with a design surface (whether it has one or more views).

> **Correct**
> HTML Designer has two views: Design and HTML.
> Web Forms Designer has two views: Design and HTML.
> XML Designer has two views: Schema and Source.

See Also: *Editor*

desire   Do not use; use *want* instead.

desktop   Refers to the onscreen work area provided by the operating system, which has the appearance of a physical desktop. Use *client area* only if necessary in documentation for software developers.

destination   General term for an end point in some user or program actions, such as the location reached when a user clicks a hyperlink, the folder to which a file is copied or moved, or the document in which a linked or embedded object is stored. Do not use *target* as a synonym.

Destination is acceptable in content for any audience. If possible, however, use a more precise term, such as *Web site* or *folder*, and use *destination* as a modifier only if necessary for clarity.

destination disk, destination drive, destination file   Not *target disk, target drive*, or *target file*. However, avoid if possible by using a word more specific to the context, as in "drag the folder to the icon for drive A or B."

device driver   Use *device driver* only in the context of a driver development kit (DDK) or in a general discussion about installing peripheral devices. If you are referring to a driver for a specific device, refer to the driver for that device, such as *mouse driver* or *printer driver*.

In content for home users and information workers, always define *driver* in the glossary.

dezoom   Do not use; use *zoom out* instead.

dialog   Do not use as an abbreviation for *dialog box*. Do not spell as *dialogue* in the context of a dialog box.

dialog box   Always use *dialog box*, not just *dialog*, and not *pop-up window*.

In content for all audiences except software developers, do not shorten to *dialog* even as a modifier. Do not hyphenate *dialog box* if you use it as a modifier. In content for software developers, it is all right, but not required, to use *dialog* alone as a modifier.

Correct for all audiences

dialog box option

dialog box title

Correct only for software developers

dialog class

dialog editor

dialog object

For more information, see *Dialog Boxes and Property Sheets* in Chapter 1, "Documenting the User Interface."

dial-up   Use as an adjective only, not as a verb or noun. Always hyphenate.

As an adjective, it defines a line, a modem, or a networking connection. It refers to a service. Do not use as a noun ("a dial up"); it is ambiguous.

Use *dial* as the verb to refer to placing a call or using a dial-up device.

different   Do not use *different* to mean "many" or "various."

In comparisons, use *different from* in most cases. Use *different than* only when the object of comparison is a clause. Avoid *different to* in American usage.

Correct

The result of the first calculation is different from the result of the second.

If the result is different from the result you expected, verify that you entered your data correctly.

Incorrect

The result of the first calculation is different than the result of the second.

Pay particular attention to parallelism in comparative statements. It is very easy to make a different comparison from the one you intend.

Correct

The result of the first calculation is different from the result of the second.

The result of the first calculation is different from that of the second.

Incorrect

The result of the first calculation is different from the second.

Constructions that use *different than* are often hard to read, even if they are grammatically correct. They work best when the subjects and verbs on both sides of the comparison are parallel. If you cannot achieve such parallelism, consider rewriting the sentence.

Correct

The taskbar looks different in Windows XP than it looked in Windows 2000.

Questionable

If the result is different than you expected, verify that you entered your data correctly.

Better

If you do not get the result you expected, verify that you entered your data correctly.

dimmed   Use *unavailable* to refer to commands and options that are in an unusable state, but use *dimmed* instead of *grayed* to describe the appearance of an unavailable command or option. (Use *shaded* to describe the appearance of check boxes that represent a mixture of settings.) Also, use *appears dimmed*, not *is dimmed*.

Correct

If the option appears dimmed, it is unavailable.

Incorrect

If the option is grayed, it is unavailable.

See Also: *gray, grayed; shaded; unavailable*

D

direction keys   Do not use; use *arrow keys* instead.

For more information, see *Key Names* in Chapter 1, "Documenting the User Interface."

directory   In general, limit use of the word *directory* to references to the structure of the file system. Use *folder* to refer to the visual representation or object in the interface. You can include *directory* as a synonym for *folder* in indexes and search topics.

See Also: *folder*

directory icon   Do not use; this term is no longer applicable. Use *folder icon* generically, if necessary.

disable   Acceptable in content for software developers in the sense of making a command or function unavailable.

Avoid in other content. Use *make unavailable* or something similar.

For more information, see *Menus and Commands* in Chapter 1, "Documenting the User Interface."

See Also: *unavailable*

disabled   Do not refer to people with disabilities as *disabled*.

For more information, see *Bias-Free Communication* in Chapter 7, "Tone and Rhetoric."

disc   Use only to refer to a CD or DVD.

See Also: *CD; disk; DVD*

discreet vs. discrete   Be sure to use these words correctly. *Discreet* means "showing good judgment" or "modest." *Discrete* means "separate" or "distinct" and is more likely to appear in technical content.

disjoint selection   Do not use. Use *multiple selection* to refer to a selection of more than one item, such as options, or *nonadjacent selection* (not *noncontiguous selection*) to make it clear that the items are separated.

disk   In general, use *disk* to refer to hard disks and floppy disks.

Unless necessary, use just *disk*, not *hard disk* or *3.5-inch disk*. Do not use fractions or symbols when specifying a disk; use decimals and spell out *inch*.

> **Correct**
> 3.5-inch disk

Do not use *diskette, fixed disk, hard drive*, or *internal drive*. Do not use *hard disk system* or *floppy disk system*. Refer to the computer specifications instead.

In general, do not use *disk* in possessive constructions, such as *disk's contents* or *disk's name*; instead, use *disk contents* or *disk name*.

When naming specific disks, use the disk names as they appear on the labels.

> **Correct**
> The utilities disk
> Disk 1

> **Note:** Do not use *disk* to refer to a compact disc.

disk resource   Use to refer to a disk or part of a disk shared on a server.

disk space   Use *disk space*, not *storage* or *memory*, to refer to available capacity on a disk.

See Also: storage, storage device

diskette   Do not use; use *disk* instead.

See Also: disk

display   Use *display* as a noun to refer generically to the visual output device and its technology, such as a CRT-based display, a flat-panel display, and so on. Use *screen* to refer to the graphic portion of a monitor.

Do not use *display* as an intransitive verb.

> **Correct**
> The program displays the document.

> **Incorrect**
> The document displays.

See Also: appears, displays

display adapter, display driver   Avoid; use *graphics adapter* instead.

    See Also: *graphics adapter*

Distributed File System (DFS)   Use initial caps to refer to Distributed File System. Use the abbreviation, which is all uppercase, after the full name has been introduced.

DNS   Spell out as "Domain Name System," not "Domain Name Server." Use to refer to the DNS networking protocol or to the Windows feature that implements the protocol. When discussing the DNS networking protocol, spell out "Domain Name System" on first use. When discussing the Microsoft Windows DNS feature, do not spell out *DNS*.

The Windows feature is *DNS*, not *DNS Server* or *Microsoft DNS Server*. If you are referring to the Windows feature and not the networking protocol, use (for example) "DNS in Windows Server 2003" or "Windows Server 2003 DNS."

Do not use dynamic DNS or DDNS.

A DNS server (lowercase s) is a computer running DNS server software.

A DNS client (lowercase c) is a client of a DNS server.

DNS Server (capital s) is the Windows service that appears in the Computer Management console. In general, refer to the service only in a discussion of stopping and starting it.

DNS Client (capital c) is the Windows service that appears in the Computer Management console. In general, refer to the service only in a discussion of stopping and starting it.

document   You can use *document* generically to refer to any kind of item within a folder that can be edited, but it's clearer to restrict its use to Word, WordPad, and text documents. Use the specific term for "documents" in other programs—for example, an Excel *worksheet*, a PowerPoint *presentation*, or an Access *database*.

Use *file* for more general uses, such as *file management* or *file structure*.

> **Correct**
>
> These demos will help you learn how to manage files and folders, print your documents, and use a network.

domain   Because *domain* has different meanings in database design, Windows, and Internet addresses, define the use or make sure that the context is clear. Always consult your project style sheet.

In database design, a domain is the set of valid values for a particular attribute. In Windows, a domain is a collection of computers sharing a common database and security policy. On the Internet, the domain is the last part of the address, following the dot. It identifies the type of entity owning the address (such as .com for commercial entities) or the country/region where the Web address is located (such as .ca for Canada).

For more detailed definitions of *domain*, see the *Microsoft Computer Dictionary*.

done   Do not use *when you are done;* it's colloquial. Use *when you have finished* instead.

DOS   Acronym for *disk operating system;* avoid. Whenever discussing the Microsoft product or the Microsoft disk operating system in general, use *MS-DOS.*

> *See Also:* MS-DOS

dot-com   Always hyphenate as an adjective to reference Web-based business issues. Do not use as a verb or noun. Do not capitalize the letter following the hyphen in headings with initial capitals.

> **Correct**
>
> dot-com company
>
> dot-com world
>
> dot-com executive
>
> dot-com stocks
>
> dot-com sector
>
> dot-com business

Do not use *dotcom*, *dot com*, *dot.com*, *.com*, or any other variation.

dotted rectangle   Avoid; use this term only if you are graphically describing the element that a user drags to select a region on the screen. Use *bounding outline* (not *marquee*) instead.

> *See Also:* bounding outline

double buffering   No hyphen. Refers as a noun to the use of two temporary storage areas. Do not use as a verb. Use a phrase such as "uses double buffering" instead.

double word   Two words. Refers to a unit of data consisting of two contiguous words (bytes). DWORD is used in code.

double-click, double-clicking   Always hyphenate. Use instead of *select* and *choose* when referring to a mouse action. Do not use *double-click on.*

> *See Also:* click

downgrade   Avoid the use of this word.

downlevel   Do not use. If possible, use a more precise definition of what you mean to say. Otherwise, use *earlier versions* or a similar construct. If you are referring to versions of third-party software as well, rewrite to make this clear.

download   Use *download* as a transitive verb to describe the process of intentionally transferring data, a file, or a program to the local computer. If necessary in context, use the passive *is downloaded*. Do not use to describe the process of opening, viewing, or switching to a Web page, even if some graphics and/or HTML files may be transferred to the user's hard disk as a result.

Correct

Design your Web page so that a user can review part of the page while your computer downloads the rest.

Incorrect

Design your Web page so that a user can review part of the page while the rest downloads.

drag   Use instead of *drag and drop*.

Do not use *click and drag*. The click action includes releasing the mouse button, and to drag an item the user must hold the button down. *Press and drag* is acceptable for inexperienced computer users.

For more information, see *Mouse Terminology* in Chapter 1, "Documenting the User Interface."

drag-and-drop   Do not use as a verb or as a noun. The action of dragging includes dropping the element in place.

It is all right to use *drag-and-drop* as an adjective to describe moving objects between windows and programs or to describe behavior a programmer wants to put in a program. In these cases, use a phrase such as "drag-and-drop editing" or "a drag-and-drop feature."

Correct

Moving files is an easy drag-and-drop operation.

You can drag the folder to drive A.

You can move the folder to drive A using a drag-and-drop operation.

Incorrect

You can drag and drop the folder in drive A.

You can use drag-and-drop to move the folder to drive A.

Drag the information from Microsoft Excel and drop it in a Word document.

drilldown, drill down   One word as a noun; two words as a verb. Do not use in documentation to refer to following a path to its files or to further analysis. It's slang.

drive   Distinguish among types of disks and disk drives only when necessary to avoid confusion. Make it clear whether you are talking about a disk or its associated drive.

Use these conventions when referring to drives:

- Use *disk* to refer to the disk. Use *drive, disk drive,* or, if necessary, *floppy disk drive* to describe the 3.5-inch disk drive in a computer.

- Use *hard disk drive,* not *hard drive,* to refer to the drive. Use *hard disk* to refer to the disk itself.

- Use *CD drive* or *DVD drive* as a general reference. Be more specific about the drive type—for example, *CD-ROM drive*—only when the distinction is important.

- Use *current drive,* not *current disk drive* or *active drive.*

- Use *drive A,* not *drive A:, drive A>,* or *A: drive.*

- Use *network drive* to refer to a logical network drive name, such as *network drive X.*

See Also: disk

drive name   Not *drive specification, designator,* or *designation.*

drop-down   Use only if necessary to describe how an item such as a menu works or what it looks like.

Drop-down is acceptable in content for software developers if necessary to describe the type of item, as in *drop-down arrow, drop-down combo box,* or *drop-down list box.*

For more information, see *Dialog Boxes and Property Sheets* and *Menus and Commands* in Chapter 1, "Documenting the User Interface."

DVD   Do not spell out *DVD.* If you refer to a DVD as a *disc,* use the correct spelling.

It is acceptable to use *DVD* alone as long as either the reference is general or there is no possibility of confusion as to what type of DVD is under discussion: video DVD, audio DVD, DVD-ROM, DVD-R, DVD-RAM, or DVD-RW. When it is necessary to be specific, be specific.

Refer to the drive for a DVD as the *DVD drive,* not the *DVD player.* If you are referring to a specific type of drive, such as a DVD-RW drive, use the appropriate name.

Do not use *DVD disc, DVD-ROM disc,* or similar constructions.

dynamic-link library (DLL)   Abbreviate as *DLL* after first mention. If you are sure your audience knows the term and that localization will not be affected, you can use *DLL* without spelling it out. Use lowercase (.dll) when referring to the file name extension.

Do not use *dynalink.*

E

earlier   Use *earlier*, *preceding*, or *previous* instead of *above* to mean earlier in a book or Help topic. In online Help, do not use any of these words to refer to a different topic that appears earlier in the table of contents. Provide an explicit cross-reference instead.

Use *earlier* instead of *lower* for product version numbers—for example, "Word 3.0 or earlier."

For more information, see *Cross-References* in Chapter 2, "Content Formatting and Layout," and *Version Identifiers* in Chapter 9, "Common Style Problems."

eBook, e-book   Use *eBook* with reference to electronic book products. For general references to electronic books, use *e-book*.

Avoid using *eBook* at the beginning of a sentence. If you cannot avoid it without creating an awkward or ambiguous sentence, use *eBook*. In headings, use *eBook*.

Use *E-book* at the beginning of a sentence and of a heading with sentence-style capitalization. In headings with title-style capitalization, use *E-Book*.

e-commerce   Use *E-commerce* at the beginning of a sentence and of a heading with sentence-style capitalization. In headings with title-style capitalization, use *E-Commerce*.

edit   Because the term can be confused with the **Edit** menu, avoid it in end-user documentation to refer to making changes in a document; use *change* or *modify* instead.

Editor   Naming convention for a window that is a code or text editor only.

> **Correct**
> CSS Editor
> Code Editor

See Also: *Designer*

edutainment   Do not use in documentation. It's marketing jargon to refer to educational software (usually multimedia or Web-based) that purports to entertain while it educates. The term can also cause difficulties for localization.

e-form   Okay to use. Spell out as *electronic form* on first use if necessary for your audience. Use *E-form* at the beginning of a sentence and and of a heading with sentence-style capitalization. In headings with title-style capitalization, use *E-Form*.

e.g.   Means *exempli gratia*. Do not use; use *for example* instead.

8.5-by-11-inch paper   Not 8.5 x 11-inch, 8 1/2 by 11-inch, or other ways of referring to the paper size.

either/or   Do not use. Fill out the construction, as in "you can either close the document or quit the program."

ellipsis button   The *ellipsis button* has been called a variety of names, including the Browse button, the Build button, and the Properties button, depending on the result of clicking the button. When possible, use a picture of the button rather than words. Always provide an image of the button at first mention for clarity, if only **(...)**. Do not capitalize the button name.

e-mail   Always hyphenate. Do not use as a verb; use *send* instead.

Use *e-mail* to refer generically to an electronic mail program or to refer collectively to e-mail messages. After you have established the context of electronic mail, it is all right to use *mail* instead of *e-mail*.

Correct

Check your e-mail for messages.

Scroll through your e-mail to find the message you want to read.

You have new mail.

Use *e-mail message* or *message* to refer to an individual piece of e-mail. Do not use *e-mail* as a synonym for *message*. If you use *message* alone, ensure that the context makes clear that you are not referring to instant messaging.

Correct

Send us an e-mail message with your comments.

You have two new messages.

Incorrect

Send us an e-mail with your comments.

E-mail us with your comments.

You have two new e-mails.

embed   Not *imbed*, which is a variant spelling.

enable, enabled   Avoid in end-user documentation. Use *you can* instead to refer to things the program makes easy or possible for the user. In addition to being vague and often inaccurate, *enable* leads to weak sentences in which the most important fact is buried in an infinitive phrase.

Correct

With Microsoft Word 2000, you can save files in HTML format.

Incorrect

Microsoft Word 2000 enables you to save files in HTML format.

In end-user documentation, do not use *enable* with reference to commands or other program features. Use *make available*, *activate*, or something similar; or rewrite the sentence.

Correct

To activate change tracking, click the Tools menu and then click Track Changes.

To track changes, click the Tools menu and then click Track Changes.

Incorrect

To enable change tracking, click the Tools menu and then click Track Changes.

In developer documentation, it is acceptable to speak of a feature or function as *enabled*. It is also acceptable in developer documentation to use *enable* when you must refer to the end user in the third person, but this usage is worth avoiding whenever possible.

See Also: allow; can vs. may

end   Use as a verb to refer to stopping communications and network connections. Use *exit* for programs.

Correct

To end your server connection, on the **Tools** menu, click **Disconnect Network Drive**.

See Also: close

end user, end-user   Avoid; use *user*, *customer*, or *you* instead.

It is all right to use *end user* in content for software developers to distinguish the developer from the user of the developer's program. It is all right to use *end user* in documentation for information technology professionals to distinguish the system administrator from the users of computers that the administrator is responsible for.

endline   One word as an adjective, as in *endline comment*.

endpoint   One word. In graphics programs, an endpoint is the beginning or end of a line segment. In content for software developers, an endpoint is a hardware port or a named pipe that a server program monitors for remote procedure calls from clients.

For information about pipes, see the *Microsoft Computer Dictionary*.

ensure, insure, assure   In common English usage, *ensure*, *insure*, and *assure* are interchangeable in many situations. To provide a consistent voice and to improve readability worldwide, make these distinctions:

- Use *insure* to mean "to provide insurance."
- Use *ensure* to mean "to make sure" or "to guarantee."
- Use *assure* to mean "to state positively" or "to make confident."

enter   Do not use as a synonym for the verb *type* except to indicate that a user can either type or click a selection from, say, a list in a combo box.

Correct

Type your password, and then press **Enter**.

In the **File name** box, enter the name of the file.

Incorrect

Enter your password, and then click **OK**.

At the prompt, enter the path and file name.

See Also: *type vs. enter*

enterprise   Acceptable in client/server documentation to mean "large company" or "corporation." Use as an adjective, if possible, as in "enterprise computing" or "enterprise networking" rather than as a noun to mean "corporation." Avoid in content for home users and information workers.

entry   Do not use as a synonym for *topic* in reference documentation.

entry field   Do not use in content for home users, information workers, or information technology professionals to refer to a text-entry field in a dialog box. Refer to the box by its label. If you must use a descriptor, use *box* instead.

It is all right to use *entry field* in a database context.

environment variable   Do not use *environment setting* or *environment string*.

erase   Do not use as a synonym for the verb *delete*. It's okay to use *erase* for specialized purposes when the program requires it, as in Paint.

et al.   Abbreviation for *et alii*, "and others." Do not use except in a text reference citation of three or more authors; use *and others* instead.

etc. Abbreviation for the Latin *et cetera*, "and the rest." Avoid *etc.* except in situations where space is too limited for an alternative, such as on a button label.

For more information, see *Foreign Words and Phrases* in Chapter 3, "Global Content."

See Also: and so on

euro (€) When referring to the currency, use lowercase. The plural of *euro* is *euros*. A euro is divided into 100 *cents*.

The euro symbol is **€**. The HTML code for the euro symbol is *€*.

When expressing an amount in euros and cents in U.S. content, use a decimal point as the delimiter. Different localities may use a decimal point or a comma, as appropriate.

Correct

€3.50

Use *supports the euro currency standard* rather than *euro-compatible* or *euro-ready*, both of which are best avoided.

Use the following phrases to refer to countries that have adopted the euro as their currency:

- European Union (EU) members trading in euros
- European Union (EU) members that have adopted the euro
- euro nations
- members of the Economic and Monetary Union (EMU)

Use references to the EMU cautiously. Many users may be unfamiliar with the organization.

> **Note:** On subsequent mentions, it is acceptable to use EU and EMU as abbreviations. It is all right to refer to EU members as EU member states and to EMU members as EMU member states.

It is all right to use *non-euro nations* to refer to EU member states that have not adopted the euro as their currency.

The terms *euroland* and *eurozone* are acceptable on Web sites in which an informal tone is appropriate. Avoid in product documentation and other formal contexts, especially if the content will be localized.

E

e-words   In general, avoid forming new words with "e-" (for *electronic*) unless you know your audience will understand. Some words that may be appropriate in certain circumstances are "e-commerce" and "e-money." *E-mail* and *e-form* are acceptable. Always hyphenate for clarity.

Use lowercase for e-words in body text and use initial capital letters in headings, titles, and at the beginnings of sentences. The word following the hyphen is capitalized in headings with title-style capitalization.

Correct

E-commerce is a very lucrative business model.

I received 120 pieces of e-mail yesterday.

How to Succeed at E-Commerce (heading)

executable file   A file with an .exe or .com extension. In content for home users and information workers, use *program file* instead. Use *executable* and *.exe* as adjectives only, never as nouns. Use the article *an*, not *a*, with .exe, as in "an .exe file."

Correct

an executable program

the .exe file

Incorrect

an executable

the .exe

execute, run   Do not use *execute* in content for home users or information workers except to follow the user interface. Use *run* instead. If the user interface includes *execute*, the user or program action is still *run*. Always use *run* in the context of macros and queries.

Correct

To run the program, click **Execute**.

You can temporarily stop Disk Defragmenter so you can run other programs at full speed.

Incorrect

You can temporarily stop Disk Defragmenter so you can execute other programs at full speed.

Execute is acceptable in content for software developers because it has become ingrained, especially in the passive voice. *Run* is preferable, however, where it does not cause any loss of meaning.

Correct

Commands are run in the order they are listed in the file.

Acceptable for software developers

Commands are executed in the order they are listed in the file.

Execution is acceptable in technical content when there is no valid alternative.

Correct

A thread is the basic unit of program execution.

See Also: *run vs. execute*

exit   Use only to refer to closing a program. Do not use to refer to closing a document or a window. Do not use to refer to switching from one program, document, or window to another.

> **Note:** In some circumstances, the Close button and the Close command function like the Exit command. Refer to the user interface elements by their correct names, but if the user is exiting the program, use *exit* to describe this action.

Correct

When you are finished, close all your documents and exit Word.

To switch to the last open program or document, press ALT+TAB.

You can click the Close button to exit Outlook.

Incorrect

When you are finished, exit all your documents and exit Word.

To exit the active window, click anywhere outside it.

You can click the Close button to close Outlook.

See Also: *close*

expand, collapse   Pertains to a folder or outline. The user can *expand* or *collapse* these structures to see more or fewer subentries. A plus sign next to a folder indicates that it can be expanded to show more folders; a minus sign indicates that it can be collapsed.

expose   Do not use in the context of the user interface. Use a term such as *make available* or *display* instead.

Expose is acceptable in the context of object-oriented programming technologies such as the Component Object Model (COM), in which it means to make an object's services available to clients.

extend   In the sense of extending a selection, use instead of *grow*.

extension, file name extension   Not *file extension*—for example, "the .bak extension."

For more information, see *File Names and Extensions* in Chapter 1, "Documenting the User Interface."

e-zine, webzine   Avoid except to connote an underground-type of electronic magazine. It's okay to use *webzine* to refer to mainstream magazines such as *Slate* or *eWEEK* that are on the Web, but it's better to call them *electronic magazines* or, if the electronic context is clear, just *magazines*. Use *E-zine* at the beginning of a sentence and of a heading with sentence-style capitalization. In headings with title-style capitalization, use *E-Zine*.

E

F

facsimile   Do not use to refer to the kind of document sent through a fax machine; use *fax* instead. Use *facsimile* only to refer to an exact reproduction of something else.

See Also: fax

fail   In end-user documentation, use only to refer to disks and other hardware. Use *stop responding* to refer to programs or the operating system. Do not use *crash* in end-user documentation and avoid *crash* in programmer documentation.

It is all right to use *fail* in programmer documentation when necessary to describe an error condition. For example, E_FAIL is a common return value in COM programs, and it is logical to say that a function that returns E_FAIL has failed to do something or other.

> **Correct**
> Backing up your files safeguards them against loss if your hard disk fails.

See Also: crash

FALSE   In general, use all uppercase to refer to a return value in content for software developers. If you are writing about a specific programming language, follow the capitalization used in that language.

Far East   Do not use. Use *Asia* instead.

far-left, far-right   Avoid; use *leftmost* or *rightmost* instead. If possible, however, avoid directional cues for reasons of accessibility.

For more information, see *Accessible Writing* in Chapter 8, "Accessible Content."

fast key   Do not use; use *keyboard shortcut* instead.

For more information, see *Key Names* in Chapter 1, "Documenting the User Interface."

favorite   Reference in Internet Explorer to a Web page or site the user may want to return to. Favorites can be added to the menu. Corresponds to "bookmark" in other browsers. Use lowercase when referring to a "favorite Web site" and uppercase when referring to the **Favorites** menu.

> **Correct**
> You can add a favorite Web site to the **Favorites** menu.
> You can display your list of favorites at any time by clicking the **Favorites** menu.

fax   Use to refer to a kind of document sent through a fax machine. Okay to use as a noun ("your fax has arrived"), an adjective ("fax machine," "fax transmission"), or a verb ("fax a copy of the order"). Do not use *FAX*.

field   Do not use to refer to a box or option in a dialog box. Okay to use to refer to Word field codes and for other technically accurate uses.

figure   Capitalize when identifying numbered art. In general reference to a figure, use lowercase.

> **Correct**
>
> Figure 5.2 compares the response times of the two versions.
>
> As the figure shows, computer prices continue to decline.

For more information, see *Art, Captions, and Callouts* in Chapter 2, "Content Formatting and Layout."

file   Okay to use generically to refer to documents and programs as well as to units of storage or file management. However, be more specific if possible in referring to a type of file—for example, the Word *document*, your *worksheet*, the WordPad *program*, and so on.

file attributes   Use lowercase for file attributes such as *hidden*, *system*, *read-only*, and *archive*.

file extension   Do not use; use *extension* or *file name extension* instead.

file name   Two words. *File name* can be used as an adjective or noun.

For more information, see *File Names and Extensions* in Chapter 1, "Documenting the User Interface."

file name extension, extension   Not *file extension*.

For more information, see *File Names and Extensions* in Chapter 1, "Documenting the User Interface."

finalize   Do not use; use *finish* or *complete* instead.

find and replace   Use *find* and *replace* as standard names for search and substitution features. Do not use *search and replace*.

Use *find* and *replace* as separate verbs. Do not use *find and replace* or *find-and-replace* as a noun. Use *find-and-replace* as an adjective. Avoid phrases like "*search* your document"; use "*search through* your document" instead.

> **Correct**
>
> Find the word "gem" and replace it with "diamond."
>
> Search through your document, and replace "cat" with "dog."

Incorrect

Do a find and replace.

Find and replace the word "gem" with the word "diamond."

Avoid the term *global* in reference to finding and replacing unless absolutely necessary. This technical jargon may not be clear to all users.

Correct

Click **Replace All** to find all occurrences of the word "gem" and replace them with "diamond."

Replace all instances of the word "gem" with "diamond."

Use *find characters* and *replacement characters* to specify what the user types into a find-and-replace text box.

finished   Use instead of *done*, as in *when you have finished*, not the colloquial *when you are done*.

firewall   Hardware, software, or a combination of the two that provides part of a security system—usually to prevent unauthorized access from outside to an internal network or intranet.

Define the term in content for home users and information workers.

fixed disk   Do not use; use *hard disk* instead.

See Also: disk; hard disk

floppy disk   Use *disk* unless you need to distinguish between *floppy disk* and *hard disk*. Do not use *floppy drive* or *floppy disk system*.

Do not use *floppy* alone as a noun to refer to a disk. It's slang.

See Also: disk

flush   In end-user documentation, do not use *flush, flush left,* or *flush right* as an adjective to describe text alignment; instead, use *even, left-aligned,* or *right-aligned* as appropriate.

In programmer documentation, *flush* as a verb is acceptable in contexts such as referring to a function that "flushes the buffer."

flush to   Avoid; use *aligned on* instead.

folder   In content about Windows, use *folder* to refer to a container for files and for other folders. If the context is MS-DOS, use *directory*. Folders are represented on the interface by a *folder icon*. It is all right to use *directory* to mean *folder* in content for software developers if necessary to match the application programming interface.

> **Note:** Not all folders represent a container for files and for other folders. For example, the Printers and Control Panel programs are also folders. Describe the nature of the folder, if necessary.

When instructing a user to click a folder, apply bold formatting to the folder name.

> **Correct**
>
> You can find the file on your hard disk in C:\Windows\System\Color.
>
> You can find the file on X:\Windows\System\Color.
>
> You can find the file in the Color folder.
>
> The system files are in the System subdirectory in the Windows directory.
>
> Click the **Windows** folder.

See Also: *directory*

folder icon   Not *directory icon*.

following   Use *following* to introduce art, a table, or, in some cases, a list.

> **Correct**
>
> The following table compares the different rates.
>
> To install the program, do the following:

If *following* is the last word before what it introduces, follow it with a colon.

See Also: *above; below*

font and font style   Use *font*, not *typeface*, for the name of a typeface design—for example, Times New Roman or Bookman. Use *font style*, not *type style*, to refer to the formatting, such as bold, italic, or small caps; and *font size*, not *type size*, for the point size, such as 12 point or 14 point.

When referring to bold formatting, use *bold*, not *bolded, boldface,* or *boldfaced*. When referring to italic formatting, use *italic*, not *italics* or *italicized*.

> **Correct**
>
> The **Bold** option makes selected characters bold or removes the bold formatting if the characters are already bold.

Incorrect

Select the **Bold** option button to bold the characters.

For more information on when to use various font styles, see *Document Conventions* in Chapter 2, "Content Formatting and Layout."

foobar, fubar   Do not use; the word is slang derived from an obscene phrase meaning "fouled up beyond all recognition." Use another placeholder file name instead—for example, *Sample* or *MyFile.doc.*

footer   In content related to word-processing and publishing programs, use instead of *bottom running head* or *running foot* when discussing page layout; however, *running foot* is acceptable as a synonym in keyword lists and indexes.

foreground program   Not *foreground process.*

format, formatted, formatting   Use *format* to refer to the overall layout or pattern of a document. Use *formatting* to refer to particulars of character formatting, paragraph formatting, and so on. Note spelling.

Fortran   Not FORTRAN (all uppercase). Do not spell out as "Formula Translation."

Fourth-generation language (4GL)   Spell out at first mention.

frame   Avoid in content for home users and information workers unless you are referring to frames in a Web page. In content for software and Web developers and for information technology professionals, use only to refer specifically to a frame, not just a section of a Web page. (Many Web sites use tables, not frames, to divide a page.)

Frame has a number of other computer-related meanings, so be sure to define it if the context is unclear.

For additional definitions, see the *Microsoft Computer Dictionary*.

frameset   A frames page is a Web page that is divided into independently scrollable regions called *frames.* The HTML document that describes the frame layout in a frames page is called the *frameset document.*

Use *frames page* to describe the page itself, but avoid this terminology for home users and information workers. In general discussions, use *frames* whenever possible.

friendly name   Do not use. Use *display name* instead to refer to a person's name as it appears in an address or e-mail list.

from   Use *from* to indicate a specific place or time as a starting point: "Paste the text from the Clipboard" or "From the time you set the clock, the alarm is active."

Use *from* to indicate a menu from which a user chooses a command if you are documenting both mouse and keyboard procedures: "From the **File** menu, choose **Open**." Use *on*, however, to indicate the starting place for clicking a command or option: "On the **File** menu, click **Open**."

from vs. than   The adjective *different* is usually followed by *from*. Use *from* when the next element of the sentence is a noun or pronoun.

Correct

The result of the first calculation is different from the result of the second.

Incorrect

The result of the first calculation is different than the result of the second.

See Also: *different*

front end, front-end   Two words as a noun; one word as an adjective. Avoid as a synonym for the desktop interface to a database or server. Such use is jargon. Instead, use the name of the *program* or *interface*, or another specific and accurate term.

FrontPage   Note spacing and internal capitalization.

function   A general term for a subroutine. In some languages, a function explicitly returns a value, which not all subroutines do.

Do not use *function* to mean *application programming interface (API)*, and do not use *API function*. Additionally, do not use *API* to mean *function*. The API is the set of classes, interfaces, functions, structures, and other programming elements that software developers use to write programs that interact with a product, technology, or operating system.

For more information about functions, routines, subroutines, and procedures, see the *Microsoft Computer Dictionary*.

G

G, G byte, Gbyte Do not use as an abbreviation for *gigabyte*. Use *GB* instead.

> *See Also:* gigabyte (GB)

gallery A gallery is a collection of pictures, charts, or other graphics that the user can select from. Refer to the items in a gallery in the same way you refer to options in a dialog box—that is, use the verb *click* or *select*.

> **Correct**
>
> Select an option from the gallery.
>
> Click the picture you want to select.

game pad Two words and lowercase.

Gantt chart Capitalize Gantt.

garbage collection, garbage collector Commonly used and acceptable terms in content for software developers. *Garbage collection* refers to the automatic recovery of heap memory or to the automatic deletion of objects that the run-time environment determines are no longer being used. The *garbage collector* is the component of a run-time environment that performs garbage collection.

gateway One word. Refers to software or a computer running software that enables two different networks to communicate.

GB Abbreviation for *gigabyte*. Use the abbreviation only as a measurement with numerals; do not use in straight text without a numeral. Spell out *gigabyte* at first mention.

> *See Also:* gigabyte (GB)

Gbit Do not use as an abbreviation for *gigabit*; always spell out.

general protection fault (GP fault) Acceptable to abbreviate as *GP fault* after first mention.

gerunds   A gerund is the *-ing* form of a verb used as a noun. Use gerunds to form the titles of procedural Help topics.

> **Correct**
>
> Managing Hardware and Software
>
> Installing New Software
>
> **Incorrect**
>
> How to Install New Software

Gerunds can sometimes create ambiguity, especially for a worldwide audience. Include whatever words are necessary to make your meaning clear or rewrite the sentence.

> **Ambiguous**
>
> You can change files using the Template utility.
>
> **Clearer**
>
> You can change files by using the Template utility.
>
> You can change files that use the Template utility.

Using gerunds to describe general concepts, such as *clustering* and *networking*, can be a problem for localization. Not all grammars allow gerunds to be used in this way, so a single word may be translated as a phrase. For example, in Dutch, *imaging* is translated as *image processing*, and *licensing* is translated as *the granting of licenses*. Further, not all gerunds are translatable in all languages, so some loss of meaning is inevitable. If you must use gerunds to describe concepts, work with your localization program manager or localization vendor to keep the impact of such words to a minimum.

For more information, see *Headings and Subheadings* in Chapter 2, "Content Formatting and Layout;" *Procedures* in Chapter 9, "Common Style Problems;" and *Verbs and Verb Forms* in Chapter 10, "Grammatical Elements."

GHz   Abbreviation for *gigahertz*. Use the abbreviation only as a measurement with numerals; do not use in straight text without a numeral. Spell out *gigahertz* at first mention.

See Also: *gigahertz (GHz)*

gigabit   Always spell out. Do not use the abbreviation *Gbit*.

gigabyte (GB)   One gigabyte is equal to 1,073,741,824 bytes, or 1,024 megabytes.

- Abbreviate as *GB*, not *G, G byte*, or *Gbyte*. At first mention, spell out and use the abbreviation in parentheses.

- Leave a space between the numeral and *GB* except when the measurement is used as an adjective preceding a noun. In that case, use a hyphen.

Correct

1 gigabyte (GB) of data

10-GB hard disk

- When used as a noun in measurements, add *of* to form a prepositional phrase.

Correct

You will need to free 1 GB of hard disk space.

For more information, see *Measurements and Units of Measure* in Chapter 9, "Common Style Problems."

gigahertz (GHz)   A gigahertz is a unit of frequency equal to 1 billion cycles per second.

- Abbreviate as *GHz*. At first mention, spell out and use the abbreviation in parentheses.

- Leave a space between the numeral and *GHz* except when the measurement is used as an adjective preceding a noun. In that case, use a hyphen.

Correct

A frequency of 11.9300 gigahertz (GHz)

11.9300-GHz communications

For more information, see *Measurements and Units of Measure* in Chapter 9, "Common Style Problems."

given   Do not use to mean specified, particular, or fixed.

Correct

Look in the specified folder.

Use the **Find** command to search for all occurrences of a specific word.

The meeting is always at a particular time.

Incorrect

Look in the given folder.

Use the **Find** command to search for all occurrences of a given word.

The meeting is always at a given time.

G

global In content for software developers, *global* refers to memory that is accessible to more than one process, to a variable whose value can be accessed and modified by any statement in a program (called a "global variable"), and to similar elements that pertain to an entire program.

Avoid *global* as a technical term in content for other audiences, especially in describing the process of replacing one text string with another throughout a document. Instead, describe the action being taken.

It is, of course, all right to use *global* to mean "worldwide."

Correct

A cascading style sheet establishes global design formats.

Use the **Find** and **Replace** commands to find all occurrences of specific text and replace it with different text.

See Also: find and replace

glyph Avoid. This is jargon when used to refer generically to a graphic or pictorial image on a button, on an icon, or in a message box. Use *symbol* instead. Okay to use in a technical discussion of fonts and characters.

See Also: icon

G

GP fault Abbreviation for *general protection fault.* Spell out at first mention.

graphic, graphical, graphics As a noun, use *graphic* to refer to a picture, display, chart, and other visual representations.

Use *graphical* as the adjectival form of the noun "graphic." Use *graphic* as an adjective only to mean "vivid" or "realistic" or in the phrase "graphic arts."

Use *graphics* to refer in general to creating pictures, displays, charts, and other visual representations using computers (for example, "graphics software").

Noun

To import a graphic from another file, click **Picture**.

Adjective

Select the graphics file you want to open.

The image is graphic and accurate.

A tutorial offers the basics in graphic design.

The graphical user interface simulates a coliseum.

graphics adapter   Use instead of *video adapter* to describe the adapter that converts image data into electronic signals processed by a computer monitor. Do not use *graphics card* or *graphics board*.

The term *video* has come to refer to moving images from devices and media such as video recorders, DVDs, and television. A computer's video system uses the graphics adapter to process video information, but the graphics adapter also processes graphics that are unrelated to video as that term is currently used.

See Also: board; card

gray, grayed   Do not use to refer to commands or options that are in an unusable state; use *unavailable* instead. Use dimmed instead of grayed to describe the appearance of an unavailable command or option. If you need to describe the appearance of check boxes with portions of a larger selection that are already selected, use *shaded*, not *grayed*.

Correct

In the **Effects** group box, names of selected options may appear shaded.

The **Print** command on the **File** menu is unavailable.

See Also: dimmed; shaded; unavailable

grayscale   One word used as an adjective or noun.

greater, better   Do not use either term to designate system requirements or versions of a program. Use *later* instead.

Correct

The program runs on Windows 3.1 or later.

You need a 486 or later processor.

Incorrect

The program runs on Windows 3.1 or greater.

You need a 486 or better processor.

See Also: later

gridline   One word.

G

group box   Two words, lowercase.

A group box is a rectangle drawn around a set of related controls in a dialog box. For example, in the **Print** dialog box of Microsoft Word, page range options are grouped in the **Page range** group box. A group box is only a visual aid; it provides no functionality.

Group box

Avoid *group box* in content for home users and information workers. It is generally unnecessary to include the name of the group box in a procedure unless a dialog box contains more than one option with the same name. In that case, use *under* with the group box name.

Correct

Under **Effects**, select **Hidden**.

Group box is acceptable in content for software developers.

For more information, see *Dialog Boxes and Property Sheets* in Chapter 1, "Documenting the User Interface."

group, newsgroup   Although these words can be synonyms, use *newsgroup* to refer specifically to an Internet newsgroup to differentiate it from other generic groups. *Newsgroup* is one word.

groupware   Use to refer to software intended to let a group of users on a network collaborate on a project.

Do not use *groupware* as a product descriptor. For example, use "Microsoft Outlook messaging and collaboration client," not "Microsoft Outlook groupware."

grow   Do not use as a transitive verb in the sense of making something larger; use a more specific verb such as *extend* instead.

Correct

If you want to increase your business ...

To extend the selection ...

Incorrect

If you want to grow your business ...

To grow the selection ...

H

hack, hacker   Use *hacker* only to refer to a programmer or computer user who attempts illegal access to a computer system or network.

Do not use *hack* in the sense of improvising a solution to a programming problem. Do not use *hacker* to mean an amateur programmer. These words are slang.

half inch   Not *half an inch* or *one-half inch*. Hyphenate as an adjective: "a half-inch margin." When space is a concern or the measurement needs to be specific, use *0.5 in*.

handheld   One word, no hyphen.

Use *Handheld PC* (and the acronym *H/PC*) to refer to the very small computer that runs Windows CE and programs developed for that system. Differentiate from *handheld computer*, which is a more general term.

Do not use *handheld* as a noun.

handle   In programming, a handle is a pointer to a pointer or a token temporarily assigned to a device or object to identify and provide access to the device. In the latter case, include a space between the word *handle* and the sequential number—for example, "handle 0," "handle 1," "handle 2."

In the user interface of various programs, a handle is an element used to move or size an object. Use *move handle* or *sizing handle*. Do not use *size handle*, *grab handle*, *little box*, or similar phrases.

handshake   One word as adjective or noun.

Handshake refers to the connection or signal established between two pieces of hardware, such as a computer and a printer; or communications software, such as the signal to transmit data between two modems. In content for home users or information workers, briefly define the term at the first occurrence.

Correct

Communicating systems must use the same flow-control (or *handshake*) method. To determine whether the systems use the same handshake method ...

hard copy   Two words. Acceptable as a noun referring to a paper version of a software document. Avoid as an adjective.

See Also: *soft copy*

hard disk   Refer to the disk itself as the *hard disk*. Be clear whether you are talking about the disk itself or the drive, which should be referred to as the *hard disk drive*, not the *hard drive*, *internal drive*, *fixed disk drive*, or *hard disk system*. Do not hyphenate *hard disk*.

> *See Also:* disk; drive

hard-coded   Use as an adjective in content for software developers or information technology professionals to describe a routine or program that uses embedded constants in place of more general user input. Avoid in content for home users or information workers.

hard of hearing   Use the phrase *deaf or hard of hearing* to refer to people who have hearing disabilities. If that phrase is too long, use *deaf* only. Do not use *hearing-impaired*.

> *See Also:* deaf or hard of hearing

> For more information, see *Bias-Free Communication* in Chapter 7, "Tone and Rhetoric."

hardware   One word.

hardwired   One word. Describes a functionality that is built into a system's electronic circuitry rather than enabled through software. Avoid this technical term in content for home users and information workers.

header   In word-processing and publishing documentation, use instead of *running head* when discussing page layout. However, *running head* is acceptable if needed for clarification or as a keyword or index entry.

> Do not use *header* as a synonym for *heading*.

> In technical documentation, *header* is an acceptable short form of the term *file header*, as in ".rtf header" or "PostScript header." Do not use *header* as a synonym for *header file*, which refers to the file at the beginning of a program that contains definitions of data types and variables used by the program's functions.

heading   Do not refer to a topic heading or chapter heading as a *head* or a *header*.

> For more information, see *Headings and Subheadings* in Chapter 2, "Content Formatting and Layout."

hearing-impaired   Do not use; use *deaf or hard of hearing* instead.

> For more information, see *Bias-Free Communication* in Chapter 7, "Tone and Rhetoric."

Help   In general, avoid *online Help;* just use *Help*. However, *online Help, definition Help, context-sensitive Help*, and *online Help files* are acceptable when necessary to describe the Help system itself or to explain how to develop a Help system.

he/she   Do not use.

> For more information about gender-neutral pronouns, see *Bias-Free Communication* in Chapter 7, "Tone and Rhetoric."

hexadecimal   Do not abbreviate this adjective as *hex*. Use *h* or *0x* when abbreviating a number, as in "Interrupt 21h" or "addresses greater than 0xFFFE." Do not insert a space between the number and *h*, and use uppercase for alphabetical characters displayed in hexadecimal numbers.

high-level   Note hyphen. Use the term carefully. A high-level language, for example, means a machine-independent language such as C++, Visual Basic, or C#.

highlight   In general, avoid using *highlight*, unless you are specifically referring to the highlighter feature in some products that users can apply to emphasize selections. Use *select* instead.

> **Correct**
>
> Drag the pointer to select the text you want to format.
>
> **Incorrect**
>
> Drag the pointer to highlight the text you want to format.

Refer to selected material as *the selection*, not *the highlight*.

> **Correct**
>
> To extend the selection, press F6.
>
> **Incorrect**
>
> To extend the highlight, press F6.

When it is necessary to be graphically descriptive, you can use *highlight* as a verb to tell the user to select text in a word-processing document, a range of cells in a spreadsheet, or fields and records in a database list view, for example. Likewise, you can use *highlight* to describe the appearance of reverse video. When using *highlight* as a verb in a procedure, include *select* in your procedure so users won't be confused when they use other products.

> **Correct**
>
> Highlight the paragraph to select it.
>
> Highlight to select the range of cells you want to copy.
>
> Programmers use reverse video to highlight special items on the screen.

high-quality   Note hyphen. Do not use *quality* alone as an adjective, only as a noun.

> **Correct**
>
> Use **AutoFormat** to create high-quality publications easily.
>
> **Incorrect**
>
> Use **AutoFormat** to create quality publications easily.

H

hint   Do not use *hint* as a heading for a type of note; use *tip* instead.

For more information, see *Notes and Tips* in Chapter 2, "Content Formatting and Layout."

hi-res   Do not use for *high-resolution*.

hit   It is all right to use *hit* to use to refer to the number of times a file from a Web page has been retrieved. Because each file associated with a Web page counts as one hit, a single page view can result in many hits. Use *page view* or *page request* to refer to the number of times a page and all its associated files have been downloaded.

Do not use *hit* to refer to the act of pressing a key on the computer keyboard. Use *press* instead.

See Also: press

home directory   Do not use. Use *root directory* instead to refer to the starting point in a hierarchical file structure. In MS-DOS, the root directory is indicated by a backslash (\).

See Also: root directory

home page   Refers to the main page of any Web site, as determined by the owner or creator of the site. One Web site can have many home pages. For example, the Microsoft Web site, *www.microsoft.com*, has a home page, but other sites within the Microsoft site have their own home pages.

Home page also refers to the Web page that is first displayed when a user starts a Web browser. Do not use *start page*.

Use lowercase to refer to the home page unless you are referring to the command.

host name   Two words.

hot key   Obsolete term. Do not use. Use *keyboard shortcut* instead.

See Also: keyboard shortcut

hot link   Do not use. *Hot link* is jargon for a connection between programs that enables information in related databases or files to be updated when information in another database or file is changed. Do not use *hot link* to refer to a hyperlink.

hot spot, hotspot   Normally two words. Use in content for software developers to refer to the specific pixel on the pointer that defines the exact location to which a user is pointing.

Avoid using otherwise except in references to Hotspot Editor, where it is one word.

Do not use *hot spot* to refer to a hyperlink.

hotfix   Use only to describe an emergency bug fix targeted at a specific customer situation and not distributed generally. Do not use *QFE* (quick fix engineering) to describe a hotfix.

For a broadly released security-related fix, use *security update*. For a broadly released security-related bug fix, use *security update*.

See Also: *patch; security update; service pack; update*

hover, mouse over   Avoid these terms, especially in end-user documentation, to refer to the action of briefly resting the mouse pointer on a button, link, and so on to see a definition or description. Instead, use *rest on, pause on*, or a similar word or phrase.

Do not use *mouse over* as a verb phrase. To describe the action of moving the mouse to a button, use a phrase such as "move the pointer over the button."

how-to vs. how to   Do not use *how-to* as a noun. Hyphenate as an adjective. Whether *how to* is hyphenated or not, do not capitalize *to* in titles.

Correct

how-to book

how-to article

How to Format Your Hard Disk

Writing a How-to Article

Incorrect

The TechNet Web site has how-tos for system administrators.

HTML   Abbreviation for "Hypertext Markup Language." Spell out as shown on first mention if necessary for your audience.

For more information, see *HTML Tag, Element, and Attribute Styling* in Chapter 5, "Web Content."

HTTP   Abbreviation for "Hypertext Transfer Protocol," the Internet protocol that delivers information over the World Wide Web. The protocol appears as the first element in the URL: "http://...." Use lowercase in the URL.

It is acceptable to eliminate "http" from a Web address if you are sure your audience will understand the context. If you are using another protocol such as FTP in an Internet address, however, you must use the protocol in the address.

In general, you do not have to spell out the meaning of the acronym at first mention unless you are discussing protocols or URLs or to clarify for your audience.

For more information, see *Protocols* in Chapter 9, "Common Style Problems."

H

hyperlink   Use *hyperlink* to describe text or a graphic that users can click to go to another document or another place within the same document. It is all right to use *link* once context has been established.

Do not use *hot spot*, *hot link*, or *shortcut* to refer to a hyperlink.

Use *go to* to describe the process of going to another page, and use create to describe writing the HTML code that forms the hyperlink.

It is all right in content for Web designers to use *followed hyperlink* or *followed link* to refer to a destination that the user has already visited. Do not use these terms in content for other audiences.

Correct

Click the hyperlink to go to another Web page.

You can create a link to almost any Web site.

For more information, see *URL, Addresses* in Chapter 9, "Common Style Problems."

H

IA-32–based   Use to distinguish computers with processors based on the Intel IA-32 architecture from computers with processors based on the Intel Itanium (formerly IA-64) architecture.

See Also: *Intel-based; Itanium-based*

I-beam   Note capitalization and hyphenation. Avoid specific references to the I-beam pointer (instead, refer simply to *the pointer*), except when necessary to describe how the pointer's shape affects its function—for example, "When you click text, the pointer looks like an I-beam."

icon   Use only to describe a graphic representation of an object that a user can select and open, such as a drive, disk, folder, document, or program.

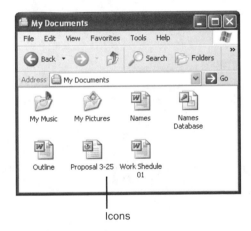

Icons

Icons

When referring to a program icon, use bold for the icon name: "Click the **Word** icon." Within programs, do not use *icon* for graphical dialog box options or options that appear on ribbons, toolbars, toolboxes, or other areas of a window.

For user interface elements that are identified by a graphic rather than label text, use the most descriptive term available, such as *button*, *box*, or *check box*. To refer to the graphic itself if there is no other identifying label, use *symbol*, as in "warning symbol."

iconize   Do not use; instead, use *shrink to an icon* or *minimize*.

i.e.   Means *id est*, "that is." Do not use; use *that is* instead.

if vs. when vs. whether   To avoid ambiguity, use *if* to express a condition; use *whether* to express uncertainty. In informal writing for the Web, it is all right to use *if* to express uncertainty. Use *when* for situations requiring preparation or to denote the passage of time.

Correct

If you do not know whether a network key is needed, contact your network administrator.

The printer might insert stray characters if the wrong font cartridge is selected.

When Setup is complete, restart your computer.

To find out whether TrueType fonts are available ...

Correct in informal contexts

To find out if TrueType fonts are available ...

Incorrect

If you do not know if a network key is needed, contact your network administrator.

The printer might insert stray characters when the wrong font cartridge is selected.

Do not use *whether or not* to express uncertainty. It is all right to use *whether ... or not* in the sense of "under any circumstances." There are often better ways to express this thought, however.

Correct

With Internet Explorer, you can save Web pages and view them later, whether you are connected to the Internet or not.

Better

With Internet Explorer, you can save Web pages and view them later, even if you are not connected to the Internet.

Incorrect

If you are unsure whether or not a network key is needed, contact your network administrator.

illegal   Use *illegal* only in specific situations, such as notices on software that say "Do not make illegal copies of this disk" or, in local content, to reference the violation of a local law, or in reference to the violation of international law. Except for certain appropriate situations, the terms *licensed* and *unlicensed* may be better.

Do not use to mean *invalid* or *not valid*.

Correct

The queue path name is not valid.

Chords cannot be composed while a segment is playing.

Incorrect

The queue path name is illegal.

It is illegal to compose chords while a segment is playing.

See Also: *invalid, not valid*

image map   Two words.

imbed   Do not use; use *embed* instead.

impact   Do not use as a verb. Use *affect* or another synonym instead.

Correct

Sending inappropriate e-mail can affect your career adversely.

Incorrect

Sending inappropriate e-mail can impact your career adversely.

in, into   *In* indicates within the limits, bounds, or area of or from the outside to a point within. *Into* generally implies moving to the inside or interior of.

Correct

A word is in a paragraph, but you move the text into the document.

Data is in a cell on a worksheet.

You edit the cell contents in the formula bar.

A file name is in a list box.

A workstation is in a domain, but resources are on servers.

You open multiple windows in a document.

You insert the disk into the disk drive.

You run programs with, on, or under an operating system, not in them.

in order to   A verbose phrase that is usually unnecessary. Use just *to* instead.

inactive, inactive state   Not *not current.*

inbound   Avoid in the sense of messages being delivered. Use *incoming* instead.

incent   Avoid. Although *incent* now appears in the *American Heritage Dictionary*, other words are available that are more widely understood worldwide. Use *motivate*, *encourage*, or whatever similar verb is most appropriate.

Correct

This pricing should encourage users to buy the new version.

Incorrect

This pricing should incent users to buy the new version.

incoming, outgoing   Use to refer to e-mail messages that are being downloaded or being sent. Avoid *inbound* and *outbound*.

increment   In content for software developers, Web developers, and information technology professionals, restrict the use as a verb to mean "increase by one or by a specified interval." As a noun, use *increment* to refer to the specified interval.

In more general material, it is all right to use *increment* in a nontechnical sense, as long as the meaning is clear in context.

indent, indentation   Use *indent*, not *indentation*, to refer to a single instance of indentation— for example, *hanging indent, nested indent, negative indent* (do not use *outdent*), *positive indent.* Do not use *indention.* Use *indentation* to refer to the general concept.

indenting, outdenting   Do not use "indenting or outdenting into the margin." Instead use "extending text into the margin" or "indenting to the previous tab stop."

independent content provider (ICP)   Use to refer to a business or organization that supplies information to an online information service such as MSN or America Online. Spell out on first mention.

index, indexes   In general use, form the plural of *index* as *indexes.* Use *indices* only in the context of mathematical expressions.

initialize   Technical term usually referring to preparing a disk or computer for use or to set a variable to an initial value. Do not use to mean start a program or turn on a computer.

initiate   Do not use to mean start a program; use *start* instead.

inline   One word, no hyphen. "Inline styles" are used in cascading style sheets to override a style in the style sheet itself. Inline styles are embedded in the tag itself by using the STYLE parameter.

input   Avoid in all content as a verb; use *type* or another appropriate verb instead. Avoid as a noun in content for home users and information workers.

> **Correct**
>
> Word moves existing characters to the right as you type new text.
>
> **Incorrect**
>
> Word moves existing characters to the right as you input new text.

input device   Use *input device* as a general reference that includes a mouse, pen, ball, stylus, keyboard, or other device that sends user input to a computer. Do not use as a synonym for *mouse*.

For more information, see *Mouse Terminology* in Chapter 1, "Documenting the User Interface."

input/output   In general, spell out at first use and then abbreviate as *I/O*. However, some technical audiences might be completely familiar with the term, in which case it is not necessary to spell out at first use.

input/output control   Acceptable to abbreviate as *I/O control* or *IOCTL* after first occurrence. Use only in technical material.

insecure   Do not use to mean "not secure." Use *not secure* instead.

insertion point   The point at which text or graphics will be inserted when the user begins working with the program. It's usually shown as a blinking line or, in character-based applications, a blinking rectangle. Use instead of *cursor* except in character-based applications, where *cursor* is acceptable. Always use the article *the*, as in "the insertion point."

inside   Use instead of the colloquial *inside of*.

install   In general, use *install* to refer to adding hardware or software to a computer system.

Do not use *install* as a noun. Use *installation* instead.

instantiate   Avoid. Use *create an instance of* [a class] instead. If you must use *instantiate*, its direct object must be the name of a class or a general reference to classes. You instantiate a class, not an object.

insure   Do not use except to refer to insurance.

See Also: assure, ensure, insure

Intel-based   Use to distinguish computers with processors based on the Intel IA-32 or Itanium architecture from computers based on other architectures such as Macintosh, VAX, or RISC.

See Also: IA-32–based; Itanium-based

I

interface   Use as a noun only, as in "user interface" and "application programming interface." Use *on* as the preposition preceding *user interface*. Use *interface* alone only if the context is clear.

Interface as a verb is jargon. Use *interact* or *communicate* instead.

Correct

It is easy to use the Internet to communicate with various interest groups.

The interface is so intuitive that even first-time users learn quickly.

The color can be adjusted on the user interface.

Incorrect

It is easy to use the Internet to interface with various interest groups.

The color can be adjusted in the user interface.

In COM-based technologies and objects in the Microsoft .NET Framework, an interface is a collection of related public functions called *methods* that provide access to an object. The set of interfaces *on* (note preposition) an object composes a contract that specifies how programs and other objects can interact with the object.

For more information, see *COM, ActiveX, and OLE Terminology* in Chapter 4, "Content for Software Developers."

Internet Connection Sharing   Technology that provides home computer users who have networked computers with the capability to share a single connection to the Internet.

Spell out on each use, using initial capital letters. You may shorten to *Connection Sharing* after first use, except in titles, chapter headings, dialog boxes, or other prominent places. Do not use *ICS* as an acronym.

Internet Explorer   Do not abbreviate.

Internet, intranet, extranet   The *Internet* refers to the worldwide collection of networks that use open protocols such as TCP/IP to communicate with each other. The Internet offers a number of services, including e-mail and the World Wide Web. Always capitalize *Internet*.

An *intranet* is a communications network based on the same technology as the World Wide Web that is available only to certain people, such as the employees of a company. Do not capitalize.

An *extranet* is an extension of an intranet using Internet protocols to provide authorized outside users with limited access to the intranet. Do not capitalize.

For more information, see the *Microsoft Computer Dictionary*.

Internet service provider (ISP)   Note capitalization. Spell out on first use.

Use to refer to an organization that provides customers with access to the Internet for such activities as Web browsing, e-mail, and newsgroup participation. Common ISPs are MSN, America Online, and EarthLink.

Interrupt   When discussing specific MS-DOS interrupts, spell out and capitalize the word *Interrupt* and use a lowercase *h*, as in "Interrupt 21h."

invalid, not valid   Both are acceptable, but if your document may be available worldwide, *not valid* is preferred. Automatic Web translation software may translate *invalid* incorrectly.

Both *invalid* and *not valid* are vague words that should be replaced with something more specific wherever possible.

Correct but vague

The telephone number is not valid.

More specific

The telephone number can contain only numbers and hyphens.

inverse video   Avoid; use *reverse video* instead. Use *highlighted* to refer to the appearance.

See Also: *highlight*

invoke   Do not use in content for home users and information workers to mean starting or running a program.

Invoke is acceptable in content for software developers to refer to calling a function, starting a process, and similar meanings, but a more specific term is preferable.

IP address   Spell out as "Internet Protocol address" on first use if your audience will not recognize the term.

issue   Avoid using as a verb; try to use a more specific verb instead. Do not use to refer to commands in content for home users or information workers.

Correct

Windows 2000 displays an error message.

Click **Save As** to save a file under a new name.

Incorrect

Windows 2000 issues an error message.

Issue the **Save As** command to save a file under a new name.

italic   Not italics or italicized.

For more information, see *Document Conventions* in Chapter 2, "Content Formatting and Layout."

See Also: *font and font style*

Itanium-based   Use to distinguish computers with processors based on the Intel Itanium (formerly IA-64) architecture from computers with processors based on the Intel IA-32 architecture.

See Also: *IA-32–based; Intel-based*

its vs. it's   Proofread your work to be sure you have used the correct word. *Its* is the possessive form; *it's* is the contraction meaning "it is." In general, avoid contractions. They are a problem for the worldwide audience.

Correct

The easy connection to other systems is just one of its many advantages.

J

Java, JScript, JavaScript Java is an object-oriented programming language developed by the Sun Corporation.

JScript is the Microsoft implementation of the ECMAScript scripting language specification, an open standard. Do not refer to it as *JavaScript*, which is the corresponding implementation by Time Warner.

jewel case Avoid. Use *CD case* instead.

join Do not use to mean "embed." *Join*, in database terminology, refers to a relationship or association between fields in different tables and should be reserved for that meaning in content about databases and database management systems.

> **Correct**
>
> If you join numeric fields that do not have matching FieldSize property settings, Microsoft Access might not find all the matching records when you run the query.
>
> When you add fields from both tables to the query design grid, the default, or inner, join tells the query to check for matching values in the join fields.
>
> To embed one object into another, click **Paste** on the **Edit** menu.
>
> **Incorrect**
>
> To join one object with another, click **Paste** on the **Edit** menu.

joystick One word. Joysticks have *controls* (not options) for controlling movement on the screen.

jump Do not use as a noun to refer to cross-references to other Help topics or to hyperlinks. Do not use as a verb to refer to the action that follows clicking a hyperlink; use *go to* instead.

justified Do not use as a synonym for *aligned*. Justified text is text that is both left-aligned and right-aligned. To describe alignment on one margin only, use *left-aligned* or *right-aligned*, not *left-justified* or *right-justified*.

In documents that discuss text alignment, include *justify* in the index with cross-references to *align*, *left align*, and *right align*, as appropriate.

See Also: left align, left-aligned; right align, right-aligned

K

K, K byte, Kbyte Do not use as abbreviations for *kilobyte*. Use *KB* instead. Do not use *K* as a slang expression for $1,000.

See Also: KB

KB Abbreviation for *kilobyte*. Use the abbreviation only as a measurement with numerals. Always spell out in other contexts. Spell out *kilobyte* at first mention, with or without a numeral, if your audience may not be familiar with the abbreviation. Insert a space between *KB* and the numeral, or hyphenate if a measure is used as an adjective.

Correct

360-KB disk

64 KB of memory left

In the early days of personal computers, disk space was measured in kilobytes.

See Also: kilobyte

Kbit Do not use as an abbreviation for *kilobit*; always spell out.

KBps, Kbps *KBps* is the abbreviation for *kilobytes per second*. *Kbps* is the abbreviation for *kilobits per second*. Spell out on first mention. Use the abbreviations only as a measurement with numerals. Spell out in other contexts.

Kerberos protocol Always use *Kerberos* as an adjective ("Kerberos protocol"), not as a noun ("includes Kerberos").

Always make clear on first mention what version or versions of the Kerberos protocol you are referring to. For example, the Kerberos version 5 protocol is the default authentication protocol for Microsoft Windows Server 2003, Windows XP Professional, and Windows 2000.

Correct

Microsoft Windows Server 2003 includes support for the Kerberos version 5 protcol.

Incorrect

Microsoft Windows Server 2003 includes support for Kerberos.

Microsoft Windows Server 2003 includes support for Kerberos version 5.

key combination   Do not use *key combination* as a term in content for home users and information workers; use *keyboard shortcut* instead.

Key combination is best avoided entirely, but it is acceptable in content for software developers when you must distinguish between a key combination, in which two or more keys are pressed simultaneously (such as CTRL+P), and a *key sequence*. In such cases, provide a definition for *key combination*.

For more information, see *Key Names* in Chapter 1, "Documenting the User Interface."

See Also: *key sequence; keyboard shortcut*

key sequence   Do not use *key sequence* in content for home users and information workers. Use *keyboard shortcut* instead.

Key sequence is best avoided entirely, but it is permissible in content for software developers when you must distinguish between a *key combination* and a key sequence. In such cases, use *key sequence* to denote keys that must be pressed sequentially, and provide a definition.

For more information, see *Key Names* in Chapter 1, "Documenting the User Interface."

See Also: *access key; key combination; keyboard shortcut*

keyboard shortcut   Use to describe any combination of keystrokes that can be used to perform a task that would otherwise require a mouse or other pointing device. In developer documentation or in material about customizing the user interface, it is permissible to use *access key* or *shortcut key* when it is necessary to distinguish between the two.

For more information, see *Key Names* in Chapter 1, "Documenting the User Interface."

See Also: *access key; key combination; key sequence; shortcut key*

keypad   Always use *numeric keypad* on first mention. Avoid using *keypad* alone. If you must use it alone, ensure that there is no possibility for the user to mistake the reference.

In general, avoid making distinctions between the keyboard and the numeric keypad. When the user can press two keys that look the same, be specific in directing the user to the proper key. For example, "Press the MINUS SIGN on the numeric keypad, not the HYPHEN key on the keyboard." This approach may cause problems because of differences in specific keyboards and numeric keypads. Document such resolutions on your project style sheet.

K

keypress   Do not use; use *keystroke* instead.

keystroke   One word. Not *keypress*.

kHz   Abbreviation for *kilohertz*. Spell out on first mention if your audience may not be familiar with the abbreviation. Use the abbreviation only as a measurement with numerals; always spell out in other contexts.

See Also: *kilohertz*

kilobit   Always spell out. Do not use the abbreviation *Kbit*.

kilobits per second   Always spell out on first mention. Abbreviate as *Kbps* on subsequent mention only as a measurement with numerals. Spell out in other contexts.

See Also: *KBps, Kbps*

kilobyte   One kilobyte is equal to 1,024 bytes.

- Abbreviate as *KB*, not *K, K byte*, or *Kbyte*. At first mention, spell out and use the abbreviation in parentheses if your audience may not be familiar with the abbreviation.

- Separate the numeral from the abbreviation with a space or a hyphen, depending on usage.

   Correct

   800-KB disk drive

- When used as a noun in measurements, add *of* to form a prepositional phrase.

   Correct

   The Help files require 175 KB of disk space.

For more information, see *Measurements and Units of Measure* in Chapter 9, "Common Style Problems."

kilobytes per second   Always spell out on first mention. Abbreviate as *KBps* on subsequent mention only as a measurement with numerals. Spell out in other contexts.

See Also: *KBps, Kbps*

K

kilohertz   A kilohertz is a unit of frequency equal to 1,000 cycles per second, or hertz.

- Abbreviate as *kHz*. Spell out on first mention and include the abbreviation in parentheses if your audience may not be familiar with the abbreviation.

- Leave a space between the numeral and *kHz* except when the measurement is used as an adjective preceding a noun. In that case, use a hyphen.

   Correct

   The processor accesses memory at 500 kilohertz (kHz).

   a 900-kHz processor

For more information, see *Measurements and Units of Measure* in Chapter 9, "Common Style Problems."

kludge, kludgy   Slang. Do not use to refer to a band-aid fix or poorly designed program or system.

knowledge base, Knowledge Base   Use all lowercase for generic references to the "expert system" database type. It is not necessary to precede *Knowledge Base* with the company name.

K

L

label, labeled, labeling   Do not double the final *l*.

landscape orientation   Printing orientation that aligns text with the wide dimension of the paper.

Landscape orientation

Compare with *portrait orientation*.

See Also: *portrait orientation*

laptop   One word. However, use *portable computer* in most instances because it does not refer to a specific size.

See Also: *portable computer*

later   Use instead of *below* in cross-references—for example, "later in this section."

Use instead of *higher* for product version numbers—for example, "Windows version 3.0 or later."

For more information, see *Cross-References* in Chapter 2, "Content Formatting and Layout."

launch   Do not use to mean *start*, as in "launch a program" or "launch a form." Use *start* instead.

See Also: *start, Start (the menu)*

lay out, laid out, layout   Derivatives of *lay out* are commonly used in reference to formatting. Use the correct spelling and part of speech according to your meaning.

> **Correct**
> You can lay out complex information in a table.
> Add formatting to your table after it is laid out.
> A table layout clarifies complex information.

leave   Do not use to refer to closing a program; use *exit* instead.

left   Not *left-hand*. Use *upper left* or *lower left, leftmost,* and so on. Include a hyphen if modifying a noun, as in "upper-left corner."

left align, left-aligned   Use to refer to text that is aligned at the left margin. Hyphenate *left-aligned* in all positions in the sentence. Do not use *left-justified*.

> **See Also:** *justified; right align, right-aligned*

left mouse button   In general, use just *mouse button*; use *left mouse button* only in discussions of multiple buttons or in teaching beginning skills.

> For more information, see *Mouse Terminology* in Chapter 1, "Documenting the User Interface."

left-hand   Do not use; use just *left* instead.

> **See Also:** *left*

left-justified   Do not use; use *left-aligned* instead.

leftmost   One word.

> Avoid giving directional cues for accessibility reasons. If you must, however, use *leftmost* to refer to something at the farthest left side instead of *farthest left, far-left,* or similar terms.

legacy   Do not use in content for home users or information workers to describe a previous version of a product or system.

> In all content, avoid using as an adjective, as in "a legacy system." Instead, use *previous, former, earlier,* or a similar term. Describe the earlier systems, if necessary, especially if discussing compatibility issues.

legal   Use only to refer to matters of law. Do not use to mean *valid,* as in "a valid action."

less vs. fewer vs. under   Use *less* to refer to a mass amount, value, or degree. Use *fewer* to refer to a countable number of items. Do not use *under* to refer to a quantity or number.

> **Correct**
> The new building has less floor space and contains fewer offices.
> Fewer than 75 members were present.
> Less than a quorum attended.

L

Incorrect

Less than 75 members were present.

The new building has less offices.

Under 75 members attended.

The new building has under 10 floors.

let, lets   Avoid in the sense of software permitting a user to do something. Use *you can* instead.

Correct

With Microsoft Project, you can present information in many ways.

Incorrect

Microsoft Project lets you present information in many ways.

See Also: *can vs. may*

leverage   Do not use as a verb to mean "take advantage of." Use *take advantage of*, *capitalize on*, *use*, or another more appropriate word or phrase.

life cycle, life-cycle   Two words as a noun. Hyphenate as an adjective.

like   Acceptable as a synonym for *such as* or *similar to*. Do not use as a conjunction; use *as* instead.

Correct

In a workgroup, you can work with files residing on another computer as you would on your own.

Moving a dialog box is like moving a window.

Incorrect

In a workgroup, you can work with files residing on another computer like you would on your own.

-like   In general, do not hyphenate words ending with *-like*, such as *rodlike* and *maillike*, unless the root word ends in double *l*s (for example, *bell-like*) or has three or more syllables (for example, *computer-like*).

line feed   Two words. Refers to the ASCII character that moves the insertion point or printer head to the next line, one space to the right of its current position. Do not confuse with the *newline character*, which is the same as the carriage return/line feed and moves the cursor to the beginning of the next line. Can be abbreviated *LF* after the first use, as in *CR/LF*.

L

list box　Two words. *List box* is a generic term for any type of dialog box option containing a list of items the user can select. In text and procedures, refer to a list box by its label and the word *list*, not *list box*.

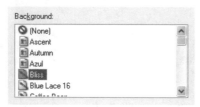

List box

Correct

In the **Background** list, click **Coffee Bean**.

Incorrect

In the **Background** list box, click **Coffee Bean**.

For more information, see *Dialog Boxes and Property Sheets* in Chapter 1, "Documenting the User Interface."

load　With the exception noted at the end of this entry, do not use *load* in content for home users or information workers. Use only to refer to dynamically calling graphics or documents, or installed programs or data—such as drivers, DLLs, scripts, registry entries, and profiles—into RAM or a program's virtual memory. Use *unload* or *remove* to refer to removing these items from memory.

Do not use *load* as a synonym for *run*, *set up*, or *download*.

Correct

Load the device driver into the upper memory area.

Loading your personal settings... [System status message]

When a user logs on, the system loads the user's profile.

Run the program in character mode.

Setting Up Word on a Network File Server

Incorrect

When a user logs on, the system adds the user's profile.

Load the program in character mode.

Loading Word on a Network File Server

Load may be acceptable in content for home users and information workers to refer to the process by which a browser processes text or graphics on an HTML page, but in most cases it would be better to choose another word or rewrite the sentence.

Acceptable

If a page you are trying to view is taking too long to load, click the **Stop** button.

Better

If a page you are trying to view is taking too long to open, click the **Stop** button.

See Also: download

localhost   The name that is used to represent the same computer on which a TCP/IP message originates. An IP packet sent to localhost has the IP address 127.0.0.1 and does not actually go out to the Internet.

lock   In general, do not use to mean *protect*, as in "protect a document from changes." Do not confuse with *write-protect*, which is what users do to disks to protect them from being over-written. Some programs (for example, Microsoft Excel and Word) use *locked* to indicate portions of a document that cannot be changed.

lock up   Do not use to describe a hardware failure or a program or the operating system that has stopped responding. Use *fail* instead for hardware, or *stop responding* for programs or the operating system.

See Also: fail

log on, log off, logon, logoff   Use *log on* or *log on to* (not *log onto*) to refer to creating a user session on a computer or a network. Use *log off* or *log off from* to refer to ending a user session on a computer or a network. Use *sign in* and *sign out* to refer to creating and ending a user session on the Internet.

Do not use *log in, login, log onto, log off of, logout, sign off*, or *sign on* unless these terms appear in the user interface.

The verb form is two words, *log on* or *log off*. As a noun or adjective, use one word, no hyphen: *logon* or *logoff*.

Correct

You must enter your password while logging on.

Some networks support this logon feature.

A single logon gives you access to all the resources of the network.

Remember to log off from the network.

When you are finished using the network, remember to log off.

Incorrect

Log in before you start Windows.

Remember to log off of the network.

Remember to log off the network.

When you logon to the network, you have access to your e-mail.

See Also: connect; sign in, sign out, sign on, sign up

look at   Avoid; use *view* instead, as in "To view the list of Help topics, click **Help**."

look up   Acceptable to use instead of *see* in cross-references to online index entries from printed documentation. If you are using common source files for both printed and online documentation, however, use *see*.

> **Correct**
>
> For more information, look up "Dial-Up Networking" in the Help index.

lo-res   Do not use; use *low-resolution* instead.

lower   Do not use to indicate product version numbers. Use *earlier* instead, as in "Word version 3.0 or earlier."

> *See Also:* *earlier*

lower left, lower right   Use as a noun instead of *bottom left* and *bottom right*. Hyphenate as adjectives: *lower-left* and *lower-right*.

lowercase   One word. Do not use *lowercased*. Avoid using as a verb.

When *lowercase* and *uppercase* are used together, do not use a suspended hyphen.

> **Correct**
>
> You can quickly change the capitalization of all uppercase and lowercase letters.
>
> Change all the uppercase letters to lowercase.

> **Incorrect**
>
> You can quickly change the capitalization of all upper- and lowercase letters.
>
> Lowercase all the capital letters.

low-level   Note hyphen. Use the term carefully; a *low-level language*, for example, means a language that is very close to machine language, such as assembly language.

> *See Also:* *high-level*

low-resolution   Note hyphen. Do not abbreviate as *lo-res*.

L

M

M, M byte, Mbyte   Do not use as abbreviations for *megabyte*. Use *MB* instead.

MAC (media access control)   It is all right to use MAC as an acronym for *media access control*. Always spell out on first mention, and always provide a glossary entry.

machine   Avoid; use *computer* instead.

machine language   Acceptable in content for software developers and information technology professionals to refer to the language of compiled code.

Macro Assembler (MASM)   A programming language. Spell out at first occurrence; after that it can be abbreviated as *MASM*.

main document   Use to refer to the document that contains the unchanging material in a merged document, such as a form letter. Do not use *core document* or other terms.

makefile   Acceptable in content for software developers. One word, lowercase.

management information systems   Abbreviate as *MIS*. In general, however, use *IS* for *information systems* instead, unless the reference is specifically to management information systems.

manipulate   Avoid in content for home users and information workers.

manual   In general, avoid *manual* as a synonym for *book*, guide, or other specific terms referring to product documentation. Use the title of the book itself if possible.

For more information, see *Titles of Publications* in Chapter 9, "Common Style Problems."

marquee   Acceptable to refer to the scrolling text feature on Web pages. Do not use to refer to the feature that draws a dotted line around a selection on the screen; use *bounding outline* instead.

See Also: *bounding outline; dotted rectangle*

master/slave   This terminology, although it is standard in the information technology industry, may be insulting to some users. Do not use in content for home users or information workers.

In content for information technology professionals or software developers, *subordinate* for *slave*. Use *master* and *subordinate* only as adjectives. You can reference the use of slave as an adjective when it is necessary to clarify the concept (for example, *also known as slave server*). You should continue to index *master server* and *slave server*.

Do not use *slave* as an adjective or a noun.

> **Correct**
>
> Each subordinate device has a unique 7-bit or 10-bit address.
>
> The architecture uses a standard master/subordinate design to replicate data from one server to many.
>
> **Correct, but not recommended**
>
> Each slave device has a unique 7-bit or 10-bit address.
>
> The architecture uses a standard master/slave design to replicate data from one server to many.
>
> **Incorrect**
>
> Each slave has a unique 7-bit or 10-bit address.

mathematical   Not *mathematic*.

matrix   Spell plural as *matrices*.

maximize   Acceptable as a verb.

Maximize button   Refers to the button with an open square (Windows 95 and later) that is located in the upper-right corner of a window that has not been maximized. The **Maximize** button performs the same function as the **Maximize** command on a window's shortcut menu.

Maximize button

Do not use *Maximize box* or *Maximize icon*. Use the phrase "**Maximize** button" to refer to the button, not just **Maximize**. It is acceptable to use *maximize* as a verb, however.

M

Correct

Click the **Maximize** button.

To fill the screen, maximize the window.

Click .

Incorrect

Click **Maximize**.

MB   Abbreviation for *megabyte*. Use the abbreviation only as a measurement with numerals. Spell out in other contexts. Spell out *megabyte* on first mention, with or without a numeral, if your audience may not be familiar with the abbreviation. Insert a space between *MB* and the numeral, or hyphenate if a measure is used as an adjective.

> **Correct**
>
> 4 megabytes (MB) of RAM
>
> 40-MB hard disk

For more information, see *Measurements and Units of Measure* in Chapter 9, "Common Style Problems."

See Also: *megabyte*

Mbit, Mb   Do not use as abbreviations for *megabit;* always spell out.

medium, media   Follow conservative practice and use *medium*, not *media*, as a singular subject. However, *media* is now gaining acceptance as a singular collective noun referring to the communications industry or the journalism profession. If usage is unclear, be conservative, but be consistent. Ensure that the verb agrees with the subject (that is, *the medium is* and *the media are*), unless you are clearly using *media* as a collective noun in the singular form.

In the computer software industry, *media* has the following meanings:

- Materials or substances, such as fiber-optic cable or wire, through which data is transmitted.

- Materials on which data is recorded or stored, such as magnetic disks, CDs, or tapes.

- The mass-communications industry and its practitioners, such as publishing or broadcasting.

- Journalists as a group, whether they are published in print, on the Web, or on broadcast media.

M

Media refers to the means of communication and should not be used to mean the content of the communication; use *media content*, *media file*, *media stream*, *media clip*, *media item*, *audio*, *video*, or *music* instead.

Correct

The media include online broadcasts as well as newspapers, magazines, radio, and television.

The media covers news of the computer industry.

The medium now used for many large computer programs is the DVD-ROM.

Do not use *media* as a shortened form of *multimedia*.

Incorrect

When the consumer plays the media ...

The media is downloaded ...

... technology that encrypts media with a key

meg Do not use as an abbreviation for *megabyte*. Use *MB* instead.

megabit Always spell out. Do not use the abbreviation *Mb* or *Mbit*.

megabits per second Always spell out on first mention. Abbreviate as *Mbps* on subsequent mention only as a measurement with numerals. Spell out in other contexts.

megabyte One megabyte is equal to 1,048,576 bytes, or 1,024 kilobytes.

- Abbreviate as *MB*, not *M*, *meg*, or *Mbyte*. At first mention, spell out and use the abbreviation in parentheses if your audience may not be familiar with the abbreviation.

- Leave a space between the numeral and *MB*, except when the measurement is used as an adjective preceding a noun. In that case, use a hyphen.

Correct

1.2-megabyte (MB) disk

1.2 MB

40-MB hard disk

- When used as a noun in measurements, add *of* to form a prepositional phrase.

Correct

You can run many programs with only 1 MB of memory.

For more information, see *Measurements and Units of Measure* in Chapter 9, "Common Style Problems."

M

megahertz   A megahertz is a unit of frequency equal to 1 million cycles per second, or hertz.

- Abbreviate as *MHz*. At first mention, spell out and use the abbreviation in parentheses if your audience may not be familiar with the abbreviation.

- Leave a space between the numeral and *MHz* except when the measurement is used as an adjective preceding a noun. In that case, use a hyphen.

    Correct

    The processor accesses memory at 50 megahertz (MHz).

    900-MHz processor

For more information, see *Measurements and Units of Measure* in Chapter 9, "Common Style Problems."

member function   Avoid. Use *method* instead.

memory   To avoid confusing users, refer to a specific kind of memory rather than use the generic term *memory*, which usually refers to random access memory (RAM). That is, use the more precise terms *RAM, read-only memory (ROM), hard disk*, and so on, as appropriate. It is all right to use *memory* for RAM if you are sure your audience will understand or if you have established the connection. In lists of hardware requirements, however, use *RAM*.

Follow the standard guidelines for using acronyms and abbreviating measurements such as kilobytes (KB) with reference to memory.

    Correct

    800-KB disk drive

    The Help files require 25 MB of disk space.

    Many applications now need at least 64 MB of RAM.

In the noun forms referring to memory measurements, use *of* in a prepositional phrase, as in "512 MB of RAM."

memory models   Do not hyphenate when referring to various memory models: *tiny memory model, large memory model*, and so on. Do hyphenate when the term modifies *program: tiny-memory-model program* and *large-memory-model program*.

memory-resident   Use as an adjective. Note hyphen. Use *memory-resident program*, not *TSR*, in content for home users and information workers. *TSR*, which stands for *terminate-and-stay-resident*, is acceptable in content for software developers and information technology professionals.

M

menu item   Do not use in content for home users or information workers. Use *command* instead. In content for software developers about creating elements of the user interface, *menu item* may be the best term to use.

message box   In content for software developers, use to describe a secondary window that is displayed to inform a user about a particular condition. In end-user documentation, use *message*.

For more information, see *Messages* in Chapter 1, "Documenting the User Interface."

message (e-mail)   In the context of e-mail, use *message* or *e-mail message* to refer to an item sent or received. Do not refer to a single message as an *e-mail*.

metadata   One word. Use in content for software developers, Web developers, or information technology professionals to refer to data that describes other data.

metafile   One word. Acceptable to use to refer to a file that describes or contains other files.

MHz   Abbreviation for *megahertz*. Use the abbreviation only as a measurement with numerals; do not use in straight text without a numeral. Spell out *megahertz* at first mention.

See Also: megahertz

mice   Avoid. Use *mouse devices* instead.

For more information, see *Mouse Terminology* in Chapter 1, "Documenting the User Interface."

micro-   In general, do not hyphenate words beginning with *micro-*, such as *microprocessor* and *microsecond*, unless it is necessary to avoid confusion or if *micro* is followed by a proper noun. If in doubt, refer to the *American Heritage Dictionary* or your project style sheet.

microprocessor   Use instead of *processor* to refer to the chip used in personal computers.

Microsoft   Do not use *MS* as an abbreviation for *Microsoft*.

midnight   Do not use *12 A.M.* or *12 P.M.* to specify midnight: use *00:00*, or just *midnight*.

Midnight is considered the beginning of the new day, not the end of the old one. If you are concerned about ambiguity, refer to *23:59* or *00:01*.

See Also: A.M., P.M.

millennium   Lowercase. Do not use *Millennium* to refer to Windows Millennium Edition.

minicomputer   Do not abbreviate to *mini*.

minimize   Acceptable as a verb.

M

Minimize button   Refers to the button containing a short line (Windows 95 and later) located in the upper-right corner of a window that has not been minimized. The **Minimize** button performs the same function as the **Minimize** command on a window's shortcut menu.

Minimize button

Do not use *Minimize box* or *Minimize icon*. Use the phrase "**Minimize** button" to refer to the button, not just **Minimize**. It is acceptable to use *minimize* as a verb, however.

Correct

Click the **Minimize** button.

To reduce a program to a button on the taskbar, minimize the window.

Click .

Incorrect

Click **Minimize**.

minus sign (–)   Use an en dash for a minus sign except for user input when the user must type a hyphen. In that case, the correct key should be clearly noted.

The HTML code for a minus sign is *–*.

For more information, see *Dashes* in Chapter 11, "Punctuation."

MIP mapping   Spell as shown. *MIP* is an acronym for "multum in parvo," Latin meaning "much in little." For more information, see the *Microsoft Computer Dictionary*.

mobile phone   As a general term, use *mobile phone*. If you are referring to a specific type of mobile phone, such as a cellular phone or a digital phone, it is all right to be specific.

Do not use *mobile telephone*.

monitor   The television-like hardware that includes the screen; use *screen* to refer to the graphic portion of a monitor. Use *display* as a general term for any visual output device, such as a flat-panel display on a portable computer.

Correct

Turn on the monitor.

A number of icons appear on the screen.

The newest portable computers have active-matrix LCD displays.

M

monospace One word. A monospace font is used primarily for examples of code, including program examples and, within text, variable names, function names, argument names, and so on.

For more information, see *Document Conventions* in Chapter 2, "Content Formatting and Layout," and *Code Formatting Conventions* in Chapter 4, "Content for Software Developers."

more than vs. over Use *more than* to refer to quantifiable figures and amounts. Use *over* to refer to a spatial relationship or position or in a comparison in which *more* is already used.

> **Correct**
>
> The Design Gallery contains more than 16 million colors.
>
> After you compress your drive, your disk will have over 50 percent more free space.
>
> If you want the Help topic to appear over the document you are working on, click the **On Top** button.

See Also: over

movable Not *moveable*.

movement keys Do not use; use *arrow keys* instead.

For more information, see *Key Names* in Chapter 1, "Documenting the User Interface."

MPEG Abbreviation for Moving Picture Experts Group (*not* Motion Pictures Experts Group), a working group responsible for, among other things, file formats for moving pictures, with or without audio. Files in MPEG format are used on CD-ROMs, video CDs, and DVDs. The extension for MPEG files is .mpg.

For more information, see the *Microsoft Computer Dictionary*.

MS-DOS Do not use *DOS* to refer to the MS-DOS operating system.

Do not use *MS-DOS* as an adjective before anything that is not a component or aspect of the MS-DOS operating system; use *MS-DOS-based* instead.

> **Correct**
>
> MS-DOS-based program
>
> MS-DOS-based computer
>
> MS-DOS command

M

Incorrect

DOS program

MS-DOS program

MS-DOS computer

See Also: DOS

MS-DOS prompt   Avoid; use *command prompt* instead.

MS-DOS-based program   Use instead of *non-Windows program* when discussing software that runs on the MS-DOS operating system.

In content written for software developers, it is all right to refer to programs that run only in the Command Prompt window as *console applications. Character-based application* is acceptable for generic references to programs that do not run in Windows or other graphical environments, if the audience is familiar with the term.

Note that *MS-DOS-based program* is spelled with two hyphens, not a hyphen and an en dash.

multi-   In general, do not hyphenate words beginning with *multi* unless it's necessary to avoid confusion or if *multi* is followed by a proper noun. Avoid inventing new words by combining them with *multi*. If in doubt, check the *American Heritage Dictionary* or your project style sheet. If the word does not appear there or in the list below, use *multiple* before the word instead.

Correct

multicast

multichannel

multicolumn

multilevel

multiline

multilingual

multimedia

multiprocessor

multipurpose

multitasking

multiuser

M

multiple selection

Use to refer to a selection that includes multiple items. Do not use *disjoint selection* or *noncontiguous selection*. It is all right to use *adjacent selection* or *nonadjacent selection* to emphasize that the selected items are or are not adjacent to each other.

Avoid using the verb phrase "multiply select." Most people will initially read *multiply* as a verb, not as an adverb. Instead, use a phrase such as "Select multiple items."

See Also: *adjacent selection; nonadjacent selection*

multiplication sign (×)

In general, use the multiplication sign (×), not the letter *x*, to indicate the mathematical operation. Use an asterisk (*) if required to match the user interface.

Use × to mean "by" in referring to screen resolution or to physical dimensions.

The HTML code for the multiplication sign is *×* or *×*.

For more information, see *Measurements and Units of Measure* in Chapter 9, "Common Style Problems."

multitasking

Do not use verb forms of this word; it is unacceptable jargon.

Correct

Windows 95 supports multitasking.

Incorrect

You can multitask with Windows 95.

multithreaded

Not *multithread*.

My Computer

An icon that represents a user's private, local system. To refer to the icon in printed documents, use just *My Computer* if the icon is shown; otherwise, use *the My Computer icon*. In procedures, apply bold formatting to **My Computer**.

My Computer

Correct

My Computer is visible at the upper left of your Windows desktop.

Double-click the **My Computer** icon.

M

N

n Conventionally, a lowercase italic *n* refers to a generic use of a number. You can use *n* when the value of a number is arbitrary or immaterial—for example, "Move the insertion point *n* spaces to the right." Reserve italic *x* for representing an unknown in mathematical equations (a variable) and other such placeholders.

See Also: *x*

namespace One word.

nanosecond One-billionth of a second. Always spell out.

native language Avoid when referring to a computer system's machine language; this term could be a misleading anthropomorphism. Instead, use *machine language* or *host language*.

navigate Do not use to refer to the act of going from place to place on the World Wide Web or on an intranet Web. Use *browse* instead.

To refer to the act of going directly to a Web page or Web site, whether by typing a *URL* in the Address bar of a browser or by clicking a hyperlink, use *go to*. Avoid *see* in this context.

Correct
To start browsing the Web, click any link on your home page when you start Internet Explorer.
To go to a Web page, type the address of the page in the Address bar, and then click the **Go** button.

It is all right to use *navigation* to refer to controls or buttons on the user interface (for example, *navigation* buttons) or to Help topics or Web pages that orient the reader (for example, *navigation* topics or *navigation* pages).

need Often confused with *want*. Be sure to use the term that is appropriate to the situation. *Need* connotes a requirement or obligation; *want* indicates that the user has a choice of actions.

Correct
If you want to use a laser printer, you need a laser printer driver.

Net Slang expression for *Internet*. Sometimes acceptable in informal writing. Do not use in product documentation.

network   Do not shorten to *net*. Do not use *network* as a verb to describe the action of connecting a computer to a network.

A computer is *on*, not *in*, a network, and computers on a network are linked or connected, not *networked*.

Use *network* as a verb and the noun *networking* only to refer to making personal and business connections.

network adapter   Use to describe the circuitry that connects a computer to a network, regardless of the physical form the adapter takes. Use *network interface card (NIC)* only when the distinction is important to the discussion.

See Also: *adapter; board; card*

network administrator   Use only to specifically refer to the administrator of networks. In general, use *administrator* or *system administrator* unless you must specify a particular kind.

See Also: *sysop; system administrator*

network connection   Not *local area network connection*.

network drive   Not *remote drive*.

new line, newline   Use two words as a noun phrase. Use the one-word adjective only to refer to the ASCII end-of-line code (CR/LF), which moves the insertion point to the beginning of a new line. Use *newline character* instead of *end-of-line mark* to refer to the ASCII end-of-line code.

Correct

Press SHIFT+ENTER to start a new line.

Use the newline character to move to the beginning of the next line.

newsgroup   An Internet discussion group focusing on a particular topic. Use instead of *group* in this sense. Reserve *group* for more generic uses.

non-   Do not hyphenate words beginning with the prefix *non-*, such as *nonnumeric* and *nonzero*, unless a hyphen is necessary to avoid confusion, as in *non-native*; or *non-* is followed by a proper noun, as in *non-English*. If such a construction seems awkward, consider writing around it. If in doubt about whether to hyphenate, check the *American Heritage Dictionary* or your project style sheet.

Do not use *non-* to negate an entire phrase.

Correct

security-related

unrelated to security

Incorrect

non-security related

For more information, see *Hyphens, Hyphenation* in Chapter 11, "Punctuation."

N

nonadjacent selection   Avoid. Use only in content for software developers and only if the term appears in the user interface or application programming interface. In general, if you must use a term for selected items that do not touch each other, use *multiple selection* or refer to the specific nonadjacent items instead.

Do not use *noncontiguous* to refer to such a selection.

Correct

To select multiple adjacent cells, drag across the cells that you want to select.

To select nonadjacent cells, select a single cell, and then hold down the CTRL key while you click other cells that you want to select.

See Also: *adjacent selection; multiple selection*

nonprintable, nonprinting   Use *nonprintable* to refer to an area of a page that cannot be printed on. Use *nonprinting* to refer to characters and other data that can't or won't be printed. Do not use *unprintable*, which means "not fit to be printed."

Correct

Some text extends into the nonprintable area of the page.

When you click **Show/Hide**, Word displays all nonprinting characters, including paragraph marks and space marks.

non-Windows application, non-Windows-based   Do not use; use the names of specific operating systems instead, such as *MS-DOS-based program*, *UNIX program*, and so on.

Also Incorrect

non-Windows NT-based

non-Windows 2000

normal, normally   Implies "in a normal manner," which may not be possible for everyone. Do not use to mean "often," "usual," or "typical." Instead, use *usually, ordinarily, generally,* or a similar term.

notification area   The area on the right side of the taskbar formerly called the *system tray* or *status area*. The clock and system notifications appear here.

Do not use the following terms as synonyms for *notification area:*

- system tray
- systray
- status area

It is all right to refer to the location of the notification area, but such references should not be incorporated into the name, which is always *notification area*. Do not use the word *area*

N

by itself to refer to the notification area. Avoid noun stacks and descriptions that might leave the impression that there is more than one notification area.

Correct

The clock appears in the notification area, at the far right of the taskbar.

The notification area is located at the far right of the taskbar.

Incorrect

The clock appears in the notification area of the taskbar.

The clock appears in the notification area on the taskbar.

The clock appears in the taskbar notification area.

The clock appears in the notification area at the far right of the taskbar.

The clock appears in the area at the far right of the taskbar.

For more information, see *Screen Terminology* in Chapter 1, "Documenting the User Interface."

NT   Do not use; always use *Windows NT*.

NUL, null, NULL, Null   Be sure to preserve the distinction between a *null* (ASCII *NUL*) *character* and a *zero character*. A null character displays nothing, even though it takes up space. It is represented by ASCII code 0. A zero character, on the other hand, refers to the digit 0 and is represented by ASCII code 48.

Use lowercase *null* to refer to a null value. Better yet, use *null value* to avoid confusion with the constant.

Use **NULL** or **Null** (depending on the language) only to refer to the constant.

null-terminated, null-terminating   Use *null-terminated* as an adjective, as in "null-terminated string." Do not use *null-terminating*, as in "null-terminating character"; use *terminating null character* instead.

number sign (#)   Use *number sign*, not *pound sign*, to refer to the # symbol. It is acceptable, however, to use *pound key (#)*, including the symbol in parentheses, when referring specifically to telephones or telephone numbers.

Always spell out *number;* do not use the # symbol (except as a key name) – for example, use *number 7*, not *#7*. When necessary to save space, as in tables, the abbreviation *No.* is acceptable.

numeric   Not numerical.

Use numeric keypad, not numerical keypad or numeric keyboard.

See Also: *keypad*

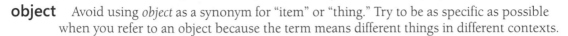

object   Avoid using *object* as a synonym for "item" or "thing." Try to be as specific as possible when you refer to an object because the term means different things in different contexts.

For example, in object-oriented programming, an object is an instance of a class. It contains both methods and data and is treated as one entity. Similarly, in COM-based technologies, an object is a combination of code and data that implements one or more interfaces. In assembly language, however, *object* refers to the object module, which contains data that has been translated into machine code.

For more information, see *COM, ActiveX, and OLE Terminology* in Chapter 4, "Content for Software Developers."

See Also: embed

Object Linking and Embedding (OLE)   Note capitalization. Spell out on first mention. Abbreviate as OLE thereafter.

For more information, see *COM, ActiveX, and OLE Terminology* in Chapter 4, "Content for Software Developers."

obsolete   Do not use as a verb. Use a phrase such as "make obsolete" instead.

of   Do not use *of* after another preposition, for example, "off of" or "outside of." It is colloquial and can be confusing for worldwide readers.

> **Correct**
>
> The taskbar is outside the main window area.
>
> Save your work, and then log off the network.
>
> **Incorrect**
>
> The taskbar is outside of the main window area.
>
> Save your work, and then log off of the network.

Office Assistant   Use *the Office Assistant* at first mention. You can shorten subsequent references to *the Assistant*.

offline   One word in all instances. Use in the sense of not being connected to or part of a system or network. Do not use in the slang sense of "outside the present context."

okay, OK   Use *OK* only to match the user interface; otherwise, use *okay*. When referring to the **OK** button in procedures, do not use *the* and *button*.

> **Correct**
>
> In the **Save As** dialog box, click **OK**.
>
> It is okay to use more than eight characters to name a file in Windows 98.
>
> **Incorrect**
>
> In the **Save As** dialog box, click the **OK** button.

on   Use *on* with these elements:

- Menus ("the **Open** command is on the **File** menu")
- Taskbar, toolbar, ruler, and desktop ("click **Start** on the taskbar")
- Disks, in the sense of a program being on a disk ("the printer drivers on Disk 4")
- User interface ("on the user interface")
- The screen itself (something appears "on the screen")
- Network ("the printer is on the network")
- Hardware platforms ("on the Macintosh")

Do not use *on* with user input actions.

> **Correct**
>
> Click the right mouse button.
>
> Click the **WordPad** icon.
>
> Click **OK**.
>
> Press ENTER.
>
> **Incorrect**
>
> Click on the right mouse button.
>
> Click on the **WordPad** icon.
>
> Click on **OK**.
>
> Press on the ENTER key.

In COM programming, an interface is implemented *on* an object.

For more information, see *Procedures* in Chapter 9, "Common Style Problems."

See Also: in, into; onto, on to

on the fly   Acceptable in content for software developers to refer to something that happens without disrupting or suspending normal operations. For more information, see the *Microsoft Computer Dictionary*.

once   To avoid ambiguity, especially for the worldwide audience, do not use as a synonym for *after*.

> **Correct**
>
> After you save the document, you can quit the program.
>
> **Incorrect**
>
> Once you save the document, you can quit the program.

online   One word in all instances.

Online is worth avoiding much of the time because it can be interpreted ambiguously. *Online* is now generally understood to refer to the Internet, but in such contexts it is better to be specific. It is also used to refer to data that resides on a computer. If you must use *online*, especially in the sense of data that resides on a computer, be explicit about your meaning so that your readers cannot misunderstand you.

> **Preferable**
>
> Many support services are available on the World Wide Web.
>
> Many products include documentation on the CDs in the package.
>
> **Acceptable**
>
> Many support services are available online.
>
> Many products include online documentation on the CDs in the package.
>
> **Incorrect**
>
> Many products include online documentation.

online Help   Avoid the redundancy of using *online* except when necessary to describe the Help system; in general, use just *Help*.

> **Correct**
>
> You have easy access to hundreds of subjects in Help.
>
> **Incorrect**
>
> You have easy access to hundreds of subjects in online Help.

on/off switch   Okay to use. Do not use *on/off button* except when referring to a remote control device.

on-screen   Hyphenate as both an adjective and adverb in all instances. However, instead of using it as an adverb, try to write around by using a phrase such as "on the screen."

> **Correct**
>
> Follow the on-screen instructions.
>
> Follow the instructions that appear on the screen.
>
> The instructions on the screen will not print.

0

on-screen keyboard   A keyboard representation on the screen that the user touches to input characters. Do not use *virtual keyboard*, *soft keyboard*, *visual keyboard*, or *keyboard display*.

> **Note:** There is an add-in for some versions of Microsoft Office called the Microsoft Visual Keyboard. This program displays the keyboard for another language on your screen so that you can either click the keys on the screen or see how the keys in the second language correspond to the ones on your keyboard. This keyboard is also referred to as an on-screen keyboard.

onto, on to   Use two words (*on to*) for the action of connecting to a network, as in "log on to the network."

Use one word (*onto*) to indicate moving something to a position on top of something else, as in "drag the icon onto the desktop."

opcode   Avoid using as a slang form of *operation code*.

open   Users open windows, files, documents, and folders. Describe the item as *open*, not *opened*, as in "an open file" and "the open document."

Do not use *open* to describe clicking a command, a menu, an icon, an option, or other similar element.

> **Correct**
>
> To open the document in Outline view, click **View**, and then click **Outline**.
>
> You double-click the Works icon to open Works.
>
> You can view your document in the open window.
>
> **Incorrect**
>
> Open the **View** menu, and then open the **Outline** command.
>
> Open the Works icon.
>
> You can view your document in the opened window.

For more information, see *Menus and Commands* in Chapter 1, "Documenting the User Interface" and *Procedures* in Chapter 9, "Common Style Problems."

operating environment, operating system   By conventional definitions, an *operating environment* (or just *environment*) includes both hardware and operating system software, whereas an *operating system* is only the software. (A *graphical environment* refers to the graphical user interface of an operating system.) In practice, however, *environment* often refers only to the operating system, as in "Visual FoxPro runs in the UNIX environment."

Various prepositions are acceptable to use with *operating system:* Programs can run *with, on,* or *under* an operating system, whichever seems most appropriate. However, do not use *run against* an operating system.

Correct

Word 2003 runs with the Windows operating system.

Microsoft Exchange Server runs on the Windows Server operating system.

Incorrect

A number of programs run against Windows XP.

See Also: platform

option, option button

In general, refer to items in a dialog box only by their labels. If you must provide a descriptor, use *option*. Capitalize the name of an option, following the interface style, but do not capitalize the word *option* itself.

With reference to an option button, you should generally refer only to the option the button controls. If you must refer to the button to avoid ambiguity, use *option button*.

Radio button is a problem term for the worldwide audience. Do not use *radio button* except in content for software developers in which the application programming interface includes the term. In that case, refer to the button as an option button, "also known as a radio button." Include *radio button* in the index with a cross-reference to *option button*.

Option buttons

Correct

In the **Sort Text** dialog box, click **No Header Row**.

Incorrect

In the **Sort Text** dialog box, click the **No Header Row** option button.

In content for software developers, it is all right to use *option* instead of *switch* to refer to a command argument or compiler option, such as **/b** or **/Za**, if your project style sheet permits.

For more information, see *Dialog Boxes and Property Sheets* in Chapter 1, "Documenting the User Interface."

See Also: control; radio button; switch

outdent

Do not use. Use *negative indent* instead.

See Also: indent, indentation

output   Use as an noun and adjective. Do not use as a verb; instead, use a term specific to the kind of output referred to, such as *write to, display on*, or *print to*, not *output to*.

> **Correct**
>
> The output provided the information needed.
>
> A printer is a standard output device.
>
> You can print a document to a file instead of to a specific printer.
>
> **Incorrect**
>
> You can output a document to a file instead of to a specific printer.

outside   Use instead of the colloquial *outside of*.

over   To avoid ambiguity, use *over* to refer to a position or location above something. For quantities, use *more than*. Do not use to refer to version numbers; instead, use *later*.

> **Correct**
>
> The [Installable ISAMs] heading appears over the list of paths to ISAM drivers.
>
> The installed base is more than 2 million.
>
> You need Windows 3.1 or later.
>
> **Incorrect**
>
> The installed base is over 2 million.
>
> You need Windows 3.1 or over.

See Also: later; more than vs. over

overtype   Use to refer to Overtype mode (note capitalization). In Overtype mode, the user *types over* existing content at the insertion point.

Do not use as a synonym for *overwrite*.

See Also: overwrite; replace

overwrite   Use only to refer to replacing new data with existing data. Use *replace* to refer to replacing an existing file with a new one with the same name.

Do not use *overwrite* as a synonym for *overtype* or *type over*.

See Also: overtype; replace

P

palette   A collection of colors or patterns that users can apply to objects, such as the color display in Control Panel.

Users click an option from a palette. The palette name should be initial cap and bold.

> **Correct**
>
> Click the color of your choice from the **Color** palette.

pane   Use only to refer to the separate areas of a split or single window. For example, in Windows Explorer, the names of all the folders can appear in one pane and the contents of a selected folder in the other pane. Use lowercase for pane names, as in "the annotation pane."

panorama   It is acceptable to use *panorama* or *panoramic view* to describe the Microsoft Surround Video technology used in Expedia and other programs. However, if the view is full circle, use instead *360-degree* or *360° view*. Use of the degree symbol is acceptable, but note that it may be difficult to see online.

> **Note:** Surround Video, despite its name, is technically not a video presentation.

parameter   Technical term referring to a value given to a variable until an operation is completed. Do not use *parameter* to mean "characteristic," "element," "limit," or "boundary."

> *See Also:* *argument vs. parameter*

parent/child   Acceptable in content for software developers and information technology professionals to refer to the relationships among processes in a multitasking environment or in content about databases to describe the relationships among nodes in a tree structure.

Do not use as a synonym for a master/slave relationship. These terms do not mean the same thing.

> *See Also:* *master/slave*

parenthesis, parentheses   Use the term *opening parenthesis* or *closing parenthesis* for an individual parenthesis, not *open parenthesis, close parenthesis, beginning parenthesis, ending parenthesis, left parenthesis,* or *right parenthesis.* It is all right to use *parenthesis* alone if it either does not matter or is unambiguously clear which parenthesis is under discussion.

For more information, see *Parentheses* in Chapter 11, "Punctuation."

patch   Do not use; use *update* instead.

> *See Also:* *hotfix; security update; service pack; update*

path   Use *path*, not *pathname*, both in general reference and in syntax. The path describes the route the operating system follows from the root directory of a drive through the hierarchical structure to locate a folder, directory, or file.

The path normally specifies only a drive and any directories below the root directory. When a path also specifies a file, it is called a *full path*.

In command syntax, *path* represents only the directory portion of the full path. For example:

copy [*drive:*][*path*]*filename*

To indicate a path, type first the drive name, followed by a colon and a backslash, and then the name of each folder, in the order you would open them, separated by a backslash. For example:

C:\Documents and Settings\user1

Use *address* or *URL*, not *path*, to refer to a location on the Internet.

In general, use *path of*, not *path to*, to refer to the location of a file.

> **Correct**
>
> The full path of my current tax form is C:\Documents and Settings\user1\My Documents\ Taxes\This year's taxes.

For information about capitalization of paths, see *Document Conventions* in Chapter 2, "Content Formatting and Layout," and *Capitalization* in Chapter 9, "Common Style Problems."

> *See Also:* *directory; folder*

PC Card vs. PCMCIA   Use *PC Card*, not *PCMCIA* or *PCMCIA card*, to refer to the add-in memory and communications cards for portable computers.

PC, PC-compatible   *PC* is the abbreviation for *personal computer*. Avoid generally. Use *computer* or *personal computer* instead. Also, because the term *PC-compatible* is vague, try to avoid it, specifying non-IBM operating environments as necessary (for example, Macintosh or UNIX).

p-code   Abbreviation for *pseudocode*. Use only in content for software developers. Spell out on first use. Capitalize as *P-Code* in titles and as *P-code* when it is the first word in a sentence.

pen   An input device that consists of a pen-shaped stylus that interacts with a computer. Use *input device* when referring generically to pens, trackballs, styluses, and so on.

Use *tap* (and *double-tap*) instead of *click* when documenting procedures specific to pen pointing devices. *Tap* means to press the screen and then lift the pen tip.

per   In the meaning of "for each," *per* is acceptable in statistical or technical contexts. In casual or colloquial contexts, however, use *a* or *for each* instead of *per*.

Correct

Users who log on only once a day are rare.

You can have only one drive letter per network resource.

Incorrect

Users who log on only once per day are rare.

Do not use *per* to mean *by* or *in accordance with*.

Correct

Find all the topics that contain a specific word by following the instructions on your screen.

Identify your computer by using the procedure in the next section.

Incorrect

Find all the topics that contain a specific word, per the instructions on your screen.

Identify your computer per the procedure in the next section.

percent, percentage   One word. In general, spell out; do not use the percent sign (%), except in tables and as a technical symbol. When spelling out *percent*, put a space between the number and the word. Always use a numeral with *percent*, no matter how small.

Correct

At least 50 percent of your system resources should be available.

Only 1 percent of the test group was unable to complete the task.

Incorrect

At least 50% of your system resources should be available.

At least 50 per cent of your system resources should be available.

Only one percent of the test group was unable to complete the task.

When describing an unspecified quantity, use *percentage*, as in "a large percentage of system resources," unless doing so would be inconsistent with the interface. For example, Microsoft Project has a **Percent (%) Complete** field.

perimeter network   A collection of devices and subnets placed between an intranet and the Internet to help protect the intranet from unauthorized Internet users. On first mention, use *perimeter network* (also known as *DMZ, demilitarized zone,* and *screened subnet*). Include *DMZ, demilitarized zone,* and *screened subnet* in the index and glossary with cross-references to *perimeter network*.

See Also: *demilitarized zone (DMZ); screened subnet*

peripheral   Avoid as a noun, especially in content for home users and information workers. Use *peripheral device* or a more specific term instead.

permissions   Use *permissions* only to refer to operations associated with a specific shared resource, such as a file, directory, or printer, which are authorized by the system administrator for individual user accounts or administrative groups. Permissions are *granted* or *assigned*, not *allowed*.

If you refer to a named permission, use title-style capitalization and roman type. Do not use *privileges* or *permission records* as a synonym for *permissions*.

> **Correct**
>
> Setting the Traverse Folder permission on a folder does not automatically set the Execute File permission on all files within that folder.
>
> Grant Read, Read and Execute, and List Folder Content permissions to the Users group.
>
> Whenever possible, assign permissions to groups rather than users.

See Also: rights; user rights

ping, PING   Do not use *ping* to refer generally to searching for a program. This usage is slang. *Ping* is acceptable when it refers specifically to using the PING protocol. The *PING protocol* is used to determine the presence of a host on the Internet. *PING* stands for Packet Internet Groper, but do not spell out. Describe if necessary.

pipe   Do not use as a verb in content for home users and information workers. Instead, use a more specific term, such as *send, move, copy, direct, redirect*, or *write*. Use as a verb only in content for software developers to refer to routing data from the standard output of one process to the standard input of another.

The symbol for a pipe in programming content is a vertical bar (|).

pixel   Short for *picture element*. One pixel is a measurement representing the smallest amount of information displayed graphically on the screen as a single dot. In content for home users or information workers, define pixel at first use.

placeholder   Do not use as a verb.

For more information about formatting of placeholders, see *Document Conventions* in Chapter 2, "Content Formatting and Layout."

plaintext vs. plain text   Use *plaintext* only to refer to nonencrypted or decrypted text in material about encryption. Use *plain text* to refer to ASCII files.

platform   Refers to hardware architecture and is sometimes used interchangeably with *operating environment* or *environment*. But because it can be ambiguous, avoid *platform*, particularly in content for home users and information workers.

Platform can be used in content for software developers if necessary to distinguish differing behaviors of a function or other API element in various operating systems, but whenever possible use *operating system* for clarity.

Cross-platform is acceptable in content for software developers or information technology professionals to refer to a program or device that can run on more than one operating system.

Use *on* to refer to a hardware platform: "on the Macintosh," but "in Windows XP."

See Also: *operating environment, operating system*

Plug and Play   Use only as a noun or an adjective. Use capitalization and spacing as shown; do not hyphenate. *Plug and Play* refers to a set of specifications developed by Intel for automatic configuration of a computer to work with various peripheral devices.

For more information, see the *Microsoft Computer Dictionary*.

plug-in   A component that permits a specific browser to recognize and support the file format of an object embedded in an HTML document. Do not use as a synonym for *add-in* or *add-on*.

point to   Use *point to* in procedures involving submenus that do not need to be clicked.

Correct

Click Start, point to All Programs, and then click Windows Update.

Also use *point to* to refer to positioning the mouse pointer at the appropriate location on the screen—for example, "Point to the window border." "Move the mouse pointer to" is acceptable phrasing only when teaching beginning skills.

pointer   Use *pointer* to refer to the arrow or other shape that moves when the user moves the mouse or other pointing device. Although the pointer can assume many shapes, do not use descriptive labels to refer to the pointer. It is all right to use descriptive labels in a discussion of the different appearances the pointer can take. For more information about pointer shapes, see *Official Guidelines for User Interface Developers and Designers* available at *http://msdn.microsoft.com*. In a programming context, a pointer is a variable that contains a memory location. In the rare cases where both types of pointer are under discussion, use *mouse pointer* and *pointer variable* as necessary to avoid ambiguity.

For more information, see *Mouse Terminology* in Chapter 1, "Documenting the User Interface."

P

pop-up   Do not use as a noun. Avoid as a verb; instead, use a term that more accurately describes the action, such as *open* or *appear*.

It is all right, if necessary to follow the application programming interface, to use *pop-up menu* in content for software developers to describe the menu that appears when the user right-clicks an item. If you must use a term to describe this type of menu in content for home users or information workers, use *shortcut menu*.

Pop-up window is acceptable in references to windows that pop up in context-sensitive Help. Do not use *pop-up window* as a synonym for *dialog box*.

Correct

Answer the questions in the wizard as they appear.

Some commands carry out an action immediately; others open a dialog box so that you can select options.

A pop-up window gives additional information about an option.

If you want to print the information in a pop-up window, right-click the window, and then click **Print Topic**.

Incorrect

Answer the questions in the wizard as they pop up.

Some commands carry out an action immediately; others open a pop-up window so that you can select options.

See Also: *shortcut menu*

port   As in *printer port* or *communications port*. Use the verb forms *port to* and *port for* only in content for software developers and information technology professionals in reference to portability. Avoid them in content for home users and information workers.

portable computer   Whenever possible, use the generic term *portable computer* in discussions about notebook, laptop, and other portable computers. In general, avoid these other designations because each refers specifically to a particular size and weight range. For more information about sizes, see *Microsoft Computer Dictionary*.

Do not use *portable* as a noun.

portrait orientation   Printing orientation so that the page is longer than it is wide.

Portrait orientation

Compare with *landscape orientation*.

post Use *post* to refer to the act of sending a message to a newsgroup or public folder, as opposed to sending it to a person.

Avoid using *post* as a noun to refer to the item sent, unless necessary for consistency with the user interface. (The use of *post* as both a noun and a verb in commands under one menu can be confusing.) Instead, use *article*, *message*, or another specific term, depending on the context, to refer to the material sent.

Avoid using *post* as a synonym for *publish*, especially when referring to publishing material on the Web.

post office vs. postoffice One word, lowercase, when referring to the component of an e-mail system; otherwise, use two words.

pound key, pound sign (#) Do not use either term to refer to the keyboard key name; use *number sign* instead. It is acceptable, however, to use *pound key (#)* when referring specifically to telephones or the telephone keypad.

See Also: *number sign (#)*

power cord Not *power cable*.

power down, power up; power off, power on Do not use; use *turn off* and *turn on* instead. Do not use *shut down* to refer to turning off a computer.

See Also: *shut down, shutdown, Shut Down; turn on, turn off*

power user Avoid outside the context of the Power Users administrative group in Windows. *Power user* as a classification of expertise is vague. To some it may mean somebody who can write a macro; to others it may mean somebody who can edit the system registry by hand. It is far safer to identify the specific knowledge or skill you are referring to.

pre- In general, do not hyphenate words beginning with *pre*, such as *preallocate* and *preempt*, unless it is necessary to avoid confusion, as in *pre-engineered*, or if *pre* is followed by a proper noun, as in *pre-C++*. If in doubt, check the *American Heritage Dictionary* or your project style sheet.

preceding Use *preceding*, *previous*, or *earlier* instead of *above* to mean earlier in a book or Help topic. In online Help, do not use any of these words to refer to a different topic that appears earlier in the table of contents. Provide an explicit cross-reference instead.

For more information, see *Cross-References* in Chapter 2, "Content Formatting and Layout."

Preface Do not use "Preface" as the title of the introductory material in documentation. Use "Introduction" or a more descriptive title appropriate to the audience, such as "Before You Begin."

press   Differentiate among the terms *press, type, enter*, and *use*. Use the following guidelines:

- Use *press*, not *depress* or *type*, when pressing a key initiates an action within the program or moves the user's position within a document or worksheet—for example, "press ENTER" or "press N." Use *pressed in* and *not pressed in*, not *depressed* and *not depressed*, to refer to the position of 3-D toggle keys.

- Use *use* in situations when *press* might be confusing, such as when referring to a type of key such as the arrow keys or function keys. In such cases, *press* might make users think they need to press all the keys simultaneously—for example, "use the arrow keys to move around the document."

- Use *type*, not *enter*, to direct a user to type information that will appear on the screen—for example, "type your name."

- Do not use *strike* or *hit*.

- Do not use *press* as a synonym for *click*.

  Correct

  Type your name, and then press ENTER.

  Press CTRL+F, and then type the text you want to search for.

  To save your file, press Y.

  To move the insertion point, use the arrow keys.

  Incorrect

  To save your file, use CTRL+S.

  Hit ENTER to begin a new paragraph.

print, printout   Use *print*, not *print out*, as a verb. It is all right to use *printout* as the result of a print job, if necessary, but try to be more specific.

print queue   Not printer queue.

privileges   Do not use as a synonym for *permissions* or *rights*.

  See Also: permissions; rights

program file   Acceptable, especially if necessary to avoid *executable file* in content for home users and information workers, but use the specific name of the file whenever possible.

program vs. application   Whenever possible, refer to a product by its descriptor, such as *database management system, spreadsheet,* or *publishing toolkit*, rather than as *program* or *application*. For example, refer to Microsoft Visual FoxPro as a "relational database development system."

If that is not possible, follow these general guidelines:

- Use *program*, not *application*, in material written for home users and information workers.

- Use *application* only in content for software developers and information technology professionals, especially to refer to a grouping of software that includes both executable files and other software components, such as a database.

- Do not use *program application*.

If in doubt, consult your project's style sheet.

See Also: applet

progress indicator   A control that displays the percentage of a particular process that has been completed, such as printing or setting up a program. Do not refer to it as a "slider."

Progress indicator

prohibition sign   Use to describe the circle with a line through it that is commonly superimposed over another symbol to indicate an activity that is not permitted.

Prohibition sign

prompt   Do not use *prompt* as a synonym for *message*. A prompt is a signal, which may or may not be a message, that a program or the operating system is waiting for the user to take some action. In general, restrict the use of *prompt* as a noun to the command prompt.

Use *prompt* as a verb to describe the act of requesting information or an action from the user.

Correct

If you receive a message that the association information is incomplete ...

When you run Setup, you are prompted to insert disks one by one.

Incorrect

If you receive a prompt that the association information is incomplete ...

See Also: command prompt

prop   Do not use as a slang form of *propagate*, as in "propping files to a server" or "propping information to a database."

properties   Properties are attributes or characteristics of an object used to define its state, appearance, or value. For example, the Special Effect property in Microsoft Access determines the appearance of a control on a form, such as sunken, raised, or flat.

Outside a programming context, *property* can be a vague term. Avoid using it except for a specific reference to something named as a property. Use *value* or *setting* instead to refer to a specific characteristic a user can set (such as the specific color of a font) or *attribute* for the general characteristic (such as "color is an attribute of fonts").

In syntax descriptions, properties are often bold, but always check your project style sheet.

See Also: attribute

property sheet, property page   *Property sheet* refers either to a secondary window that displays the properties of an object after carrying out the **Properties** command or to a collection of tabs or *property pages* that make up a dialog box.

In general, do not use the terms *property sheet* and *property page* in content for home users or information workers; use *dialog box* or *tab* instead. If your product uses *property sheets*, see your project style sheet for specific usage of the term.

For more information, see *Dialog Boxes and Property Sheets* in Chapter 1, "Documenting the User Interface."

protected mode   Not *protect mode*. Use only in technical documentation.

pull quote   Two words. Refers to a brief excerpt visually set off from the main text, usually in large type, to draw the reader's attention to the content.

pull-down   Do not use as a noun. Avoid in describing menus except in content for software developers.

See Also: drop-down

purge   Do not use because of negative associations in ordinary English usage. Use *delete*, *clear*, or *remove* instead.

push button, push-button   Two words, hyphenated as an adjective.

Avoid in all contexts. If you must use a technical term to refer to a button, use *button* or *command button*. In content for software developers, *push button* can be included parenthetically and in indexes, if necessary.

For more information, see *Dialog Boxes and Property Sheets* in Chapter 1, "Documenting the User Interface."

See Also: command button

push-to-talk   Do not capitalize in text. In titles, capitalize as *Push-to-Talk*.

Q

quality   Do not use *quality* alone as an adjective.

Correct

Microsoft Word is a high-quality word processor.

Incorrect

Microsoft Word is a quality product.

quarter inch   In general, use *a quarter inch*, not *quarter of an inch* or *one-quarter inch*.

quick key   Do not use; instead, use *keyboard shortcut*.

See Also: *keyboard shortcut*

quit   Avoid. Use *exit* instead to refer to the user action of closing a program. Use *close* to refer to the user action of closing a document or a window. Use *close* to refer to the action a program takes to close itself. Use *log off* to refer to ending a user session on a computer or on a network or Internet connection.

See Also: *close; exit; log on, log off, logon, logoff*

R

radio button   For globalization reasons, do not use in content for home users, information workers, or information technology professionals. Refer to the option button by its label or use *option* instead. If necessary to avoid ambiguity, use *option button*.

Avoid in content for software developers. If *radio button* appears in the application programming interface, refer to the button itself as an option button, "also known as a radio button." Include *radio button* in the index with a cross-reference to *option button*.

For more information, see *Dialog Boxes and Property Sheets* in Chapter 1, "Documenting the User Interface."

See Also: option, option button

radix, radixes   Do not use *radices* as the plural.

ragged right   Acceptable to refer to the uneven right edge in documents. Opposite of *right-aligned*.

RAM   Acronym for *random access memory*. Spell out at first mention if your audience is unfamiliar with the term.

See Also: memory

range selection   Avoid. In content for home users and information workers, use a phrase such as "a range of items" to refer to a selection of adjoining pages, cells, and so on.

Use the same type of phrasing in content for software developers and information technology professionals, but if you are describing the feature, use *adjacent selection*.

The selection of more than one nonadjacent item is called a *multiple selection*.

See Also: adjacent selection; multiple selection; nonadjacent selection

re-   In general, do not hyphenate words beginning with the prefix *re-* unless it is necessary to avoid confusion or *re-* is followed by a word that is ordinarily capitalized. If in doubt, check the *American Heritage Dictionary* or your project style sheet.

> **Correct**
> reenter
> recover [to get back or regain]
> re-cover [to cover again]
> recreate [to take part in a recreational activity]
> re-create [to create anew]

Avoid using *re-* words (such as *resize* or *restart*) unless you mean that a user should redo or repeat an action. The root word (*size* or *start*) is often enough.

read-only   Always hyphenate.

Correct

read-only memory

This file is read-only.

read/write   Use *read/write*, not *read-write*, as in "read/write permission."

read/write permission   Not *read/write access*. Files and devices have read/write properties, but users have the permission to access those files and devices.

real time, real-time   Two words as a noun. Hyphenate as an adjective.

Correct

Real-time operations happen at the same rate as human perceptions of time.

In chat rooms, users communicate in real time.

reboot   Do not use; use *restart* instead, and take care to establish that it is the computer, not a program, that is restarting.

Correct

After Setup is complete, restart your computer.

Incorrect

After Setup is complete, reboot your computer.

Restart after Setup is complete.

If the user interface or application programming interface uses *reboot* in a label or element name, it is all right to reproduce the label or element name, but use *restart* to refer to the action described.

Correct

The **Reboot** method shuts down the computer and then restarts it.

recommend   It is all right, but not required, to make recommendations directly by using a phrase such as *we recommend*. Alternate phrasings are also acceptable. Do not use *recommend* when something is required. Avoid *it is recommended*.

Correct

We recommend at least 256 MB of RAM to run this program.

This program performs best with at least 256 MB of RAM.

You must have at least 128 MB of RAM to run this program, but for best performance you should have at least 256 MB.

Incorrect

It is recommended that you have at least 256 MB of RAM to run this program.

See Also: *should vs. must*

Recycle Bin
Use with the article *the*, as in "the Recycle Bin." In Windows 95 and later, the Recycle Bin is a temporary storage place for deleted files. Apply bold formatting in procedures.

Recycle Bin

refresh
Use *refresh* to refer to updating a Web page. Avoid using in documentation to describe the action of an image being restored on the screen or data being updated; instead, use *redraw* or *update*. To refer to the **Refresh** command, use language such as: "To update the screen, click **Refresh**."

registry, registry settings
The *registry* is a database that stores configuration data about the user, the installed programs and applications, and the specific hardware. The registry has a hierarchical structure, with the first level in the path called a subtree. The next level is called a *key*, and all levels below keys are *subkeys*.

Use lowercase for the word *registry* except when it is part of a named system component, such as the Registry Editor. The first-level subtrees are system-defined and are in all uppercase letters, with words separated by underscores. Registry subtrees are usually bold.

Correct

HKEY_CLASSES_ROOT

HKEY_LOCAL_MACHINE

Keys are developer-defined and are usually all uppercase or mixed caps, with no underscores. Subkeys are usually mixed case.

Correct

SOFTWARE

ApplicationIdentifier

Application Identifier *Name*

stockfile

the new program subkey

An entire subkey path is referred to as a *subkey*, not a *path*. This is a typical subkey:

Correct

\HKEY_LOCAL_MACHINE\SOFTWARE\Microsoft\Jet\3.5\Engines\Xbase subkey

For a subkey, the items in the **Name** column are *entries*. The items in the **Data** column are *values*.

R

reinitialize   Do not use to mean *restart*.

> *See Also:* *initialize*

release notes   Use this term to refer to information about test and beta versions of a product. For more information, see *Readme Files and Release Notes* in Chapter 9, "Common Style Problems."

REM statement   Short for "remark statement," which is the term for a comment in BASIC and some other programs. Do not use generically to refer to a comment. Use *comment* instead.

For more information, see *Code Comments* in Chapter 4, "Content for Software Developers."

remote   Acceptable to describe a person or computer at another site. In programming, a remote computer is usually a computer connected, directly or indirectly, to the computer a program is running on. Do not use *remote drive* to describe a disk drive on a remote computer. Use *network drive* instead.

Do not use *remote* as a noun except to refer to a remote control device, such as that used to operate a TV set.

remove   Do not use *remove* to mean *delete*. *Remove* is correct in the following contexts:

- As a preferred synonym for *uninstall*
- As a synonym for *unload*
- To refer to taking an item off a list in a dialog box that has **Add** and **Remove** buttons
- To refer to taking a toolbar button off a toolbar, or hiding displayed data without deleting the data, such as columns in Windows Explorer

> *See Also:* *delete; load; uninstall*

replace   Do not use as a noun.

Correct

You can replace all instances of an incorrect term at one time.

Incorrect

You can do a global replace of an incorrect term.

In general, use *replace*, not *overwrite*, in instances of replacing a file.

Correct

Replace the selected text with the new text.
Replace the file with the changed file.

> *See Also:* *find and replace*

restore   Use to refer to restoring an item that was deleted. Do not use *undelete*.

See Also: *undelete*

Restore button   Do not use *Restore box* or *Restore icon*. Refers to the button containing the image of two windows. It appears in the upper-right corner of a window near the **Close** button and can replace either the **Minimize** or, more often, the **Maximize** button. Clicking it restores a document to its previous size.

Restore button

right   Not *right-hand*. Use *upper right* or *lower right, rightmost*, and so on. Include a hyphen if modifying a noun, as in *upper-right corner*.

right align, right-aligned   Use to refer to text that is aligned at the right margin. Hyphenate *right-aligned* in all positions in the sentence. Do not use *right-justified*.

See Also: *justified; left align, left-aligned*

right mouse button   In most content, use this term rather than *secondary mouse button*, *mouse button 2*, or other terms. Even though a user can program a mouse to switch buttons, usability studies show that most users understand this commonly used term.

For more information, see *Mouse Terminology* in Chapter 1, "Documenting the User Interface."

right-click   Acceptable to describe clicking the secondary (normally right) mouse button. For very basic content, define the term if necessary.

Correct
Using the right mouse button (right-click) ...
Right-click to select the file.

right-hand   Do not use; use just *right* instead.

See Also: *right*

rightmost   One word.

Avoid giving directional cues for accessibility reasons. If you must, however, use *rightmost* to refer to something at the farthest right side instead of *farthest right, far-right*, or similar terms.

rights   Use *rights* only in a nonspecific way to refer to system actions that are authorized by the system administrator. For specific references, use *user rights*.

Do not confuse *rights*, which apply to system operations, with *permissions*, which apply to specific system resources such as files or printers.

Do not use *privileges* as a synonym for *rights*.

> **Correct**
>
> Domain administrators should use a primary user account, which has basic user rights in the domain.

See Also: *permissions; user rights*

rip   Avoid in the sense of transferring music or video from a CD or DVD to a hard disk. If you must use *rip*, define on first mention and provide a glossary entry.

ROM   Acronym for *read-only memory*. Spell out at first mention, unless you are positive that your audience knows the term.

See Also: *memory*

roman   In general, don't use *roman type, light type,* or *lightface* unless you need to define or describe the font style; instead, use just *roman*. Do not use as a verb. Note that it is not capitalized.

> **Correct**
>
> Use roman, rather than italic, for most text.

For more information, see *Document Conventions* in Chapter 2, "Content Formatting and Layout."

See Also: *font and font style*

root directory   Use this term, not *home directory*, to refer to the directory or folder (indicated in MS-DOS with a backslash: \) from which all other directories or folders branch. Do not shorten to *root* when you mean the directory.

> **Correct**
>
> Change to the root directory and type
>
> **edit autoexec.bat**

See Also: *directory; folder*

run time, runtime, run-time   *Run time* is the time during which an application is running.

> **Correct**
>
> You can enter and modify data at run time. During design time, you create objects and modify their design.

A *runtime* is an environment that is required to run programs that are not compiled to machine language. Do not use *runtime* as a synonym for reader programs such as Microsoft Office file viewers.

The adjective *run-time* describes a thing that is occurring or relevant at run time.

> **Correct**
>
> Microsoft Access file viewer
>
> The common language runtime is a key element of the .NET Framework.
>
> run-time error
>
> run-time state
>
> **Incorrect**
>
> Microsoft Access runtime

In headings that use title-style capitalization, capitalize as *Run Time*, *Runtime*, and *Run-Time*.

run vs. execute   Avoid using *execute* to refer to running a program or macro. Use *run* instead.

In content for software developers or information technology professionals, it is acceptable to use *execute* to refer to programming processes, especially if required by the user interface or the application programming interface, but *run* is still preferable.

> **Correct**
>
> While Windows defragments your disk, you can use your computer to carry out other tasks.
>
> You can temporarily stop Disk Defragmenter so you can run other programs at full speed.

run vs. run on   A computer runs an operating system such as Microsoft Windows NT Server, but a program runs on the operating system.

Correct

Many companies are configuring their computers to run Windows NT Server.

They have to install upgraded programs to run on Windows NT Server.

running foot, running head   Use *footer* and *header* instead; *running foot* and *running head* are acceptable if needed for clarification or as keywords or index entries.

See Also: *footer; header*

R

S

(s) Do not add (*s*) to a singular noun to indicate that it can be singular or plural. In general, use plural, but be guided by meaning. Alternatively, if it's important to indicate both, use *one or more*.

> **Correct**
>
> To add rows or columns to a table, ...
>
> To add one or more rows to a table, ...
>
> **Incorrect**
>
> To add a row(s) or column(s) to a table, ...

sample vs. preview   A *sample* is a graphic representation of something that might show up on screen, not an exact representation of what is in the file the user is working on.

A *preview* is a graphic representation of exactly what the user will see on screen.

save   Do not use as a noun.

> **Correct**
>
> Before you turn off your computer, save your files.
>
> **Incorrect**
>
> Before you turn off your computer, do a save of your files.

Use these prepositions with save: "save *on* a disk," "save *to* a file," and "save *for* a rainy day."

scale up   In general, use *scale up*, not *upsize*, even though the jargon *upsize* is becoming common in client/server products.

scan line   Two words. Refers to either the row of pixels read by a scanning device or one of the horizontal lines on a display screen.

screen   Use instead of *screenful* or *full screen*. It is all right, however, to say that a program is running in *full-screen mode*.

Use *screen* to refer to the graphic portion of a visual output device. Use *display* as a general term for visual output devices, such as "CRT-based display" or "flat-panel display."

See Also: display; monitor

screen resolution   Use *number×number*, not *number by number*, as in "640×480," not "640 by 480." Use the multiplication sign, not an *x*.

> *See Also:* *multiplication sign*

screened subnet   Do not use, except on first mention, in which case use *perimeter network* (also known as *DMZ, demilitarized zone,* and *screened subnet*). On subsequent mention, use perimeter network. Include DMZ, demilitarized zone, and screened subnet in the index and glossary with cross-references to perimeter network.

> *See Also:* *perimeter network*

ScreenTip   Generic term for any on-screen tip, such as a ToolTip. Used especially in end-user documentation in Office.

script, scripting language   Whenever possible, refer to a script generically. That is, just use *script* when you are referring to the code.

> *See Also:* *Java, JScript, JavaScript; scriptlet*

scriptlet   Use only to refer to the Web component called a scriptlet. Use *script* in all other cases or use a more specific term if necessary.

scroll   *Scroll* does not take a direct object. Use directional signals or prepositions with *scroll*.

If the concept of scrolling is already clear, use a verb phrase such as *move through*.

With the IntelliMouse pointing device, the user scrolls within the document by rotating the wheel of the mouse. It is all right to use *scroll up* and *scroll down* to describe this behavior.

Correct

> You can scroll through the document to get to the end.
> Drag the scroll box to move through the information.
> Scroll down until you see the new folder.

Incorrect

> You can scroll the document to get to the end.
> Drag the scroll box to scroll the information.

scroll arrow, scroll bar, scroll box   Use these terms specifically to refer to the interface element shown. Do not use *arrow* to refer to the *scroll arrow*; it can be confused with an up or down arrow.

Scroll arrow   Scroll box

Scroll arrow and scroll box

Do not use *gray* or *shaded area* to refer to the *scroll bar*.

Do not use *slider* or *slider box* as a synonym for *scroll box*.

search engine   Acceptable in content for software developers or information technology professionals to refer to a program that searches for keywords in documents or in a database. The term is now used most often in connection with services and programs that search the Internet.

Avoid in content for home users and information workers. Refer instead to the action itself ("Search for interesting Web sites") or use *search service* or *search page*.

search, search and replace   Do not use for the search and substitution features; use *find* and *replace* instead.

Use search, find, and replace as verbs, not nouns. Avoid *search your document*; use *search through your document* instead.

> **Correct**
>
> Find the word "gem" and replace it with "jewel."
>
> Search through your document for comments in red.

> **Incorrect**
>
> Do a search and replace.
>
> Search your document for comments in red.

See Also: *find and replace*

secondary menu   Avoid; use *submenu* instead.

See Also: *submenu*

security update   A broadly released fix for a product-specific security-related issue.

See Also: *service pack; update*

select   Use *select* to refer to marking text, cells, and similar items that will be subject to a user action, such as copying text. Items so marked are called *the selection, selected text, selected cells*, or whatever.

Use *select* to refer to adding a check to a check box or to clicking an item in a list box or a combo box. Do not use *select* as a general term for clicking options in a dialog box.

Do not use *highlight* as a synonym for *select*. Selecting is a standard procedure, and *highlight* can often be confused with product features such as text highlighters that only provide visual emphasis.

Do not use *pick* as a synonym for *select*.

See Also: *choose; click; highlight*

selection cursor   In general, avoid this term, which refers to the marker that shows where the user is working in a window or dialog box or shows what is selected. Use *insertion point* or *pointer* instead.

See Also: *insertion point*

S

service pack   Use to refer to a cumulative set of all hotfixes, security updates, updates, and critical updates that address problems found in all components of a product since its original release.

Service release is an obsolete term. Use *service pack* instead.

It is all right, but not required, to abbreviate *service pack* as *SP* to identify a particular service pack. If you spell out *service pack* in this case, capitalize the term.

Always spell out *service pack* in other contexts.

Correct

This program requires Windows 2000 SP3 or later.

This program requires Windows 2000 Service Pack 3 or later.

This service pack addresses all known security vulnerabilities.

Incorrect

This SP addresses all known security vulnerabilities.

Do not confuse *service pack* with *update rollup*, which contains multiple bug fixes but is not as comprehensive as a service pack.

See Also: update

set up, setup, Setup (the program)   Two words as a verb, one word as an adjective or a noun. Capitalize the Setup (one word) program. Do not hyphenate.

Verb

Have everything unpacked before you set up your computer.

Adjective

The setup time should be about 15 minutes.

Noun

Your office setup should be ergonomically designed.

Run Setup before you open other programs.

Insert Setup Disk 1 in drive A.

See Also: install

set vs. specify   It is worth avoiding words like *set* and *specify* that make general reference to user actions. A better approach is to be specific about the action the user should take.

Correct

Color an appointment or meeting.

Right-click an appointment or meeting, point to **Label** on the shortcut menu, and then click a color in the list.

Avoid

Specify the color of an appointment or meeting.

Right-click an appointment or meeting, point to **Label** on the shortcut menu, and then specify a color in the list.

Do not use *set* to indicate the user action of entering or selecting a value in a dialog box. Because *set* has so many potential meanings, it is a difficult word for non-native speakers of English. If you must make a general reference to such a user action, use *specify* instead.

Programmers are accustomed to, and expect to see, references to getting and setting properties, so it is all right to use *set* in content for software developers to indicate the developer action of entering or selecting the value of a property, whether in source code or through the user interface.

setting   Use *setting* or *value* in content for home users and information workers to refer to a specific value that the user can set, such as the specific color of a font.

Correct

You can choose blue as the setting for your font.

Differentiate from *attribute*, which is the general characteristic that can be set.

Correct

Color is one attribute of fonts.

Avoid *property* in general content unless you are discussing something that is specifically identified as a property.

See Also: *properties*

set-top box   Standard industry term for the computer that sits on top of a television set to create two-way communication. Note hyphen. Do not use the abbreviation *STB*.

shaded   Use *shaded*, not *grayed* or *dimmed*, to describe the appearance of a check box that may occur when there is a mixture of settings for a selection in a group of options. The shaded appearance indicates that some previously checked options may make parts of the selection different from the rest.

Shaded options

See Also: *dimmed; gray, grayed*

shell   Acceptable as a noun in content for software developers or information technology professionals. Avoid in other contexts.

Avoid using *shell* or *shell out* as a verb. Use more precise terminology instead, such as "create a new shell" or "return to the operating system."

shortcut   One word, lowercase, as a noun or an adjective. Exception: Capitalize for the Outlook Shortcuts that appear on the Office Shortcut Bar.

Do not use as a synonym for *hyperlink*.

shortcut key   Do not use in content for home users or information workers. Use *keyboard shortcut* instead.

Shortcut key is best avoided entirely, but it is permissible in developer documentation or in material about customizing the user interface when you must distinguish between an access key and a shortcut key. In such cases, use *shortcut key* to denote a key combination used to perform a command, and be sure to provide a definition.

If you must use *shortcut key*, use the singular form when only one key is required: "the shortcut key F1." Otherwise, use the plural: "the shortcut keys CTRL+N."

For more information, see *Key Names* in Chapter 1, "Documenting the User Interface."

See Also: *access key; key combination; keyboard shortcut*

shortcut menu   The shortcut menu appears when the user right-clicks an item. It lists commands pertaining only to the item that the user clicked.

Shortcut menu

In general, it should not be necessary outside a programming context to use a term for the shortcut menu. If you must, use *shortcut menu*, not *context menu* or *pop-up menu*.

Correct

Right-click the selected text, and then click **Copy**.

Avoid

Right-click the selected text, and then click **Copy** on the shortcut menu.

should vs. must

Use *should* only to describe a user action that is recommended but optional. Use *must* only to describe a user action that is required.

Correct

You should periodically back up your data.

You must have at least 128 MB of RAM to run this program, but for best performance you should have at least 256 MB.

Windows does not provide for multiple versions of a file with the same name. To save different copies of a document, you must save each copy under a different file name.

Avoid using *should* to indicate probability. Wherever possible, express certainty. When that is not possible, use *may* or rephrase.

Correct

When you click **Submit**, the data is sent to the company, and you will get a confirmation e-mail message within 24 hours.

Incorrect

When you click **Submit**, the data is sent to the company, and you should get a confirmation e-mail message within 24 hours.

It is all right, and often better, to use alternate ways of specifying recommendations or requirements. For example, for required actions, you can use the imperative mood; for optional actions, you can use a phrase such as *we recommend*. In either case, you can rephrase the sentence entirely. Avoid *it is recommended*.

Correct

We recommend at least 256 MB of RAM to run this program.

See Also: *can vs. may*

S

shut down, shutdown, Shut Down

Two words as a verb, one word as a noun or an adjective. The **Shut Down** command on the **Start** menu of some versions of Windows is two words, capitalized.

Shut down refers to the orderly closing of the operating system. Do not use *shut down* to refer to turning off the power to a computer. Do not use *shut down* as a synonym for *close* or *exit*.

Correct

Shut down your computer before you turn it off.

This action shuts down Windows so that you can safely turn off the computer power. Many computers turn the power off automatically.

The accidental shutdown may have corrupted some files.

Before you turn off your computer, click **Start**, and then click **Shut Down**.

See Also: *close; exit; turn on, turn off*

sign in, sign out, sign on, sign up

Use *sign in* and *sign out* to refer to creating and ending a user session for an Internet account. You *sign in to* (not *sign into*) a Microsoft .NET Passport account, an Internet service provider account, or an XML Web service. Use *log on* and *log off* to describe creating and ending a user session for a computer or intranet user account.

Use *connect*, *make a connection*, and similar phrases to refer to the act of physically attaching a computer to a network, whether intranet or Internet.

Use *sign on* only as part of the term *single sign on* (SSO). The user action is still *signing in*, even though the technology is called *single sign on*. Use *sign off* only informally to refer to getting approval. Otherwise, do not use *sign on* and *sign off* unless these terms appear in the user interface.

Use *sign out* to refer to closing a user session on the Internet.

Use *sign up* to refer to enrolling in a service.

Hyphenate these terms only when they are used as adjectives, not as verb phrases.

Correct

Type your sign-in name here.

Sign in here.

You can sign up for Internet Explorer by filling in the following information.

You can connect your server to the Internet.

See Also: *log on, log off, logon, logoff*

simply

Avoid. It is generally unnecessary and can sound condescending if the user does not find the task as simple as the writer does.

site map   Two words.

size   Acceptable as a verb, as in "size the window." It is also acceptable to use *resize* to mean "change the size of."

slider   Control that lets users set a value on a continuous range of possible values, such as screen brightness, mouse-click speed, or volume. In content for software developers, sometimes referred to as a *trackbar control*.

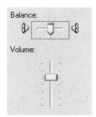

Sliders

Do not refer to the scroll box or a progress indicator as a slider.

> **Correct**
> Move the slider to the left to decrease pointer speed.

For more information, see *Dialog Boxes and Property Sheets* in Chapter 1, "Documenting the User Interface."

See Also: progress indicator

small caps   Do not use small caps in documentation for key names or A.M. and P.M; they are awkward to designate in code such as HTML.

You can use the term *small caps* in documents. If necessary for clarity, refer to them as *small capitals* first, followed by a phrase such as "often referred to as 'small caps.' "

smart card, Smart Card   Use lowercase for generic references to smart cards or smart card technology. Capitalize as part of proper names, but not in general references to smart card implementations.

snap-in   A program that runs in the context of Microsoft Management Console.

soft copy   Avoid; it is jargon formed by analogy with *hard copy*. Use a more specific term, such as *electronic document* or *file*, instead.

software update   Use to describe any update, update rollup, service pack, feature pack, critical update, security update, or hotfix used to improve or fix a software product.

S

spam   *Spam* is a problem for the global audience, and not all readers interpret it in the same way. Nevertheless, it is in wide use and is acceptable in certain circumstances.

Use *spam* only to refer to unsolicited commercial e-mail. Do not use *spam* to refer generally to commercial e-mail, such as bulk e-mail sent to a customer list. Do not use *spam* to refer to an inappropriate posting to a large distribution list, newsgroup, or listserv.

Do not use *spam* as a verb.

specification   Capitalize *specification* when it is part of the title of a document, as in *The Network Driver Interface Specification*. Avoid the informal *spec* in documentation.

speed key   Do not use. Use *keyboard shortcut* instead.

See Also: shortcut key

spelling checker   Refer to the tool as the *spelling checker*, not *spell checker* or *Spell Checker*. Do not use *spell check* as a verb or noun.

Correct

Use the spelling checker to check the spelling in the document.

Incorrect

Spell check the document.

Run the spell checker.

spider   Refers to an automated program that searches the Internet for new Web documents and places information about them in a database that can be accessed by a search engine. Define on first mention, and include a glossary entry if your audience may be unfamiliar with the term.

spin box   Use only in content for software developers to describe a control that users can move ("spin") through a fixed set of values, such as dates.

Spin box

In general content, refer to a spin box by its label, for example, the **Start time** box.

For more information, see *Dialog Boxes and Property Sheets* in Chapter 1, "Documenting the User Interface."

split bar   Refers to the horizontal or vertical double line that separates a window into two panes. In some programs, such as Windows Explorer, the window is already split, but the user can change the size of the panes. In other programs, such as Word or Excel, the user can split the window by using the split box. The term is acceptable in both technical and end-user documentation.

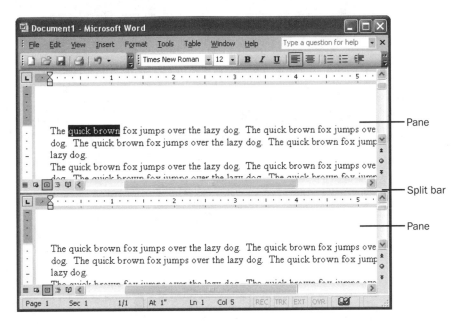

Split bar separating two panes

For more information, see *Screen Terminology* in Chapter 1, "Documenting the User Interface."

split box   Refers to the control at the top right of the vertical scroll bar (for horizontal splitting) or far right of the horizontal scroll bar (for vertical splitting). Users point to the split box to drag the split bar. The term is acceptable in all documentation.

Split box on a vertical scroll bar

spoofing   Refers to various practices that conceal the identity of a user account, an e-mail account, or a computer's Internet Protocol (IP) address that is taking some action. For example, e-mail spoofing involves forging the header of an e-mail message so that the message appears to come from someone other than the true sender.

Spoofing is a valid technical term, and it is all right to use it if you are sure your audience will understand your meaning. If you have doubts, especially in content for home users or information workers, define the term in place and add it to your glossary, or write around the term.

Where appropriate to avoid ambiguity, use a modifier to be as specific as possible about the kind of spoofing you are referring to, such as e-mail spoofing or IP spoofing.

spreadsheet   Do not use as a synonym for *worksheet*. A spreadsheet is a computer accounting program, such as Microsoft Excel; a worksheet is the document produced by a spreadsheet program.

SQL   When referring to Structured Query Language, SQL is pronounced "es-cue-el" and takes the article *an*—for example, "an SQL database."

As part of the name Microsoft SQL Server, SQL is pronounced "sequel."

stand-alone   Use as an adjective. Do not use as a noun.

Correct

You can use Word either as a stand-alone word processor or on a network.

Incorrect

Some early word processors were stand-alones.

start page   Do not use to refer to the Web page that appears when the user starts the browser. Use *home page* instead.

See Also: *home page*

start, Start (the menu)   In general, use *start*, as in "start a program," instead of *boot*; *initiate*; *initialize*; *issue*; *launch*; *turn on, turn off*; and similar words and phrases.

Capitalize references to the Start menu and the Start button on the taskbar, and always specify which one you are referring to. In procedures, refer to the Start button simply as **Start**, and use bold.

Do not refer to the Start button as the *Windows Start button*.

Correct

You have no doubt already noticed the new look of the Start button and other desktop elements.

Start Windows, and then click **Start** to start your programs.

On the taskbar, click **Start**, and then click **Run**.

Incorrect

Start Windows, and then click the **Start** button to start your programs.

On the taskbar, click the Windows **Start** button, and then click **Run**.

startup, start up   Avoid *start up* as a verb. Use *start* instead.

Avoid *startup* as a noun in content written for home users or information workers. Write around it if possible. It is all right to use *startup* as a noun in content written for developers or information technology professionals.

It is all right to use *startup* as an adjective in phrases such as *startup disk* and *startup screen*.

Correct

To start the program, click the icon.

When the program starts, a startup screen appears.

If there is a catastrophic failure, use the emergency startup disk to start Windows.

Incorrect

To start up the program, click the icon.

On startup, a splash screen appears.

If there is a catastrophic failure, use the emergency boot disk to start Windows.

See Also: *bootable disk; start, Start (the menu)*

status bar   Not *status line* or *message area*. Refers to the area at the bottom of a document window that lists the status of a document and gives other information, such as the meaning of a command. Messages appear on, not in, the status bar.

Correct

The page number is displayed on the status bar.

Follow these guidelines for writing effective status bar messages

- Use parallel constructions and begin the message with a verb.

  The message describing the **View** menu, for example, should read something like "Contains commands for customizing this window" and the message describing the Internet folder icon should read something like "Changes your Internet settings."

- Use present tense.

  For example, use "Changes your Internet settings," not "Change your Internet settings."

- Make sure the text is constructive. Try to avoid repeating the obvious.

  For example, even though the **File** menu is quite basic, a message such as "Contains commands for working with the selected items" gives some useful information with the inclusion of the phrase "selected items."

- Use complete sentences, including articles, and end with a period.

For more information, see *Screen Terminology* in Chapter 1, "Documenting the User Interface."

stop   Acceptable to use to refer to hardware operations, as in "stop a print job." Use *exit* with programs.

See Also: *exit*

storage, storage device   Do not use *storage* to refer to memory capability; use *disk space* instead. *Storage device* is acceptable as a generic term to refer to things such as disk and tape drives.

stream, streaming   Acceptable as a noun or verb to refer to video or other graphics coming to a browser or media player over the Internet. *Stream* is also an I/O management term in C.

Avoid other metaphorical uses.

strike   Do not use to refer to keyboard input; use *press* or *type* instead.

See Also: *press*

strikethrough   Not *strikeout* or *lineout*. Refers to the line crossing out words in revisions.

struct   Do not use in text to refer to a data structure identified by the **struct** language keyword. Use *structure* instead.

style sheet   Two words. Can refer to a file of instructions for formatting a document in word processing or desktop publishing, or to a list of words and phrases and how they are used or spelled in a particular document.

In Internet use, refers to a cascading style sheet (a .css file) attached to an HTML document that controls the formatting of tags on Web pages. The browser follows rules (a "cascading order") to determine precedence and resolve conflicts.

In an XML context, *XSL* is the abbreviation for Extensible Stylesheet Language. Even so, refer to an .xsl file as a *style sheet*.

See Also: *cascading style sheets*

sub-   In general, do not hyphenate words beginning with *sub-*, such as *subheading* and *subsection*, unless it is necessary to avoid confusion or if *sub* is followed by a proper noun, as in *sub-Saharan*. If in doubt, check the *American Heritage Dictionary* or your project style sheet.

subaddress   Do not use to refer to parts of an address that go to a specific place in a file, such as a bookmark. Use the specific term instead.

subclass   Do not use as a verb. Use a standard verb, such as *create a subclass*.

submenu   Describes the secondary menu that appears when the user selects a command that includes a small arrow on the right. Avoid in end-user documentation if possible, for example, by referring only to what appears on the screen. The term is acceptable in programmer documentation.

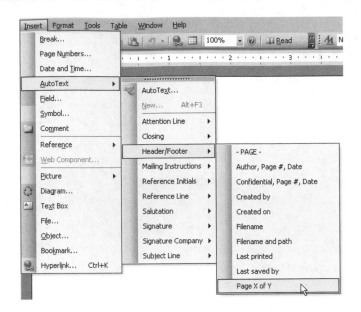

Submenus

Avoid the terms *cascading menu*, *hierarchical menu*, and *secondary menu*.

Correct (in a procedure)

On the **Edit** menu, point to **Clear**, and then click the item you want to clear.

For more information, see *Screen Terminology* in Chapter 1, "Documenting the User Interface."

Super VGA, SVGA
Use *Super VGA (SVGA)* on first mention. After that, it is all right to use *SVGA*. There is no need to spell out VGA in either case.

surf
To browse the Web. Generally implies a more random browsing than the less informal *browse*. Acceptable in informal contexts if accurate.

switch
Acceptable to use as a verb, as in "switch to another window." Use instead of *activate* or *toggle*.

Correct

To embed the new object, switch to the source document.

You can easily switch between open windows.

Incorrect

To embed the new object, activate the source document.

You can easily toggle between open windows.

Acceptable as a noun in content for software developers to refer to command-line and compiler options, such as **/Za**, if your project style sheet permits.

symbol   Use the word *symbol* to refer to a graphic or special character that represents something else, but differentiate a symbol from an icon. (An icon represents an object that the user can select and open. A symbol can appear on an icon.)

Follow these guidelines for discussing symbols:

Write out the name of the symbol in text and, if the symbol itself is important, enclose the symbol in parentheses. Use symbols alone only in tables and lists where space is at a premium or in mathematical expressions.

Correct

You can type a backslash (\) to return to the previous entry.

Only 75 percent of the students attended.

Incorrect

You can type a \ to return to the previous directory.

Only 75% of the students attended.

For screen elements such as buttons, you can use only a graphic of the button after it has been named once or if clicking it brings up a definition.

Correct

Click Minimize.

Click [_] .

Spell out *plus sign*, *minus sign*, *hyphen*, *period*, and *comma* when referring to them as key names.

Correct

Press COMMA.

Type a comma.

Press the PLUS SIGN (+).

Incorrect

Press ,.

Press +.

Write out plurals of symbols, showing the use in parentheses. Do not add s or 's to a symbol.

Correct

Type two backslashes (\\) to show a network connection.

Incorrect

Type two \'s to show a network connection.

Type two \\s to show a network connection.

Do not insert a space between a number and the symbol that it modifies.

Correct (to conserve space)

75%

<100

Incorrect

75 %

< 100

For more information, see *Measurements and Units of Measure* and *Names of Special Characters* in Chapter 9, "Common Style Problems."

sysop   Even though *sysop* is jargon for "system operator," it is acceptable in referring to the person who oversees or runs a bulletin board system or online communications system in content about such products. Define first. Avoid in all other documentation.

system   Use generically to refer to computer hardware configurations, not the computer alone. The system includes the computer and peripheral devices. It is not synonymous with, but can include, the *system software*.

See Also: *system software*

system administrator   Use only to refer to the person responsible for administering the use of a multiuser computer system. Generally, use *administrator* unless you must specify a particular kind. Use *network administrator* only to specifically refer to the administrator of networks.

system prompt   Do not use; use *command prompt* instead. If necessary, be specific in naming the command, as in "MS-DOS prompt."

See Also: *command prompt*

system software   Not *systems software*. Use generically to refer to an operating system or software that extends operating system functionality.

system tray   Do not use. Use *notification area* instead.

See Also: *notification area*

T

tab   Do not use as a verb.

Because multiple uses can be ambiguous, especially for the worldwide audience, use the noun *tab* alone to refer only to a tab in a property sheet. For other uses, clarify the meaning with a descriptor: the TAB key, a tab stop, or a tab mark on the ruler.

Correct

Use the TAB key to move through a dialog box.

Set a tab stop on the ruler.

Click the **View** tab.

Incorrect

You can tab through a dialog box.

Set a tab on the ruler.

For more information, see *Dialog Boxes and Property Sheets* in Chapter 1, "Documenting the User Interface."

table of contents   Do not use *Table of Contents* as the heading for the list of contents at the beginning of a document or file; use just *Contents* instead. It is correct, however, to refer generically to the *table of contents*.

TB   Do not use as an abbreviation for *terabyte*, which should not be abbreviated.

See Also: *terabyte*

terabyte   One terabyte is equal to 1,099,511,627,776 bytes, or 1,024 gigabytes.

Do not abbreviate.

Leave a space between the numeral and *terabyte* except when the measurement is used as an adjective preceding a noun. In that case, use a hyphen.

Correct

36 terabytes

36-terabyte database

When used as a noun in measurements, add *of* to form a prepositional phrase.

Correct

This database contains 36 terabytes of information.

For more information, see Measurements and Units of Measure in Chapter 9, "Common Style Problems."

that vs. which   *That* and *which* are often confused. Be sure to use the appropriate word. *That* introduces a restrictive clause, which is a clause that is essential for the sentence to make sense. A restrictive clause often defines the noun or phrase preceding it and is not separated from it by a comma. In general, do include the word *that* in restrictive clauses, even though in some clauses the sentence may be clear without it. Including *that* prevents ambiguity and helps translators understand the sentence.

Correct

You will need to supply information about applications that you want to run with Windows.

Incorrect

You will need to supply information about applications which you want to run with Windows.

You will need to supply information about applications you want to run with Windows.

Which introduces a nonrestrictive clause, which is a clause that could be omitted without affecting the meaning of the sentence. It is preceded by a comma. Nonrestrictive clauses often contain auxiliary or parenthetical information.

Correct

Your package contains the subsidiary information card, which you can use to obtain device drivers or local technical support.

Do not use *that* or *which* to refer to a person; instead use *who*.

See Also: who vs. that

then   *Then* is not a coordinate conjunction and thus cannot correctly join two independent clauses. Use *and* or another coordinate conjunction or *then* with a semicolon or another conjunctive adverb to connect independent clauses in, for example, two-part procedural steps.

Correct

On the **File** menu, click **Save As**, and then type the name of the file.

Incorrect

On the **File** menu, click **Save As**, then type the name of the file.

Avoid using *then* to introduce a subordinate clause that follows an *if* clause (an "if ...then" construction).

Correct

If you turn off the computer before shutting down all programs, you may lose data.

Incorrect

If you turn off the computer before shutting down all programs, then you may lose data.

thread   Acceptable to describe a series of articles or messages on the same topic in a newsgroup or e-mail discussion. In content for software developers, *thread* is acceptable in the context of threaded programming models.

three-dimensional, 3-D   *Three-dimensional* is preferred, but *3-D* is acceptable. Spell out at first mention. Use *3-D* in tables and indexes and where space is a problem, as well as to reflect the product interface.

Hyphenate both the spelled-out and abbreviated versions. Use *3D* (no hyphen) only as specified by product names.

time bomb   Two words.

time stamp   Two words.

time-out, time out   Always hyphenate as an adjective or noun. Do not hyphenate as a verbal phrase.

Correct

A time-out occurs if the connection can't be made.

If the connection isn't made, a time-out event occurs.

The connection timed out.

title bar   The horizontal bar at the top of a window that shows the name of the document or program. Acceptable term for all audiences.

Title bar

titled vs. entitled   Do not use *entitled* as a synonym for *titled;* instead, use *entitled* to mean "is owed." Books are *titled;* a user may be *entitled* to a set of documentation.

Titled usually leads to wordy phrases. If you must use it, it is not followed by a comma.

Correct

Look in the book titled *User's Guide,* which accompanies your software.

Look in the *User's Guide* that accompanies your software.

357

toggle   Use as an adjective, as in *toggle key*. A toggle key turns a particular mode on or off.

Do not use *toggle* as a verb; instead, use *switch, click,* or *turn on* and *turn off* to describe the action. For example, use the specific name of a toggle key or command to refer to what the user should do to switch between modes.

Correct

Use the CAPS LOCK key to switch from typing in capital letters to typing in lowercase.

To turn the Ruler on or off, click **Ruler** on the **Edit** menu.

Incorrect

Toggle the CAPS LOCK key on or off to switch from capital letters to lowercase.

To turn the Ruler on or off, toggle Ruler on the Edit menu.

tone   Avoid; use *beep* as a noun to refer to a sound, as in "when you hear the beep," unless the user can choose a particular sound.

See Also: beep

tool   Use *tool* to describe a feature that aids in accomplishing a task or set of tasks.

Do not use *utility* as a synonym for *tool* except in indexes and search vocabularies. By using different terms for the same thing, we encourage users to look for differences where none exist.

toolbar   Not *command bar* except in documentation for software developers.

In referring to a toolbar by name, do not capitalize *toolbar*.

The main toolbar that is on by default and contains buttons for basic tasks, such as opening and printing a file, is called the "standard toolbar."

In general, refer to toolbar buttons by the name that appears in the corresponding Tool-Tip. If you must use a term to refer to the buttons on a toolbar, use *toolbar buttons*.

Correct

1. Select the words you want to format as bold, and then click **Bold**.

2. On the **Drawing** toolbar, click **Insert WordArt**.

Incorrect

On the standard toolbar, click **Bold**.

toolbox   Generically, a toolbox is a collection of drawing or interface tools such as paint-
brushes, lines, circles, scissors, and spray cans. In programming applications such as
Visual Basic, the toolbox also includes controls that users can add to programs, such as
command buttons and option buttons. Tools in a toolbox differ from the commands on a
toolbar in that the shapes or controls often can be dragged to a document and manipu-
lated in some way.

Toolbox

Treat elements in a toolbox like any other options in dialog boxes. That is, in procedures
tell users to click a particular option and use bold for toolbox labels. Do not capitalize *toolbox* except to match the interface or if it's a specifically named product feature.

> **Correct**
>
> Insert a **Combo Box** control in the dialog box.

For more information, see *Dialog Boxes and Property Sheets* in Chapter 1, "Documenting
the User Interface."

toolkit   One word.

ToolTip   One word, with both *T*s capitalized, to refer to the feature.

> *See Also:* *ScreenTip*

top left, top right   Avoid; use *upper left* and *upper right* instead, which are hyphenated as
adjectives.

topic   As in *Help topic*; do not use *article* or *entry*.

toward   Not *towards*.

trailing   Acceptable to mean "following," as in *trailing period*, *trailing slash*, or *trailing space*.

TRUE   In general, use all uppercase to refer to a return value in content for software developers. If you are writing about a specific programming language, follow the capitalization used in that language.

turn on, turn off   Use instead of *power on, power off; start;* or *switch on, switch off* to mean turning the computer on and off.

Do not use to refer to selecting or clearing check boxes in procedures. Use *select* and *clear* or *click to select* instead. It is acceptable to use in text to refer to the status options such as multimedia on Web pages (as in, "You can turn off graphics").

turnkey   Always one word.

tutorial   Not *CBT* (for *computer-based training*). Use *online tutorial* to distinguish from a printed tutorial if necessary.

two-dimensional, 2-D   *Two-dimensional* is preferred, but *2-D* is acceptable. Spell out at first mention. Use *2-D* in tables and indexes and where space is a problem, as well as to reflect the product interface.

Hyphenate both the spelled out and abbreviated versions.

type vs. enter   Use *type*, not *type in* or *enter*, if information that the user types appears on the screen. An exception to this rule is that you can tell users to "enter" a file name, for example, in a combo box when they have the choice of typing a name or selecting one from a list. You can also use a combination of words such as "type or select" if space is not an issue.

Correct

Type your password.

Enter the file name.

Type the path to the server or select it from the list.

Incorrect

Type in your password.

Enter your password.

See Also: *press*

U

U.K.   Acceptable abbreviation for *United Kingdom* as a noun or adjective, but avoid except in tables or to save space. If you use the abbreviation, it is not necessary to spell out at first mention. Always use periods and no space.

un-   In general, do not hyphenate words beginning with *un-*, such as *undo* and *unread*, unless it is necessary to avoid confusion, as in *un-ionized*, or unless *un-* is followed by a proper noun, as in *un-American*. If in doubt, check the *American Heritage Dictionary* or your project style sheet.

unavailable   Use *unavailable*, not *grayed* or *disabled*, to refer to unusable commands and options on the interface. Use *dimmed* only if you have to describe their appearance.

> **Correct**
> You cannot use unavailable commands until your file meets certain conditions, such as having selected text. These commands appear dimmed on the menu.

For more information, see *Menus and Commands* in Chapter 1, "Documenting the User Interface."

See Also: *dimmed; disable*

uncheck, unmark, unselect   Do not use for check boxes or selections; use *clear the check box* or *cancel the selection* instead.

undelete   Do not use except to reflect the user interface or the application programming interface. Use *restore* instead.

Even if the product interface uses *undelete*, the action is still to *restore*.

> **Correct**
> To restore the deleted text, on the **Edit** menu click **Undelete**.

See Also: *restore*

underline, underscore   Use *underline* to refer to text formatting with underlined characters or to formatting. Use *underscore* to refer to the underscore character (_).

undo   Do not use the command name *Undo* as a noun to refer to undoing an action, especially in the plural. Write around instead, as in "to undo multiple actions" or "select the actions that you want to undo." It is acceptable to say that a command *undoes* an action.

uninstall   Do not use except to match existing user interface or, in programmer documentation, to refer to a particular type of program. Use *remove* instead.

Universal Naming Convention (UNC)   The system for indicating names of servers and computers, such as *Servername**Sharename*. Spell out on first mention. Use only in content for software developers or information technology professionals.

unprintable   Do not use; use *nonprinting* instead.

unregister   Acceptable term in content for software developers.

update   Use *update* as a noun to describe a broadly released bug fix for a problem that is not related to security. For a bug fix for a problem that is not related to security but that can affect the core functionality of a product, use *critical update*.

Do not use *patch* or *hotfix* to describe an update.

Do not use *update* as a general term for any change to a product. Use the specific term that is appropriate for the kind of change under discussion.

Do not use *update* to refer to a product upgrade.

Use *update rollup* to refer to a cumulative set of hotfixes, security updates, updates, and critical updates that are packaged together for easy deployment. An update rollup often targets a specific area, such as security, or a specific product component, such as Internet Information Services. Do not confuse with *service pack*, which refers to a cumulative set of all such fixes for defects found in all components since the original release of a product.

Use *update* as a verb to describe the action of installing a hotfix, security update, update, or service pack.

Use *software update* to refer to any update, update rollup, service pack, feature pack, critical update, security update, or hotfix used to improve or fix a software product.

Also use *update* as a verb instead of *refresh* to describe the action of an image being restored on the screen or data in a table being updated.

Correct

To update the appearance of your screen, click **Refresh**.

See Also: *hotfix*; *patch*; *refresh*; *security update*; *service pack*; *upgrade*

upgrade   Use to refer to installing a new version of a previously installed product. For example, a user might upgrade the operating system on her computer from Windows 2000 Workstation to Windows XP Professional.

Upgrade is acceptable as a noun, a verb, or an adjective.

Do not use *upgrade* as a synonym for *update*, *service pack*, or any other release that occurs between product versions.

> **Correct**
>
> To upgrade your operating system to Windows XP Professional, place the CD in the drive.
>
> To install the upgrade version, you must already have a previous version of the program on your computer.
>
> The upgrade was successful.

upper left, upper right   Use instead of *top left* and *top right*. Hyphenate as adjectives.

uppercase   One word. Do not use *uppercased*. Avoid using as a verb.

uppercase and lowercase   Not upper- and lowercase.

> *See Also:* *lowercase*

upsize   Avoid. Use *scale up* instead.

upward   Not *upwards*.

U.S.   Acceptable abbreviation for *United States* only when used as an adjective. Do not use *US*, *USA*, or *U.S.A.* Avoid except in tables or to save space.

If you use the abbreviation, it is not necessary to spell out at first mention. Always use periods and no space.

Spell out *United States* as a noun except when third-party legally required content specifies otherwise.

usable   Not *useable*.

Usenet   Use this term to refer to the collection of computers and networks that share news articles. It overlaps with the Internet, but is not identical to it. The term is from "User Network" and is sometimes seen all capped.

U

user name   Two words unless describing a label in the user interface. If the user interface uses *username*, use the one-word form only to describe the interface element.

Correct

In the **Username** box, enter your user name.

Incorrect

In the **Username** box, enter your username.

user rights   Use *user rights* to refer to Microsoft Windows security policies that apply to individual user accounts or administrative groups. The system administrator manages user rights through the User Rights Assignment snap-in. User rights are *assigned*, not *granted* or *allowed*.

If you refer to a named user right, use sentence-style capitalization and bold type for the name itself.

If an operation requires that the user be logged on to an account that is a member of a specific administrative group, refer to the group rather than to the associated user rights.

Do not use *privilege* as a synonym for *user right*.

Correct

You must have the **Perform volume maintenance tasks** user right to perform this task.

You must be logged on as a member of the Administrators group to perform this task.

Incorrect

You must have the **Perform volume maintenance tasks** privilege to perform this task.

using vs. by using   To accommodate the worldwide audience and to reduce the possibility of ambiguity, use *by using*, even if the preposition seems unnecessary. Be careful to avoid a dangling or misplaced modifier.

Ambiguous

You can change files using the Template utility.

Clearer

You can change files by using the Template utility.

You can change files that use the Template utility.

Using the Template utility, you can change files.

For more information, see *Dangling and Misplaced Modifiers* in Chapter 10, "Grammatical Elements."

See Also: using vs. with

using vs. with   Avoid *with* to mean "by using"; it is ambiguous and makes localization more difficult.

> **Correct**
>
> You can select part of the picture by using the dotted rectangle selection tool.

> **Incorrect**
>
> You can select part of the picture with the dotted rectangle selection tool.

With is acceptable in some marketing materials and sometimes with product names.

> **Correct**
>
> With Home Essentials, you can create professional documents quickly and easily.

See Also: *using vs. by using*

utility   Do not use. Use *tool* instead.

See Also: *tool*

utilize   Do not use as a synonym for *use*. Use only to mean "to find a practical use for."

> **Correct**
>
> Some applications are unable to use expanded memory.
>
> If a form contains many fields that use the same information, you can repeat the information with the ASK and REF fields.

U

V

value axis   In spreadsheet programs, refers to the (usually) vertical axis in charts and graphs that shows the values being measured or compared. For clarity, refer to it as the *value (y) axis* at first mention; *y-axis* is acceptable for subsequent mentions. You can also use *vertical (y) axis* in documentation for novices.

> *See Also:* *category axis*

VCR   Abbreviation for *videocassette recorder*. It is not necessary to spell out the term at first use.

versus, vs.   In headings, use the abbreviation *vs.*, all lowercase. In text, spell out as *versus*.

> **Correct**
>
> *Daily vs. Weekly Backups*

VGA and related terms   Do not spell out *VGA* and related graphics specifications such as *SVGA, XGA, UXGA, SXGA,* and *QXGA.*

Do not use *VGA+* to describe graphics specifications of higher resolution than VGA; there is no such thing.

It is all right to use the abbreviation for a graphics specification as a modifier for a graphics device such as an adapter or a monitor.

> **Correct**
>
> QXGA graphics adapter
>
> SVGA monitor
>
> VGA device

For more information, see Chapter 12, "List of Acronyms and Abbreviations."

via   *Via* implies a geographic context. Avoid using *via* as a synonym for *by, through,* or *by means of.* Use the most specific term instead.

video adapter   Obsolete term. Use *graphics adapter* instead.

> *See Also:* *graphics adapter*

video board   Do not use. Use *graphics adapter* instead.

video display   Do not use; use *screen* to refer to the graphic portion of a monitor and *display* to refer generically to a visual output device.

> *See Also:* *display; screen*

viewport   One word. Refers to a view of a document or image in computer graphics programs.

virtual   Avoid in content for home users and information workers.

In other contexts, use to describe a device or service that appears to the user as something it actually is not or that does not physically exist. For example, a virtual disk performs like a physical disk, but is actually a part of the computer's memory. Some other virtual devices or services are virtual machine, virtual memory, and virtual desktop. Use the term only to refer to a specific element.

For more information, see the *Microsoft Computer Dictionary*.

virtual root   Acceptable to use to refer to the root directory that the user sees when connected to an Internet server. It is actually a pointer to the actual root directory. Do not use *virtual directory* as a synonym.

virtual server   Acceptable in content for software developers and information technology professionals to refer to a server that appears to a browser like a physical server. Sometimes used as a synonym for *Web site*. Use *Web site* instead if possible in context.

virtualize   Do not use in content for home users or information workers.

In other contexts, do not use as a synonym for *simulate*. If you must use *virtualize*, use it only to mean creating a virtual implementation. For example, "to virtualize storage" would mean to create virtual storage, which makes many physical storage devices appear to be one device.

visit   In the context of the Internet, use *visit* only to talk about going to a Web site for the purpose of spending time at that site. You may also use *go to* in this context.

To talk about going to a specific Web page, use *go to*.

Correct

Visit our Web site at *www.microsoft.com*.

For information about Microsoft Windows and Microsoft .NET programming, visit the Microsoft Developer Network Web site.

When you visit a retail Web site, you can often put items you want to purchase into a shopping basket.

For information about Microsoft Windows and Microsoft .NET programming, go to the Microsoft Developer Network Web site.

To learn how to convert text to numbers in Microsoft Excel 2002, go to *http://support.microsoft.com/default.aspx?scid=kb;en-us;Q291047&sd=tech*.

Incorrect

To learn how to convert text to numbers in Microsoft Excel 2002, visit *http://support.microsoft.com/default.aspx?scid=kb;en-us;Q291047&sd=tech*.

voice mail   Two words. Do not abbreviate as *v-mail* or *vmail*.

vulnerability   *Vulnerability* can refer to any product flaw, administrative process or act, or physical exposure that makes a computer susceptible to attack by a hostile user. Because *vulnerability* covers so many types of security problems, its misuse can easily confuse readers on a very sensitive topic. Follow the guidelines in this topic to ensure that readers do not misunderstand the security-related information you are giving them.

Behavior that is by design is not a vulnerability; do not describe it as such.

On first use in a given topic, always be specific as to what kind of vulnerability you are discussing:

- **Product vulnerability.**   A security-related bug in a product. A product vulnerability is always addressed either by a security bulletin on *http://www.microsoft.com /security* or by a product service pack. If a security issue is not addressed in either of these ways, do not refer to it as a product vulnerability.

- **Administrative vulnerability.**   Failure to observe administrative best practices, such as using a weak password or logging on to an account that has more user rights than the user requires to perform a specific task.

- **Physical vulnerability.**   Failure to provide physical security for a computer, such as leaving an unlocked workstation running in a workspace that is available to unauthorized users.

After context is established, it is all right to use *vulnerability* without a modifier. It is, however, a good idea to reestablish context by occasionally using the modifier throughout the topic.

It is all right to use *vulnerability* on first mention without a modifier only in the most general sense. If the reader would be wrong in interpreting this use of *vulnerability* to mean any or all specific types of vulnerabilities, use one or more specific phrases to make your meaning unambiguous.

For other security issues, use the most specific term that describes the issue, taking care to define the term if it might be unfamiliar to members of your audience. If there is no specific term, use *security issue*.

V

Correct

Because there have been vulnerabilities related to the handling of HTML e-mail, you should consider using group policies to assign HTML e-mail to the Restricted sites zone.

In Active Directory, the administrator of any domain within a forest is trusted to control any other domain within the forest.

Do not expose your system to administrative vulnerabilities. For example, do not log on as an administrator unless you are doing a task that requires the user rights of an administrator.

Incorrect

There is a vulnerability within Active Directory that can allow the administrator of any domain within a forest to gain control of any other domain within the forest.

W

W3C   Abbreviation for World Wide Web Consortium, the organization that sets standards for the Web and HTML. Spell out on first mention.

want   Not *wish*. Do not confuse with *need*. Be sure to use the term that is appropriate to the situation. *Need* connotes a requirement or obligation; *want* indicates that the user has a choice of actions.

> **Correct**
>
> If you want to use a laser printer, you need a laser printer driver.

> **Incorrect**
>
> If you wish to format the entire word, double-click it.

we   In general, do not use, except in the phrase *we recommend*.

> For more information, see *Person* in Chapter 10, "Grammatical Elements."

Web   Always capitalize *Web*, even if you are referring to an intranet Web.

> It is all right to use *Web* alone to refer to the World Wide Web, as long as the context is clear. For inexperienced computer users, use *World Wide Web* on first mention, and then shorten to *Web*.
>
> When used as a modifier, capitalize the W and use two words, with the following exceptions used throughout the industry:
>
> - web-centric
> - webcam
> - webcast
> - webmaster
> - webzine
>
> > **Correct**
> >
> > Web address
> > Web browser
> > Web page
> > Web site

web-   Words beginning with the prefix *web-* are common nouns and appear in lowercase. Normal rules of capitalization apply in titles and at the beginning of a sentence.

> **Correct**
>
> The webcast is scheduled for Tuesday at 20:00.
>
> **Incorrect**
>
> The Webcast is scheduled for Tuesday at 20:00.

Web page   Two words. *Web* is capitalized; *page* is not.

Web site   Two words. *Web* is capitalized; *site* is not.

Weblication   Jargon for "Web application." Do not use. It could be confused with "Web publication."

where   Use to introduce a list, as in code or formulas, to define the meaning of elements such as variables or symbols.

> **Correct**
>
> Use the following formula to calculate the return, where:
>
> r = rate of interest
>
> n = number of months
>
> p = principal

while   Use to refer to something occurring in time. Avoid as a synonym for *although*, which can be ambiguous.

> **Correct**
>
> Fill out your registration card while you wait for Setup to be completed.
>
> Although the icon indicates that the print job is finished, you may have to wait until a previous job is finished.
>
> **Incorrect**
>
> While the icon indicates that the print job is finished, you may have to wait until a previous job is finished.

white paper   Always two words.

white space, white-space   Two words as a noun, hyphenated as an adjective.

who vs. that   Although there is no linguistic basis for not using *that* to refer to people, as in "the man that was walking," it is considered more polite to use *who* instead of *that* in references to people. Therefore, use *who*, not *that*, to introduce clauses referring to users.

> **Correct**
>
> Custom Setup is for experienced users who want to alter the standard Windows configuration.

> **Incorrect**
>
> Custom Setup is for experienced users that want to alter the standard Windows configuration.

wildcard character   Always use the word *character* with *wildcard* when referring to a keyboard character that can be used to represent one or many characters, such as the * or ?

Wildcard is one word.

window   Do not use as a verb.

Windows Explorer   Do not use as a synonym for Internet Explorer. Windows Explorer is a feature of Windows operating systems that shows the hierarchical structure of the files and folders on a computer. Do not precede with *the* and do not shorten to *Explorer*.

Windows Installer   Initial capitals.

Windows, Windows-based   Do not use *Windows* to modify the names of programs, hardware, or development methods that are based on or run on the Windows operating system. Instead, use *Windows-based* or *running Windows*. To avoid a ridiculous construction, the term *Windows user* is acceptable.

> **Correct**
>
> Windows-based application
>
> Windows-based device
>
> a computer running Windows

> **Incorrect**
>
> Windows application
>
> Windows computer

W

Winsock   Acceptable to refer to the Windows Sockets API. Avoid *Sockets*.

wireframe   One word. Refers to a type of three-dimensional graphic.

wizard   Always use lowercase for the generic term *wizard*. Capitalize *wizard* if it is part of a feature name that appears in the user interface.

> **Correct**
>
> When you first install Word on your computer, the Setup program makes many wizards and templates available.
>
> You can create a Web page or frames page with the Web Page Wizard.

Refer to an individual screen within a wizard as a *page*.

word processing   Hyphenate word-processing words according to part of speech, as shown:

- Word-processed (adj.), word-processing (adj.)
- Word processor (n.), word processing (n.)

Avoid using *word process* as a verb. Use *write, format*, or another more specific term instead.

wordwrap   One word. It's acceptable to use *wordwrapping*, as in "turn off wordwrapping."

work area   Two words. Do not use *work area* unless the term has a specific meaning in a particular product. Use *workspace* to refer to the area within a window where the user interacts with the program.

workgroup   One word.

working memory   Do not use; use *available memory* instead.

worksheet   Do not use as a synonym for *spreadsheet*. A spreadsheet is a computer accounting program, such as Microsoft Excel; a worksheet is the document produced by a spreadsheet program.

workspace   One word. Refers to the area within the window where the user interacts with the program. Use *client area* only if necessary in content for software developers.

workstation   One word. Use to refer to a personal computer used by an individual in a network. A workstation is the client in a client/server system.

World Wide Web   Spell on first mention in material for novices, and then use *the Web*.

Use *on* to refer to material existing on the Web. You can use *to* or *on* to refer to the action of creating and publishing something *to the Web* or *on the Web*.

write-only   Always hyphenated. Related to *read/write*, but *write-only* and *read-only* refer to properties of files, and *read/write* refers to a level of permissions granted to users, not an adjective that defines files or other objects.

write-protect, write-protected   Always hyphenated. Use *write-protect*, not *lock*, to refer to the action of protecting disks from being overwritten.

> **Correct**
>
> to write-protect a disk
>
> a write-protected disk
>
> a disk that is write-protected

WWW   Abbreviation for World Wide Web. Acceptable if it appears in the product interface, but in general use *the Web* instead.

See Also: *World Wide Web*

W

X

x   Use a lowercase italic *x* as a placeholder number or variable. Do not use to refer to a generic unspecified number; use *n* instead. Do not use to refer to a multiplication sign.

> **Correct**
>
> version 4.*x*
>
> R4*x*00
>
> **Incorrect**
>
> Move the insertion point *x* spaces to the right.

Do not use *80x86*. Refer to the specific processor. If necessary, a construction such as "80386 or higher" is acceptable.

See Also: *multiplication sign (×); n*

x86   A generic name for the series of Intel microprocessor families that began with the 80286 microprocessor. x86 microprocessors include the 80286 series, the 386DX/SX/SL family, the 486DX/SX/DX2/SL/DX4 family, and the Pentium family. Use only in content for high-end technical users when you need to refer to Intel processors only from 80286 or later.

x-axis   In general, use *category (x) axis* to refer to the (usually) horizontal axis in charts and graphs that shows the categories being compared. Include a reference to the horizontal axis if it will clarify the meaning. Note lowercase, hyphen, and roman.

Xbase   Not *xBASE*.

x-coordinate   Lowercase, hyphenated, and roman.

XON/XOF   All uppercase letters with slash mark. Refers to the handshake between two computers during transmission of data.

Y

y-axis   In general, use *value (y) axis* to refer to the (usually) vertical axis in charts and graphs that shows the values being measured or compared. Include a reference to the vertical axis if it will clarify the meaning. Note lowercase, hyphen, and roman.

y-coordinate   Lowercase, hyphenated, and roman.

Z

z-   Hyphenate all words referring to entities that begin with *z* used as a separate letter, such as *z-axis*, *z-coordinate*, *z-order*, and *z-test*. Follow your project's style sheet for capitalization.

z-axis   In 3-D charts, the z-axis shows depth. It generally represents values. Refer to the z-axis as the *value axis*, where both the x-axis and y-axis are category axes, but include *z-axis* in parentheses if it will clarify the meaning. Note lowercase, hyphen, and roman.

zero character   In the ASCII character set, a zero character represents the digit 0 but is ASCII code 48. Differentiate it from the NUL character (ASCII code 0).

> *See Also:* NUL, null, NULL, Null

zero, zeros   Not *zeroes*.

> In measurements, when the unit of measurement is not abbreviated, zero takes the plural, as in "0 megabytes."

Zip Code   Avoid in general text; instead, use the generically international *postal code*. In forms or fill-in fields include *postal code* as well as Zip Code capitalized as appropriate. It is acceptable to combine the two terms to save space.

> **Correct**
> ZIP Code/Postal Code: _____
> ZIP/Postal Code: _____
> Postal Code: _____

zoom in, zoom out   Do not use *dezoom* or *unzoom*.

Index

Symbols and Numbers

& (ampersand), 45, 208
* (asterisk), 212, 306
@ (at sign), 212
... (ellipses), 181–82
... (ellipsis button), 220, 252
— (em dash), 179–80
– (en dash), 180, 303
€ (euro), 255
- (minus sign), 303
× (multiplication sign), 129, 132, 306, 338
(number sign), 310, 323
% (percentage sign), 319
| (pipe symbol), 320
" " (quotation marks), 176–77
/ (slash marks), 182
_ (underscore), 361
2-D (two-dimensional), 360
3-D (three-dimensional), 357
3.5-inch disk, 245
4GL (Fourth-generation language), 263
8.5-by-11-inch paper, 252

A

abbreviations. *See also specific abbreviations*
  globalization, 61, 62, 63, 67
  index entries, 102
  list of acceptable, 183–96
  measurements, 129–31
  plural forms, 166
  possessive forms, 168
  protocols, 137
  time zones, 141
  Web page titles, 88
-able, 199
abort, 199
above, 200
accelerator key, 200
access, 200
access key, 201
access privileges, 202
access rights, 202

accessibility. *See also* people with disabilities
  art, 29, 30
  assistive technology, 212
  cognitive impairments, 114, 115
  hearing impairments, 108, 114, 239, 272
  online content, 30, 35
  physical impairments, 108
  visual impairments, 29, 30, 35, 108, 114, 115
accessible, 201
accessory, 201
accessory programs, 37
accounts receivable, 202
acknowledgement, 202
acronyms. *See also specific acronyms*
  formatting and layout, 37
  globalization, 61, 63
  index entries using, 102
  list of acceptable, 183–96
  plural forms, 167
  possessive forms, 168
  Web page titles, 88
action bar, 202
action button, 202
activate
  enable vs., 253
  guidelines for using term, 202
active, 203
active and passive voice
  described, 160–61
  globalization, 61
  guidelines for choosing, 157
  modifiers, 170
  second person and active voice, 164
active content, 81
active document, 81
active script and active scripting, 81
active server pages, 81
Active Server Pages, 81
ActiveX terminology, 80–86. *See also* Component Object Model (COM)
ad hoc, 204
adapter, 203

add-in and add-on
  applet vs., 209
  guidelines for using term, 203
  plug-in vs., 321
address, 203
adjacent selection
  guidelines for using term, 204
  range selection vs., 329
adjectives
  -able and -ible suffixes, 199
  globalization, 61
  hyphenation, 178–79
administer, 204
administrator, 204
Administrator program, 204
ADO (ActiveX Data Objects), 82
adverbs
  globalization, 61
  hyphenation, 179
affect vs. effect, 204
after, 313
afterward, 205
against, 205
alarm, 205
alert, 205
align and aligned on, 206
alignment, 78
allow, 206
alpha, 206
alphabetical, 207
alphanumeric, 207
alt text, 30, 60, 207
alternative methods of procedures, 118, 122–23
although, 372
A.M., 207
among vs. between, 207
ampersand (&)
  guidelines for using term, 208
  headings and subheadings, 45
and, 208
and/or, 208
and so on, 208
anthropomorphism, 111–12
antialiasing, 209
antivirus, 209
API (application programming interface), 264
apostrophes, 174

N

Microsoft
Press

Learn how to get the job done every day—
faster, smarter, and easier!

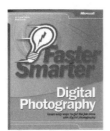   

**Faster Smarter
Digital Photography**
ISBN: 0-7356-1872-0
U.S.A. $19.99
Canada $28.99

**Faster Smarter
Microsoft® Office XP**
ISBN: 0-7356-1862-3
U.S.A. $19.99
Canada $28.99

**Faster Smarter
Microsoft Windows® XP**
ISBN: 0-7356-1857-7
U.S.A. $19.99
Canada $28.99

**Faster Smarter
Home Networking**
ISBN: 0-7356-1869-0
U.S.A. $19.99
Canada $28.99

scover how to do exactly what you do with computers and technology—faster, smarter, and easier—with FASTER SMARTER
oks from Microsoft Press! They're your everyday guides for learning the practicalities of how to make technology work
e way you want—fast. Their language is friendly and down-to-earth, with no jargon or silly chatter, and with accurate how-
information that's easy to absorb and apply. Use the concise explanations, easy numbered steps, and visual examples
understand exactly what you need to do to get the job done—whether you're using a PC at home or in business,
pturing and sharing digital still images, getting a home network running, or finishing other tasks.

Microsoft Press has other FASTER SMARTER titles to help you get the job done every day:

Faster Smarter PCs
ISBN: 0-7356-1780-5

Faster Smarter Microsoft Windows 98
ISBN: 0-7356-1858-5

Faster Smarter Beginning Programming
ISBN: 0-7356-1780-5

Faster Smarter Digital Video
ISBN: 0-7356-1873-9

Faster Smarter Web Page Creation
ISBN: 0-7356-1860-7

Faster Smarter HTML & XML
ISBN: 0-7356-1861-5

Faster Smarter Internet
ISBN: 0-7356-1859-3

Faster Smarter Money 2003
ISBN: 0-7356-1864-X

To learn more about the full line of Microsoft Press® products, please visit us at:

microsoft.com/mspress

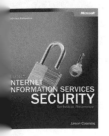

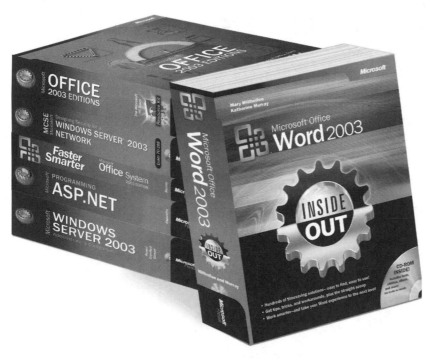